P9-AOD-978

OUTRAGE
in Ohio

OUTRAGE
in Ohio

A Rural Murder, Lynching, and Mystery

———◆———

DAVID KIMMEL

Indiana University Press

This book is a publication of

Indiana University Press
Office of Scholarly Publishing
Herman B Wells Library 350
1320 East 10th Street
Bloomington, Indiana 47405, USA

iupress.indiana.edu

© 2018 by David Kimmel
All rights reserved

No part of this book may be reproduced or utilized in any form or by any means, electronic or mechanical, including photocopying and recording, or by any information storage and retrieval system, without permission in writing from the publisher. The Association of American University Presses' Resolution on Permissions constitutes the only exception to this prohibition.

Manufactured in the United States of America

Library of Congress Cataloging-in-Publication Data

Names: Kimmel, David (David Paul), [date] author.
Title: Outrage in Ohio : a rural murder, lynching, and mystery / David Kimmel.
Description: Bloomington, Indiana : Indiana University Press, [2019] |
    Includes bibliographical references.
Identifiers: LCCN 2018009921 (print) | LCCN 2018012745 (ebook) | ISBN
    9780253034250 (e-book) | ISBN 9780253034236 (cl : alk. paper) | ISBN
    9780253034229 (pb : alk. paper)
Subjects: LCSH: Secaur, Mary, -1872. | Murder—Ohio—Mercer County—Case
    studies. | Lynching—Ohio—Mercer County—Case studies.
Classification: LCC HV6533.O5 (ebook) | LCC HV6533.O5 K56 2019 (print) | DDC
    364.152/309771415—dc23
LC record available at https://lccn.loc.gov/2018009921

1 2 3 4 5   23 22 21 20 19 18

For Bevan

CONTENTS

ACKNOWLEDGMENTS

I would like to thank staff members at the following institutions: Mercer County Recorder's office, Mercer County Clerk of Courts office, Mercer County District Library, Shanes Crossing Historical Society, Rutherford B. Hayes Presidential Library, Allen County Public Library Genealogy Center, Westmoreland County Recorder of Deeds, Baltzer Meyer Historical Society, Ohio Genealogical Society Library, Holmes County Recorder's office, Fairfield County District Library, and Beeghly Library at Heidelberg University. The following people contributed to my work by sharing information and access to artifacts: Helen Almendinger, Lew and Barb Boggs, Sharon Schaadt Cowen, Karen Feasby, Harrison Frech, Carl Kimmel, Tim Kimmel, Mary Krugh, and Tom Pryer; please forgive me if I have forgotten anyone! Heidelberg University Colleagues helped me with writing the dialect for my French, German, and Irish neighbors: Robert Berg, Nainsi Houston, and Marc O'Reilly. Heidelberg University colleagues Kate Bradie and Ruth Wahlstrom read an earlier version of the book for me, and my wife, Sandy Kimmel, has proofread it again and again. This work was partially supported by sabbatical leaves and summer grants from Heidelberg University.

INTRODUCTION

Two bodies slowly turn on the ends of ropes. A soiled ribbon rests on a table. A young man sits in a cell, measuring out the days, weeks, and months. A mother and father set out a black-draped photo of their foster daughter. Hogs rooting in the hot undergrowth smell blood, sense food is near. A crowd retraces its steps, puffs of dust clinging to shoes, to legs. Riders race into a town square with pistols drawn. The pages of an open testament ruffle in the slight breeze. A hand transcribes a dying wish. Somewhere in this heap of broken images the truth lies.

⊱─━━━━━─⊰

Celina, Mercer County, Ohio—Sunday, June 30, 1872[1]

George shifted uncomfortably on the hard wooden bench in the front row of the tiny courthouse. He moved his feet, and the iron shackles clanked against the floor. The air hung with sweat and warm wool and nerves. In the windows, George could see the faces of townspeople and farmers peering into the gloom of the courthouse from the bright afternoon sunshine.

Behind the faces in the windows, more faces, some in trees, all strained for a glimpse of the proceedings. He turned around and looked back into the courtroom, all eyes turning to him in curiosity. He looked past them for his parents. At last he saw his mother, her face barely visible through the intervening heads and shoulders. She was looking down to her left, probably attending to Peck or Charlie. *Look up, look over here,* he commanded to no avail. Through the heads he could make out his father staring straight ahead.

To George's right on the bench sat one of the guards, and beyond him was Jake. In the first row directly in front of Jake sat McLeod and Ab. All three looked scared and much the worse for having spent two nights in the county jail. George imagined he didn't look much better. McLeod stared straight ahead, but Absalom gawked at the crowd. George saw Jake look around the guard at him. He gave his brother a thin-lipped smile, but Jake turned away. George's ears burned at the slight.

A sudden murmur swept the crowd behind him as a group of men in black robes strode into the room. All were large men, trim if graying, probably about the age of his father and definitely—from the looks of their sunburnt faces—farmers, no matter what else they might be at the moment. A voice high above the crowd announced the three justices. George rose to his feet along with the rest of the people, and then sat down with them.

George watched the glare on the large head of the man introduced as Justice Snyder who rose to address the courtroom. "I hereby call this hearing to order. Just to be official, this is a hearing to consider the case of Alexander McLeod and Absalom Kimmel, who are charged, as if anyone didn't know, with the abduction, violation, and murder of Mary Arabelle Secaur on Sunday, June 23, 1872, in Liberty Township of Mercer County, the State of Ohio. I remind all present that this is a hearing only, and that should the case against the defendants be deemed sufficient, their case will be taken up by the Circuit Court of Common Pleas when it arrives in Mercer County in November. The prosecution may now open its case."

"Child Found Dead." *Mercer County Standard*, Thursday, June 27, 1872[2]

On Monday afternoon last, the body of a highly respected little girl, aged about thirteen years, by the name of Mary Secore, who has been making her home with Mr. John Sitterly for some time past, was found about half a mile west of the residence of Mr. Strouse May, in Liberty township, this county, in a most horrible and mangled condition; the head being entirely separated from the body and the skull broke in several pieces, the flesh eaten from the body by hogs which had found it before search was made. The little girl had attended Sabbath school Sabbath afternoon, and was probably on her road home. We have learned nothing definite as to what caused her death, but from the many rumors afloat, suppose that some fiendish person had attempted an outrage, and fearful of being detected, committed an atrocious murder. If a murder it be, the perpetrator of the heinous act should be ferreted out and suffer the penalty of the law in its most rigid form.

Liberty Township, Mercer County, Ohio—Saturday, June 23, 1877

Daniel Mahoney[3]

I first knew of the horror when Johanna came stumbling along through two rows of young corn, shouting and waving her arms. I stopped hoeing and wiped the grit off my own neck and face. She made a lot of noise before getting close enough to make any sense. By then she was so out of breath she could hardly speak.

"Yerrah, girl, catch yourself."

"Come help ..." she puffed. Her face was red with the exertion. "The men're waiting."

"What men? Hold on now. What is it?"

"Mary, she's gone!" Johanna got out, finally.

"Our Mary?" I dropped my hoe and set off for the house at a run.

"Nah, 'tisn't our Mary. Stop a second so a body can talk." Johanna bumped into my back as I pulled up.

I turned and grabbed her shoulders. "Speak sense, then, woman. Who is it? What's happened?"

"Young Mary Secaur's after disappearing."

"Mary Secaur? Is it Strouse's granddaughter lives with the Sitterlys?"

"She never came home from the church, you know, and her folks fear the worst."

I looked in the direction of the house but saw no one. "Who'd you say is at the house?"

"Wells, Sitterly, May and his son, and few others. You be running on and doing the necessary, Daniel."

I looked at the tears welling up in her green eyes. I pulled her to myself and then set off for the house at a dead run. Six neighbors stood in our front yard.

"Come quick," said Wells. He turned with the others, and we set off. "Johanna tell you what happened?"

"That she did. The grim business, it is."

It took us a quarter of an hour to walk to the churchyard, where we met another four local farmers. Henry Hinton took charge, as always. He organized us into teams, and we set off down the road, retracing the girl's steps from the previous afternoon.

It's a good two miles from the church to Sitterly's farm, and it'd be a hard walk on any hot summer day, but looking into every ditch, asking at every doorway, and peering into every thicket along the way took a good deal out of me. By four, I was hot, jaded, and growing more and more anxious with every step. It's hard work looking for something you hope you won't find.

I'm glad it wasn't me who found her. I was clear on the other side of the road, poking around some bushes, when I heard Meizner shout out.

⊢─◆─○─◆─⊣

Tiffin, Ohio—June 23, 2017

David Kimmel

Mary Secaur was a very real girl, and her death rocked her rural community in Western Ohio 145 years ago. The Kimmels were a very real family, original settlers whose descendants reach out from the past to this day. I am no innocent bystander. I am no objective observer. I am historian, detective, storyteller, family member. That last is vital.

My father grew up in Rockford, a small town just miles from the scene of these events. Though his aunts and uncles knew of Mary Secaur's case, he was innocent until the mid-1990s, when, like many newly retired people, he turned from the world of work to the work of tracing his roots. Tucked inside a letter from one of his Western Ohio cousins, one paragraph caught his eye—a paragraph of rape, murder, retribution, and regret. That was all he had, but it was enough to pique his interest. Dad did some more checking, both with relatives and online, and he was able to glean more information, including a photocopy of James Day's 1872 booklet, *Lynched!* which recounted the case in sensational, graphic terms. When Dad died in the fall of 1997, I inherited the case. The murder and what followed make for a gripping story, but that only partly explains why over the years—at the expense of other work I should have been doing—I have returned to this project again and again.

Outrage in Ohio is an exploration of an 1872 case of murder and lynching in western Ohio. I have investigated the facts of the case, the lives of the participants, and the community in which the events took place, as well as the time period, but I have also explored the inner lives of the participants, the larger social implications of the events, and the dynamics within this Western Ohio community. What you will not find here is a straightforward novel, marching onward from beginning to end in pursuit of a single narrative. Narratives have a way of dictating the truth of an event, of cutting off the what-ifs and perhapses of a situation as their authors make their way down the forking paths of storytelling. Instead of a single story, here is a collection of narratives—contemporary, historical, and fictional. The contemporary voices are provided by newspaper accounts, an unpublished journal, and the semiofficial booklet published just after the lynchings. Occasionally, I step in as narrator to tidy up loose ends or to provide some analysis of the case. The fiction comes in two flavors: some are fictionalized versions of real, documented events, while some I have imagined in order to explore real situations and people and relationships. Along the way I carefully note my sources and any departures from hard facts. So here is what I have discovered—and partially what I have imagined—about the Secaur-McLeod-Kimmel murders.

MAPS

Map 1. Ohio and Pennsylvania, showing counties referenced in the story. Map by David Kimmel.

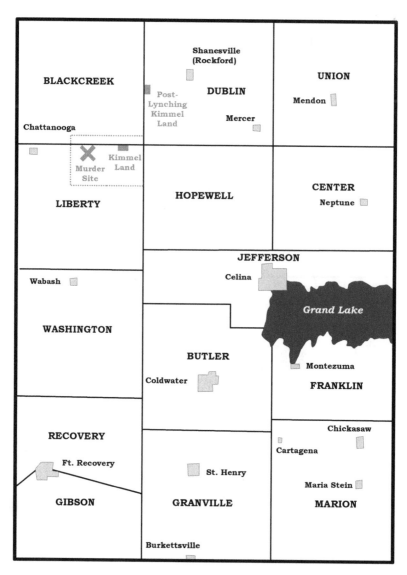

Map 2. Location of Liberty Township within Mercer County, Ohio. Map by David Kimmel.

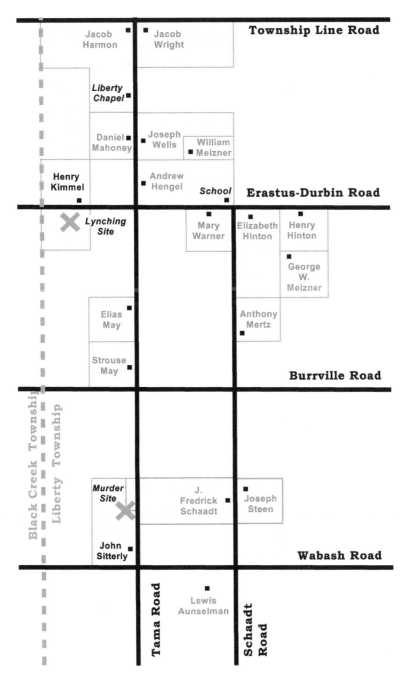

Map 3. Residents of portions of Black Creek and Liberty Townships c. 1872. Map based on *Map of Mercer County Ohio*. Philadelphia: Chas A McConahy, 1876, and 1870 US Census. Map by David Kimmel.

PEOPLE

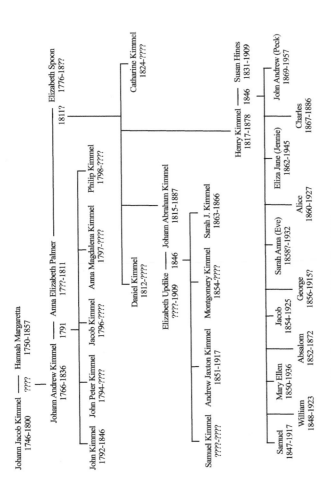

Figure 0.1. Kimmel family tree. Graphic by David Kimmel.

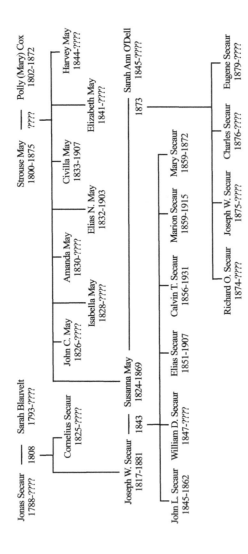

Figure o.2. Secaur family tree. Graphic by David Kimmel.

OUTRAGE
in Ohio

1

MURDER

"A Little Girl Murdered." *Van Wert Bulletin*. June 28, 1872

Mr. Gabriel Lockart, a merchant in Shane's Crossings, a little town thirteen miles South of Van Wert, in Mercer county, has given us the following particulars of one of the most revolting outrages ever perpetrated:

On Sunday last, a little girl named Secar, *who lived with a family near Shane's Crossings, attended Sunday School and Church, as was her custom. She had not returned to her home on Monday morning, but the family were not alarmed, believing that she had stayed over night with some of the neighbors. At noon search was made for her, and failing to learn her whereabouts, the alarm was given and the neighbors were called together. Some twelve or fifteen men went to the Church and traced her to a point where the road passes through the woods, with a large space without a house. The last that could be heard of her was that a family living near this place saw her about half past twelve, on Sunday, on her way home. A search was made in the fields and woods along this road. Near a clump of bushes two pieces of her hat were found, and one of the men, who was attracted by the noise of some hogs in the bushes, walked around to the side where the hogs were and found them fighting over the little girl's body which they were devouring.*

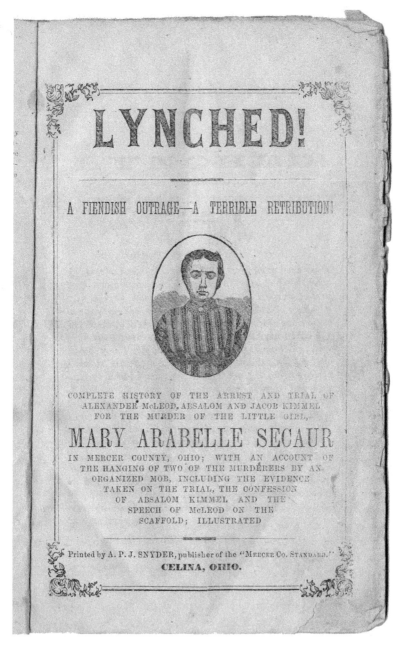

LYNCHED!

A FIENDISH OUTRAGE—A TERRIBLE RETRIBUTION!

COMPLETE HISTORY OF THE ARREST AND TRIAL OF
ALEXANDER McLEOD, ABSALOM AND JACOB KIMMEL
FOR THE MURDER OF THE LITTLE GIRL,

MARY ARABELLE SECAUR

IN MERCER COUNTY, OHIO; WITH AN ACCOUNT OF
THE HANGING OF TWO OF THE MURDERERS BY AN
ORGANIZED MOB, INCLUDING THE EVIDENCE
TAKEN ON THE TRIAL, THE CONFESSION
OF ABSALOM KIMMEL AND THE
SPEECH OF McLEOD ON THE
SCAFFOLD; ILLUSTRATED

Printed by A. P. J. SNYDER, publisher of the "MERCER CO. STANDARD."
CELINA, OHIO.

Figure 1.1. Title page of James H. Day's *Lynched!* Ohio History Connection.

Liberty Township, Mercer County, Ohio—Monday, June 24, 1872

Mary Ellen Kimmel[1]

I was working in the garden after supper with Anna and little Peck when Charlie ran up to the fence, panting hard.

"There's a girl ate by hogs down the road!" he yelled as soon as he caught enough wind to get it out.

Anna and I stopped where we were. "What are you talking about?" I asked.

Charlie spoke again, slowly and emphatically, with the surety and superiority of a five-year-old who knows something his elders don't. "There's a girl they found the hogs ate." He made a horrible face to emphasize the last words.

I looked at Anna, who mirrored what I assumed was my own puzzled expression.

"It's awful, it's awful. Come quick!" gasped Charlie and broke into tears. I dropped my hoe and crossed the garden to the fence where he stood bawling. I leaned over the wooden rails and lifted him. He was growing heavy—I didn't pick him up much anymore, so his weight was a surprise. He clasped me around the neck and, still sobbing, buried his face in my shoulder.

"Anna, go fetch Mother," I said, hugging Charlie close to me. She ran down the path and into the back of the house. Charlie continued to cry loudly into my shoulder. Peck sat in the dirt staring at us, his lower lip trembling as he debated whether he should cry, too.

Mother hurried from the house, drawn directly to Charlie's cries. Anna, Alice, and Jennie followed her out the door and stood in a little clump at the back of the house. Charlie turned from me and reached for Mother, who pulled him from me and gathered him in, he burying his face in her neck and growing silent, except for a few sobs that continued to shake his frame. Mother patted his back and shushed him as she rocked back and forth. At the sight of Mother, Peck also let loose, so I went to him and picked him up. He was much lighter than his older brother but only that much louder for not understanding why he was crying. We finally got the two of them quieted down, and Charlie wriggled out of his mother's arms to stand independently on the ground before us. Try as she might, though, Mother could get nothing more from him.

She turned to me. "Give me Peck, and run on up to the crossroads to see if you can find out what's happened. You girls stay here," she added to the group by the back door.

I followed her directions and was quickly out of the garden, around the side of the house, over the turnstile, and walking down the road. It had been dry for the past few weeks, so thick clouds of dust puffed up as my feet struck the roadway. I entered the tunnel of second-growth woods towering along both sides of the road between our clearing and the crossroads. It was cooler in the shade, but closer, too. Up ahead, the bright evening light illuminated knots of women and men standing at the crossroads.

An empty house stood off to the right, its fields and yards filling with weeds. I waved to the women as I approached, and Johanna Mahoney waved back. Around her was gathered every woman in the neighborhood, it seemed: Arrela Wells, Elizabeth Hengel, Mary and Susan Warner, Abigail and Sophie Harmon from way down on the Township Line Road, and Susannah and Mary May. Even ancient Susan Meizner had emerged from her backset cabin off behind the Hengels' lot. Their husbands and older sons stood in a group about fifty feet off, and the children swirled around the crossroads, running and laughing and stirring up dust that glowed orange in the late afternoon light.

The adults weren't laughing. I joined the group of women. They looked serious and worried. "Have you heard about Mary Secaur?" Johanna asked me.

"Mary Secaur?" I asked. "The Sitterlys' girl?"

"The very one," said Johanna. "She disappeared on the way home from church, and the men found her in the bushes this afternoon."

"Her head was cut off," said Arrela.

"And her clothes were gone," said Susannah.

I made a face. I knew what that meant.

Mary Warner spoke in a low voice, more to the road than to the rest of us. "I can't imagine how she suffered."

A shudder ran through the group. We were quiet for a moment. I tried to block the thoughts and images that came unbidden to my mind, but then I remembered what Charlie had said.

"Charlie said something about ..."

"Hogs," said Johanna.

"Horrible," said Susannah.

"Awful," said Mary.

"Don't surprise me none," came a creaking voice. It was Susan Meizner. "I lived here in the woods nigh on thirty years. Nothing no animal or *man*"—she laid a heavy emphasis on that last word while looking over at the clot of men standing across the road from us—"might do surprises me no more."

"You don't mean Mary's death doesn't shock you?" asked Arrela.

"Shock me? Sure. Surprise me? No." She looked around at the women in the circle. "You know what happens."

Unfortunately, we did, out here in the country with farms full of young men and teenage boys. Not that old men were above suspicion. I looked over at the three oldest daughters knotted to one side of the group. Susan Warner and Sophie Harmon, hands clasped, leaned closer together. Mary May, just two years older than the dead cousin who shared her name, hugged herself and stared uncomfortably at the roadway beneath her feet.

"And it'll only be worse once they get worked up." Susan Meizner nodded in the direction of the men, whose voices were a loud murmur in the growing dusk. The farmers stood in a loose group, gesturing wildly as they spoke.

"Well, I'm glad of the men and their protection," said Elizabeth Hengel in her thick German accent. "They will find out what happened and take action. They'll root out the guilty." She was looking straight at me as she said this. I ignored her. There was bad blood between our families.

"Where's your Andrew?" asked Johanna.

"Down the road, talking with Henry Hinton," said Elizabeth. We all looked toward a distant clump of figures standing to the south.

"Himself is worked up, I'll wager," said Johanna.

"Something to organize," said Susannah. "And people to boss."

Mary Warner laughed dryly. "And don't we know how Henry loves to take charge?"

"Henry Hinton is all the law we have in this township," said Elizabeth. "Someone has to keep the peace. And he's a veteran."

"Which he don't let anyone forget," said Susannah.

"If some of our husbands won't protect us, I'm glad to know there's them what will," said Arrela.

"Whose husband are you talking about?" asked Susannah. "Yours is no veteran, either."

"I ain't talking about no veterans. I'm talking about bad seed." Arrela looked me in the eye for a full moment. "Some folks should watch out, is all."

I opened my mouth to ask her what she meant, but changed my mind.

By now the sun had dipped below the trees, and darkness was gathering quickly. Mosquitos were rising from the weeds along the side of the road, and the women around me had been absently slapping themselves for the past few minutes. As by an invisible signal, the conversation halted and the groups broke apart. Couples and children headed back to their homes together. I walked alone down the darkening road toward home. I had plenty to tell my mother—and plenty to think about.

⊢⊶⊙⊷⊣

"The Liberty Township Murder." *Celina Journal.* July 4, 1872

As it has been stated, she was killed some time on Sunday afternoon, 23d ult. [of last month], and was found the following Monday about 4 P.M. . . . The scene of the tragedy lies in the northwestern part of the county on an east and west road running past Liberty U. B. Church, and about 2½ miles east of the state line, and 2 miles west of the church. At the fatal spot is a thick undergrowth of briery box wood very near the narrow road; a fence also runs north and south and along the road for some distance, and when nearing the first corner, she was met, evidently by more than one person, with pre-conceived evil intent and dragged,

amid smothered screams and prayers, behind the above-mentioned bushes, some
40 feet from the road. The first object in thus taking her there, can be imagined
with better clearness than we can state it.

⊷•◦•◦•⊷

Mercer County Courthouse, Celina, Mercer County, Ohio—Sunday, June 30, 1872

The crowd rustled and craned for a view as LeBlond, the head of the prosecution team, stood and addressed the bench. "Your Honors, at noon today, Absalom Kimmel made a confession to two persons ..." The rest of LeBlond's statement was drowned out as a sudden burst of conversation flooded the courtroom. It took several minutes of gavel-banging by Judge Snyder before the crowd settled down enough for LeBlond to continue. "As I said, at noon today, Absalom Kimmel made a confession, which I hold here in my hand. The prosecution would like to submit this confession as its first evidence in the case."

The defense team jumped to its feet, shouting objections that were blown back in their faces by shouts and threats from the crowd. "Quiet! Quiet in the court!" Judge Snyder continued to bang the gavel as the crowd ignored him. He raised his voice. "I said quiet, you pack of clodhoppers! I'll clear this court if you don't pipe down!" The roar subsided into a murmur of indignation at Judge Snyder's words. "That's better. I remind the courtroom and those sitting in the trees outside that this is an official hearing of a court of the United States of America. You are present by the sufferance of this court, and we can rescind that privilege at any time."

George Kimmel had little idea what Judge Snyder meant and guessed that neither did most of the crowd, but his words created their desired effect. In the ensuing calm, Snyder motioned for both teams of lawyers to approach the bench. The crowd strained in an attempt to overhear the discussion between the lawyers and the three judges. LeBlond handed Snyder a page, and the judge read it before handing it off to the defense. They spoke amongst themselves in disappointingly low voices. After some time, the teams returned to their seats, and Snyder called on Absalom to stand and address the court. After being nudged by the lawyer nearest him, Absalom stood hunched before the judge.

As Snyder spoke, he held up the sheet of paper. "Absalom Kimmel, the prosecution has submitted this confession it claims was deposed by you at noon today. Do you confirm the veracity of this claim?" Absalom stared blankly at Snyder, then looked over at the defense lawyers. They shook their heads at him, and he turned and looked helplessly at George and his other brothers. "Absalom Kimmel," said Snyder, clearly irritated, "did you confess to Sheriff Thornton Spriggs and Prosecuting Attorney William Miller?" Absalom nodded. "Speak up, son."

"Yeah … yes," said Absalom. Once again, conversation ruffled the air. Snyder hammered it into stillness. He again addressed Absalom, "And did these two, as the defense claims, hold out inducements in return for your confession?"

Again, Absalom stared back at Snyder. The judge sighed audibly. "Dang it, boy, did the sheriff offer to make a deal with you?"

Absalom's face cleared. "Yes, sir. He said I could go home if I signed his paper."

"And are you aware of the contents of the paper you signed?" asked Snyder.

Absalom turned around and looked back at the sheriff, who was seated back behind them to the right of the room. George noticed the sheriff nodded at Absalom.

"Well?" asked Snyder.

"I guess so," said Absalom. "I mean, yes."

"Can you even read?" asked Snyder.

George saw Absalom's ears turn red. "Yes."

"And did you read this document?" asked Snyder, gesturing with the paper. Absalom didn't move. Snyder waited a good ten seconds before sighing audibly. "You may sit down, son," he said. The judges huddled together. After a few minutes, Judge Snyder banged his gavel for quiet and addressed the room. "The court sustains the objections of the defense. This confession will not be considered as evidence in this case."

At this the crowd shouted threats against the defendants, the defense team, and the judges. Snyder banged and banged his gavel repeatedly for silence. Finally, the room quieted enough for him to be heard.

"The court reminds this audience that the judges may at any time exercise their right to clear the room and conduct this hearing in private." Shouts pealed across the room at this. "And then you and your wives will have plenty to complain about. Sheriff, stand by!"

‹—•◦—◦—◦•—›

"The Brutal Murder at Celina. Capture of the Murderers." *Van Wert Bulletin*. July 5, 1872

Absalom Kimble, another member of this family, now under arrest, voluntarily confesses that he, with Andrew McCloud and others whom he refuses to name, met Mary Secore on her way home from Sabbath school in the deadening of a strip of woods. They approached and enticed her into a thicket, some distance from the road, and there McCloud seized her, choked her until she fell feinting. They tore off her clothing, and committed the fiendish deed. During its commission, the unconscious victim showed signs of reviving, when McCloud again choked her. He left her for dead, but, on looking back, he perceived signs of life, and, with the exclamation of "What, not dead yet? Damn you, I'll settle you!" he struck the murderous blow with a heavy stick of wood, breaking her skull.

"Horrible Crime." *Cincinnati Commercial Tribune*. July 3, 1872

At this sickening spectacle Absalom Kimble says, "I could stand it no longer, and walked off." This confession was ruled out on some technicality, at the preliminary examination held at Celina on the 30th.

‹—•◦—◦—◦•—›

Tiffin, Ohio—June 23, 2017

David Kimmel

Sorting through a tangle of reports, rumors, and conjectures is a challenge, so it might prove helpful to summarize the basic facts of the murder. At nine o'clock on Sunday morning, June 23, 1872, thirteen-year-old Mary Arabelle Secaur left the home of her foster parents, John and Sarah Sitterly, for Sunday school, heading east on what is now Tama Road, to the Liberty United Brethren Church just two miles from home.[2] The service following Sunday school ended at noon, and Mary walked west with a large group of parishioners, including one or two of her brothers and her grandfather, Strouse May.[3] The body split at the first crossroads (now Erastus-Durban Road), some heading south and some north. Mary, her grandfather, and "two little girls" continued west. After crossing the bed of a branch of Little Black Creek, the party reached Strouse May's house, where he remained at his front gate to watch the girls home.[4] "A few rods further on," Mary left the little girls at their home, probably that of C. E. Stephans,[5] and her grandfather watched her walk west, her feet undoubtedly kicking up dust into the dry air,[6] until she disappeared from view in a slight depression.[7] A neighbor just down the road later reported having seen her pass by "at about half past twelve."[8] This was the last time her family or friends saw Mary alive.

Assuming that Mary had stayed on at her grandparents' after church, the Sitterlys began to worry about Mary only when she failed to return by the next morning.[9] After inquiring at the Mays' home and then around the neighborhood, John Sitterly gathered neighbors to help look for his foster daughter. A search party of twelve to fifteen men set out from the church around noon, retracing Mary's steps and inquiring at each house along the way.[10] It took four hours before G. W. Meizner found her body within two feet of a thicket just off the road near the Sitterlys' house.[11] Strouse May later described the body as "horribly mangled" with the head "entirely separated from the body" and the skull "crushed in and parts of it gone."[12] The body had lain in the late-June heat for over twenty-seven hours, and the neighborhood's free-ranging hogs had fed on the corpse. Her parasol and testament lay nearby, along with a heavy, bloodied club.[13] Mary's pink church dress was found "fast to the body around the waist"; the rest of her clothing was near her body.[14]

▸─◆─○─◆─◂

Mercer County Courthouse, Celina, Mercer County, Ohio—Sunday, June 30, 1872

Eventually, the crowd's agitation dropped, and the prosecution was able to begin its exhaustive examination of evidence and witnesses. The testimony began tamely enough, with an account of Mary Secaur's last morning delivered by the girl's grandfather. The crowd then leaned forward expectantly as Joseph Steen, a local painter and part of what George's father called "the Hinton crowd," told the court about seeing the girl's body when George Meizner found it Monday afternoon.

"I seen her dead in the thicket, on the road between Strouse May's and John Sitterly's on the north side of the road at the southeast corner of a wheat field." Steen paused for a moment, as if considering whether to continue or what to include in his account. "How much you want? It's terrible stuff, and not the sort of thing to discuss before ladies." The air in the room rustled with voices and whispers.

"Go ahead, Mr. Steen," said LeBlond. "Anyone here, male or female, should know what to expect from the testimony."

"Yes, sir. Well, I knew her body when I seen it. I mean to say that I knew whose body it was. Now, here's the awful part; I still have dreams about this. It was torn and eaten by hogs, the head was off and all in pieces. I found the under jaw and back part of skull. There was no flesh on either of them. The skull looked like it had been broken by a heavy club." The buzzing quieted to a barely audible whisper.

"I see," said LeBlond. "Now, what happened to the body after its discovery?"

"We left the body lay until a jury of six men was summoned to hold an inquest. I was at the inquest, and I never saw the body afterward."

"One more question, Mr. Steen. How was the body attired when you discovered it?"

"Her clothing was torn off, and most of it laid at her side, partly under her. A pink dress was fast to the body around the waist." Steen finished looking less confident and smug than he had at the beginning of his testimony. Articulating what he had seen and done the week before seemed to make it more real for him.

George imagined the scene, and it turned his stomach. It was better not to think too much about it. He would never be able to go up there if he started to consider the girl. Still, as one witness after another was called forward, George felt ill and couldn't keep his mind away from the images Steen had described.

Unbidden and unwanted, the image of his younger sister, Sarah, came to his mind. He saw her lying in the bushes, her dress torn off, her head scattered around the field. George chased the thought from his head. Blood and death were nothing new to him. He had slaughtered plenty of animals in his lifetime. Still, those fingers with the bite marks. He looked out of the corner of his eye at his brothers and McLeod. McLeod sat impassively, taking it all in. Absalom at that moment was staring up at the ceiling, his mouth hanging open. George looked around the guard at Jake, who watched the testimony. Then Jake turned, and George jerked his eyes to the floor. He couldn't stand to have Jake look at him that way.

⊱•⊰

"Child Found Dead." *Mercer County Standard*. June 27, 1872

A jury was impaneled on Monday by Esq. Hinton, who made report that the deceased came to her death by the hands of some person unknown.

James H. Day, *Lynched!*

The remains were then gathered up and taken to the house of Mr. Citterly and kept until the next day, Tuesday, June 25th, when they were taken to the Liberty Chapel Church yard, and, in the presence of a large concourse of people and her sorrowing friends, were entombed close by the grave of her mother.[15]

"The Liberty Township Murder." Celina Journal. July 4, 1872

On Wednesday of last week it was deemed prudent to hold a physicians' post mortem examination, and for that purpose Drs. Jones, Parrott, Touvelle, Miller, Richardson, and Brandon, together with Sheriff Spriggs, Prosecuting Attorney Miller, a Journal reporter, and several others from Celina, repaired to the scene....

When the body was found, the hogs had made a sickening, mangled mass of her once beautiful form. And at the grave, when her body was exhumed for the purpose of examination, it presented the most revolting, sickening, and horrid specimen of inhuman butchery that eye ever gazed upon. One could not long look upon her without thinking from his inmost soul, that death, however it may be given, could not appease this most damnable murder, "foul and unnatural."

It is the accepted opinion that she fought hard and bravely for her chastity, receiving severe blows on her arms and body, as in self-defense, there being three scars on the left arm, having been given fully six hours before death. After their more than beastly passions were satiated, death was the next surest thing to silence the crime they had already committed. The skull was beaten and broken into fragments by a huge club, which was found and had the appearance of such use. A few pieces of the skull and jaw bone were found some 15 feet from the body with the flesh and everything eaten off. The throat showed unmistakable signs of being cut, to "make assurance doubly sure," and the neck was eaten and torn into shreds. Her body was entirely nude, the abdomen and entrails being torn and destroyed—her hands and arms were chewed, scratched, and mangled; finger-nail marks were visible on the right shoulder, and the breast, near the right collarbone, was struck with some heavy instrument after life had passed away. These latter suppositions are the opinions of the physicians, who made the examination for the purpose of establishing the fact that she was killed by human violence, which is beyond a doubt. The examination was conducted in a proper legal form.

⊱─◦─⊰

Liberty Township, Mercer County, Ohio—Saturday, June 23, 1877

Daniel Mahoney[16]

That Wednesday following the murder, the women occupied the center of the crossroads, as was their due. Across from us and beyond the women stood a group of older boys and young men, whose loud and boisterous talk carried over to us on the evening air. We squatted in a rough semicircle at the edge of the weed and brush, picking at pebbles in the silence broken occasionally by a hawk and a spit ... or a sentence. While the women were discussing the rumors and tales that made their way up the pike from the hearing in Celina, we were debating the same.

Wright and Harmon had walked the mile from the next crossroads at the township line. They told us their neighbors across the line were worked up and ready for action, only looking to us to hand up the guilty parties.

"Hand over them criminals, and the boys'll take care of the rest," said Wright.

"*Oui*, but who are the criminals?" asked Harmon.

"That's easy enough to tell," said Wright, nodding up the road toward the Kimmels' homestead. "There's only one family ornery enough for this business."

"Careful, now," said Wells. "They's kin of my Sarah, may she rest in peace."

"They already questioned Absalom. He's got the alibi," I said.

"That was Anselman they questioned, not Absalom," said Wells. "You got your facts cockeyed."

"Anselman, who lives by Leininger?" asked Harmon. "Which Anselman? Not the old man?"

"Charles, the queer one," said Wells.

"No, it was Absalom, I'm sure of it," I said. "Your own Arrela told my Johanna," I said to Wells.

"I can't account for everything our wives get mixed up in their heads," said Wells, and the group laughed. "It was Anselman, or I'm an Irishman. Oh, sorry."

I ignored the slight. "But why Anselman?"

Wells looked toward the women and lowered his voice. "Some say the girl and him was more than neighbors."

"Careful what you say about my niece," said May. "That girl was my sister's daughter and pure as the driven snow. Anyone says otherwise is going to answer to me."

"Of course, Elias, easy. I didn't say I believed it. It was just what I heard," said Wells. He carefully avoided eye contact with May.

"This ain't about Anselman, no how," said Wright. "He proved his alibi. He was at their place all afternoon, so he couldn't a hurt the girl, even if he had reason." He said this last with a slight challenge to his voice, directed at May. "There's only one family around wicked enough for something like this."

Wells looked thoughtful at this, but he kept silent.

"It was Absalom had the alibi. The sheriff stopped there Tuesday, and he seemed satisfied with the boy's story," I said.

"There's more Kimmels than Absalom," said Wright.

"And there was the tin peddlers," said May.

"That's right. They showed up Saturday night," said Wells. "Thomas said he saw them with the Kimmel boys at the election."

"These peddlers, who were they?" asked Harmon.

"Henry Kimmel's nephew from over the line in Indiana," said Wells. "Plus some other feller from Fort Wayne."

"I seen them on their way out of the state Monday morning," said May. "Heading west about six or seven, near Jacob Leininger's. They had two wagons. The stranger and Jacob was together; the nephew and Absalom was in the other wagon."

"Yeah," said Wright. "Why would they pull stakes so early and head out of state?"

"Troth, May was out that early," I suggested. The group made immediate unhappy sounds at that.

"What are you saying?" asked May, a slight edge to his voice.

"Nothing, only it doesn't seem so odd tin peddlers would be on the road at seven in the morning," I said.

"But with them two Kimmel boys?" asked Wright.

"Who was with the stranger at church on Sunday," said May. "I seen them with my own eyes. Nine or ten in the morning at Sunday school—with the rest of the Christians in the neighborhood."

I kept my own peace at that insult. Our Catholicism was a sore point amongst my neighbors, especially Harmon. Huguenots have long memories.

"My Thomas says he seen the stranger and Absalom together at church," said Wright. "This was pert near eleven o'clock. He seen them go across the road into the woods and come back again. They both left church together, at least a half hour before it was out. Bill and Jake was at church, too."

"To think the murderers were at our own church, and on what is my land, after all!" said Harmon.

"Going to church don't make nobody a murderer," said Wells.

"Aye is it. 'Tis any one of us it could be . . . or our sons," I said, and I immediately regretted speaking. The group turned a chill wind onto me. Harmon, Wright, Wells, and May—they all had sons in their late teens and early twenties. My own son being nine made my comment an accusation.

May spoke first. "I seen Jacob and Absalom watering horses at two or three in the afternoon, Sunday."

The group considered the fact. "It would give them enough time to commit the murder and return home," said Harmon.

"What if they was washing at the pump and not just watering horses?" asked Wright.

"That's right," said May.

"Wait, but you said … ," I started but was shouted down.

"They was at the pump with McLeod, washing something off their hands, wasn't it?" asked Wright.

"Washing at the pump, that's serious," said Harmon. "And they were seen leaving church early. Did anyone see them after church?"

"They was mixed in with the crowd walking west," said Wright.

"But did anyone see them?" asked Wells.

"They was there," said May. "And then headed out west at crack of dawn the next day. The question is, what do we do about it?"

Our conversation halted as we noticed Hinton and Hengel walking toward us from the south. Far off behind them I could see clots of men and women standing at the next crossroads. The pair squatted down among us, and the group stared at the dirt a moment before Hinton spoke. "Gentlemen, this is evil business, grim business." We all grunted in acknowledgment. "We have the murder of one of our dear sweet girls, a belle of the neighborhood. When I think of my little Effie or my sister, Mary, or my wife or my mother …" He paused for effect, knowing he had our attention. "Or your daughters or wives. I opine there's not one member of the fairer sex in this township—in the whole county—who's safe with such chicanery on the loose."

"But how do we know who done it?" asked Wells.

"Quite sure we know!" said Hengel, his thick German accent emphasizing each word. He pointed meaningfully up the road. "We all know where the threat is. There is only one family do this." We all looked up the road in the direction he pointed. A dip in the road just before it reached Kimmel's homestead kept it from view.

"But there are no witnesses," I said. I winced. When would I learn to keep my own mouth shut?

"They were seen at church and after church walking in the direction of the murder," said Harmon.

"And washing at the pump in the afternoon," said Wright.

"Washing at the pump?" asked Hinton. "That's a considerable important clue. I'll be sure the sheriff hears of that."

"And I seen them heading out of state Monday morning," said May. "And Jake and Absalom was with them."

"This here Absalom is really a scourge," said Hengel. "It is not one of us who cares not for our women when that man-child roams the forest. And the other boys are not much better from the upbringing they had."

Hinton cleared his throat. "If we are ever to rise above the beasts of the field, we will need to excise our community of such as the Kimmels. Drunken, shiftless, lecherous, violent—I think we all know what any Kimmel is capable of. And a traveling tin peddler! He may be carrying out his designs on other unsuspecting innocents this very minute. If he's brazen enough to attack a maiden at high noon on the Sabbath—within yards of her own front door—there's little that will stop him but the hangman's noose. While we parry here, I tell you, the guilty are laughing at us. Gentlemen, this is a struggle for civilization against anarchy and bestiality."

There were sounds of approval from Wright, Harmon, and May at this. I looked at Wells, who squatted silently. The sun had set completely, and the darkness was growing thick. It was becoming difficult to make out anything beyond our immediate circle but the whites of our women's clothes.

"We must now act!" said Hengel, his voice louder than necessary. He pounded his fist into his open palm on the last word.

"It's too late for anything now," said Wells. "Anyway, we can't take the law into our own hands."

"Of course not," said Hinton. "Let the law take its course. It's what sets us apart from the likes of the Kimmels, after all. But we must hurry, or the law won't have that chance. The law moves slowly, but the criminals move quickly." There was a murmur of agreement. "I'll ride off to town in the dark to notify the sheriff. It's my duty as justice of the peace. Then he can set off west to find the peddlers in the morning."

With that, we broke up and reformed into family knots on our ways back to our homes.

<hr />

A $500 reward—that, whereas, a most horrible and atrocious outrage and murder was committed on the person of one Mary Secaur, a young lady of thirteen years of age, in Liberty Township, Mercer County, Ohio, on June 23, 1872, I, therefore, offer a reward of $500 for the apprehension and conviction of the perpetrator or perpetrators of said crime.

Thornton Spriggs,
Sheriff of Mercer Co., Ohio.
Celina, Ohio, June 26, 1872[17]

<hr />

Tiffin, Ohio—June 23, 2017

David Kimmel

Sheriff Thornton Spriggs and a small group of deputies—D. T. Spriggs, William Johnson, and William Moore—raced off Thursday morning,[18] catching up with the peddlers Friday morning in the center of Fort Wayne's business district.[19] Spriggs and his men hustled McLeod and Andrew Kimmel back to Ohio, stopping on their way through Liberty Township to arrest Absalom Kimmel and two of his brothers—seventeen-year-old Jacob and sixteen-year-old George—at the crossroads near the family farm before locking all five men in the Celina jail at around nine o'clock in the evening.[20]

<hr />

Indiana Herald. July 10, 1872[21]

On last Friday morning, about half-past 8 o'clock, four men rode up Calhoun street in an open carriage at a rapid pace, and, when at the corner of Washington street, two of them alighted and presented their revolvers at the heads of two individuals who were passing by. The two persons accompanied the others to the carriage, which was driven off in a southerly direction at an almost break-neck gait. This was a somewhat remarkable affair, to say the least, to take place in broad day light on the principal street of the city; and a Gazette reporter set to work diligently to learn the circumstances before speaking of the matter, and after two days' active search succeeded in getting a clue to the arrest. . . .

Several detective officers, induced by the reward [for the murderers of Mary Secaur], went to work to get a clue to the villains who had committed the crime, and have already succeeded in arresting five persons suspected of complicity in the affair, two of whom are the parties taken in this city on Friday. These fellows are named respectfully Alexander McCloud and A. J. Kimmel. The former has been in the employ of A. J. Dillingham, Rag and Tinware Dealer, for about a year, as the "conductor" of a peddler wagon, and the latter has been acting in the same capacity since last autumn. They were out with their wagons in Ohio, last Sabbath, which seems to lend color to their alleged participation in the outrage.

Both of them have been regarded by Mr. Dillingham as good men, Kimmel being a son of Dr. Kimmel, of Huntington. The detective officers who made the arrest managed the affair with great pluck and nerve especially considering the probable fact that they had no legal authority to take the men, not having any requisition on the Governor.

◦──◦──◦──◦

Tiffin, Ohio—June 23, 2017

David Kimmel

Andrew Kimmel secured his release from prison Saturday morning, June 29, by signing an affidavit against the other four being held for trial and posting $500 bond toward an appearance at the next district circuit court session in November.[22] On Sunday, a special preliminary examination of the case against Alexander McLeod and Absalom Kimmel convened in the county courthouse. The packed courtroom heard testimony from Mary Secaur's relatives, from members of the search party that found her body, from the doctors who conducted the autopsy, from the sheriff and one of his deputies, and from Andrew and George Kimmel.[23]

◦──◦──◦──◦

Celina, Mercer County, Ohio—June 30, 1872

The testimony continued on into the late afternoon. The prosecution's interminable discussion of the bloody ribbon had becalmed the audience, but they fluttered with new interest when LeBlond called Andrew Kimmel, the cousin of the accused who had turned state's evidence against McLeod and Jacob, Absalom, and George Kimmel. As he walked to the stand, Andy looked over at George and gave him a weak smile. George was puzzled at this, just as he had been puzzled by the news that Andy had testified against them all in return for his freedom. *Don't think for a moment that we'll forget this*, thought George.

Andy, who wore a clean shirt and had shaved and combed his hair recently, was questioned methodically by LeBlond about his occupation, his partnership with McLeod, the bloody ribbon found on McLeod's bridle, his memories of the comings and goings of the defendants on the Sunday of the murder, and their departure for Indiana on Monday morning. Eventually, LeBlond stepped down to be replaced by Murlin, head of the defense team.

"Mr. Kimmel, could you please explain why you included George Kimmel in your affidavit against the Kimmels? Do you infer that he was guilty of the crime?"

"I did not mean that George Kimmel was guilty. I objected to making the affidavit against George, but Miller told me it was only a form and the only object was to get at the guilty parties; with that understanding, I filed the affidavit." George felt relieved. He had always liked Andy, and he had been shocked when he found out that it was Andy's testimony that had led to his arrest. He missed Murlin's next question, but he refocused just in time to hear Andy say, "I sat next to McLeod at dinner; I did not see any blood on his shirt at that time." With that, Andy left the stand, and George started at his own name ringing out loudly in the courtroom.

⊢⊷⊶⊙⊷⊶⊣

"The Secor Murder. Interview with A. J. Kimmel."
Indiana Herald. July 10, 1872

On Monday, it was reported that he had returned to his home near this place; and we believing it desirable that the gross misrepresentations of the facts which had appeared in the daily papers should be corrected, at our request Andrew J. Kimmel called at this office on Monday evening, and made the statements upon which this article is based.

His parents live at the old toll-gate on the Warren plank-road, a little over a mile from Huntington. He has been employed for some time driving a peddling-wagon for A. J. Dillingham, of Ft. Wayne. On the Thursday previous to the murder (June 20), he went to Ohio with his wagon. About 4 p.m. on Friday, at a cross-road, some four miles from the scene of the murder, he accidentally met Alexander McCloud, who was driving another of Dillingham's teams, and with whom he was well acquainted. It was their custom to meet—according to the exigencies of their business—sometimes once a week, and at others from two to four weeks; but this meeting was purely accidental. Being in the neighborhood of the residence of Henry Kimmel, Andrew's uncle, they drove thither, and remained over night. Saturday morning, Andrew hitched in his team and got ready to leave, paying his bill; but yielded to the solicitations of his relatives to remain over the Sabbath.

On Saturday, they attended a railroad election in Liberty township, returning to his uncle's about five or six o'clock in the afternoon, remained about the premises all evening, and slept there. Andrew slept with McCloud on the nights of Friday and Saturday. Sunday morning, June [23], (the day of the murder) McCloud, together with seven members of Henry Kimmel's family—boys and girls—went to Sunday School at Liberty Church, and all remained to hear the preaching. Andrew, being ill with neuralgia, stayed at the house. At about half-past eleven a.m. he was sitting on the porch talking with his uncle, when his cousin Absalom Kimmel and McCloud returned to the house together, leaving the rest of the party which had accompanied them at the church. In reply to an inquiry, McCloud said they were tired of the preaching. Directly afterward, Andrew went upstairs, and feeling unwell, lay down on the bed, without removing his clothing. About 12 o'clock, noon, the rest of the party returned from church, and it is Andrew's opinion that at that time McCloud and Absalom Kimmel had left the house, although, from his being upstairs, he cannot positively assert that such was the case. About 2 p.m., they returned, and it is supposed the murder was committed between these hours—12 p.m. and 2 p.m.—but it was not discovered until Monday.

They stayed at Henry Kimmel's that night, leaving on Monday morning, the murder being yet unknown, and Andrew ignorant that anything of the kind had occurred.

[Andrew tells of their sales trip through eastern Indiana, ending in Fort Wayne Thursday evening.] The next morning, between eight and nine o'clock, they were arrested on Calhoun street, Ft. Wayne, by the sheriff of Mercer county and three deputies. McCloud was inclined to resist the officers, while Andrew advised submission, saying they had done nothing which need make them afraid to go anywhere. They were forced into the vehicle, McCloud cursing and protesting, and saying when some three miles out of the city, that he thought there was "some

G-d d—d mob." At Decatur they got dinner, and were separated—the party proceeding in two buggies, one of the prisoners being carried in each. They passed through Wilshire, Van Wert County, Ohio, and proceeded at once to the scene of the murder, shortly before reaching which McCloud was handcuffed. Throughout the entire trip he had been rebellious, profane and saucy. Arrived at the scene of the murder, McCloud became somewhat excited, and avowed, in substance, that he had "never committed murder or adultery on that bloody spot." It must be borne in mind that all this time the officers had not acquainted either of the men with the cause of their arrest—so Andrew says—and that up to this time he had not known of a murder having been committed. From this place they were taken to Celina, where a preliminary examination was held, and Andrew released, without having been confined in jail at all, as was incorrectly stated in some of the newspapers. He was put under $500 bond to appear at the fall term of court, as a witness, and left for home last Saturday. We believe the people of the whole county will rejoice with him and his family over the manner in which his innocence has been vindicated.

Very naturally he is anxious that the misrepresentations which have been circulated through the papers should be corrected. The statement that Henry Kimmel's family were "notoriously bad characters," as was published, was proven by the testimony of his neighbors to be false. They were all dismissed from custody, with the exception of Absalom Kimmel, who, with McCloud, is confined in the Celina jail. These two are the only ones now held for the crime. It is said Absalom has made a confession or statement to two persons, but up to the time of Andrew's departure it had not been made public. One newspaper account states that a ribbon—subsequently identified as one worn by the girl—was found attached to Andrew's bridle. This he denies, and says that the ribbon referred to in the papers was picked up from the ground—on what he afterward learned to be the scene of the murder—by one of his cousins, who handed it to McCloud, and that the latter fastened it to the bridle of one of his own horses, where it was afterward found, in Ft. Wayne, by a deputy sheriff from Mercer county.

Concerning the murder, Andrew knows nothing further than was elicited by the testimony given by various parties at the preliminary trial. The late hour at which this point was reached in our interview with him, prevented his giving the facts to us with any fullness, or our making notes of what he did say.

⊱⦿⊰

Celina, Mercer County, Ohio—June 30, 1872

Comments riffled through the room as George Kimmel made his way to the witness stand. He looked across at Deputy Johnson and Sheriff Spriggs. Johnson gave him a you-know-what-to-say nod. George's mouth tasted metallic, and he unsuccessfully sucked at the back of his throat in a vain attempt to generate some moisture. He knew what he had to do, but he was scared to do it in front of this big crowd. LeBlond asked him to recount the events of last Sunday. It was now or never.

"I was at home on Sunday with Andy Kimmel." So far, so good. "McLeod was at the house all day; he was not off the place." The room stilled a moment as the crowd processed this new information. LeBlond stared at George blankly. Now time for the bombshell. "I had no conversation with Absalom or McLeod about murdering the girl." Conversation skittered about the audience. Had George said what they thought they had heard? In the midst of the turbulence, LeBlond staggered to the prosecution's table, where he was greeted with the agitated voices of the other lawyers.

George found himself confronted with Murlin, who nodded appreciatively and pitched his voice grandly into the room. "George, you've caused quite a commotion. Could you please explain your last statement in light of your signed deposition regarding the case in question?"

George knew Murlin was only asking this to get him to say what they had discussed the day before. George began, and the rustling hushed as the people strained to hear. "I was arrested and put in jail on Friday. Saturday morning, Dan Spriggs and Bill Johnson took me out of jail and took me to the woods. When they got into the woods, they threatened to hang me. I knew they had no rope and was not afraid of hanging." He looked over at Johnson, who was giving him an evil look. "They then said they would kill me in three minutes if I didn't tell all about the murder. They had revolvers in their pockets, and I was afraid they would kill me unless I told something, so I told them that Ab and McLeod had told me that they had all the fun they wanted with the girl, and that they killed her afterward. All I told Spriggs and Johnson was a lie to get rid of them." Murlin returned to the defense table.

LeBlond was back, and this time he seemed collected and prepared. "Mr. Kimmel, would you please explain yourself? Am I to believe that you are recanting a sworn statement you made in front of several reliable witnesses?"

George spoke straight at LeBlond. "All I told Spriggs and Johnson was a lie. I saw McLeod and Absalom washing at the pump at about two o'clock. I told Spriggs and Johnson that the boys said they had killed the girl, and that they first had all the fun they wanted. I never had heard the story before but made it up as I went along."

LeBlond stared at George with a displeased look on his face. George continued. "I told them I saw blood on McLeod's shirt. That part was not a lie; I did see blood on his shirt. That was true, and it was true that they washed at the pump. McLeod took one shirt off in the afternoon, and after he came back at one o'clock or after, he put a striped shirt on over the one he had on. There was blood on the one he had on."

LeBlond no longer had the sick look on his face as he dismissed George from the stand. Back on the bench, McLeod and Jake nodded to George as he approached. Absalom stared down at his hands resting in his lap. George settled into his seat to see LeBlond questioning the sheriff on the stand.

Spriggs looked confidently at the defendants as he spoke in answer to some question by LeBlond. "We found them Friday morning in Fort Wayne, Indiana, and made the arrest. On our way there, we agreed among ourselves not to tell them what they were arrested for or to say anything in their presence from which they could infer the cause of their arrest or to what place they were to be taken to. I did not tell them, nor did anyone else to my knowledge."

LeBlond looked relieved at the sheriff's performance. "Sheriff Spriggs, could you please tell the court about the actual arrest?"

"We first saw them, McLeod and A. J. Kimmel, at the business house of Dellingham, in Fort Wayne. They seemed to be in a great hurry. We met them on the street and arrested them at once. I saw nothing wrong with Andy, but McLeod jumped back, tried to get away, and called for his friends to assist him. We forced him into our wagon and immediately started for home."

"Sheriff, did you notice any blood on the defendant's clothing at this time?"

"As soon as we got under way, I examined McLeod critically for marks of blood." Spriggs held out his own wrist to demonstrate. "He saw me, and at once turned up the wristbands of his shirt. I saw blood on his right wristband. He was greatly agitated and quivered awfully, as though he had an ague."

"Was there any other blood on his person?"

"I also saw blood on one of his boots—the left one, I think—and on his pants. He tried to cover up the blood on his boot by placing his other boot over it. The blood on his pants looked to me as though he had attempted to wash it off."

LeBlond seemed satisfied. "Sheriff, was McLeod made aware of the charges against him when he was arrested?"

"At Decatur, we stopped nearly half a mile out of town, for fear if we took him into town while we were getting fresh teams, he might hear what crime he was charged with and why he was under arrest. We were very careful at all times that they should hear nothing of a murder having been committed, and I am sure no one told them in my presence or hearing."

Spriggs performed like a trained dog, every statement conforming to LeBlond's leading questions. The two were a perfect team. "Sheriff, did McLeod make any incriminating statements during the ride from Indiana?"

"After we left Decatur, I asked McLeod where he was on Sunday. He halted, quivered again, and then evaded the question and did not answer. He told me afterward that he was at Kimmel's on Sunday and was with Andy all the time. Then he said he was at church and came away before it was out. Then he said Andy was not at church. He contradicted himself several times."

LeBlond turned partway to the audience and said loudly, "He contradicted himself!" He paused for dramatic effect and then returned to Spriggs. "Please tell the court about McLeod's behavior at the scene of the crime."

"When we neared the residence of John Sitterly, William Moore came forward from the rear carriage, and said, 'Andy has told us all about it.' McLeod trembled, cried, and said, 'My God, it can't be possible Andy has gone back on me,' and he was terribly agitated. McLeod said to me, 'I didn't hurt the gal.'"

LeBlond let this statement sink in before asking, "And this was at the murder site?"

Spriggs shook his head. "He said this before we got to the place of the tragedy. When we got there, he stared at the spot intently."

"He stared right at the murder scene without any explanation on your part?" Spriggs nodded, and LeBlond asked, "Could you please tell the court of McLeod's behavior on the ground at the murder site?"

"I then took him to the place," said Spriggs. "He cried bitterly and said he was innocent. I told him then that we knew all about the matter, and he'd better tell the truth."

"And how did McLeod react to this news?"

"When I said this, he turned to the fence of a field nearby crying and said, 'I never committed adultery here or anything else. I never saw this bloody spot before.' There was no blood on the ground that could be seen."

Again, LeBlond turned to the crowd and spoke in a voice pitched for the farthest reaches of his audience. "So, McLeod, unprompted by you, mentioned adultery *and* called the scene of the murder a 'bloody spot'?" He paused before continuing. "About what time was it now, and where did you travel next?"

Spriggs looked thoughtful for a moment. "I'd estimate it was around six o'clock when we left the murder scene. We then drove on to Henry Kimmel's house and stopped. While at the Kimmels', he pled earnestly for a few minutes private talk with Kimmel, which I refused. After we left Kimmel's, I turned on him very suddenly and said, 'McLeod, who was with you out in the woods about two o'clock on Sunday?' He seemed to be frustrated and faltered out, 'Ja-Jake-Abs.' We then went on south about a half-mile and arrested the other three Kimmel boys. When he saw the boys, he was very anxious to have a short, private talk with them, and asked me to allow him the privilege, which of course I refused."

"Naturally," said LeBlond. "Sheriff Spriggs, I'd like to thank you for your direct and informative answers. No further questions, Your Honor."

"But I'm not done, yet," said Spriggs. The crowd reacted with a rumble of comment. LeBlond was already three steps toward his seat when Spriggs halted him in his tracks. He turned back to the sheriff, who looked pleased with himself. "I have more evidence."

"It looks like a day for surprises," said Judge Snyder to laughter from the room. "Mr. LeBlond, please return to your witness." More chuckles.

LeBlond walked back to Spriggs a little warily. "You have more for us, Sheriff?" he said for the room to hear. "What are you doing?" George heard him whisper to Spriggs.

Spriggs rummaged around in his jacket and pulled out a large penknife. "This!" he said dramatically as he pulled open the blade and held it up for the room to see. There was clearly blood on the large blade. Conversation burst from the crowd.

"Objection!" Murlin was on his feet instantly. The crowd grew louder.

Snyder held up a hand to Murlin and conferred silently with the other two justices. Finally, he said, "Objection overruled, at least for now. Let's see how the cat jumps."

LeBlond, still perplexed by the sheriff's behavior, stood staring at the knife for a moment before shaking himself and saying, "And what is this that we're looking at, Sheriff Spriggs?"

Snyder spoke. "Looks like a knife to me." The crowd laughed.

Spriggs looked intently around the room. "I took this knife from the pocket of McLeod when I arrested him. And that's not all." He reached back into his pocket and fished out a pocket handkerchief, which he waved open with a flourish. The red-patterned handkerchief was spotted with brown dots. "There's this!"

LeBlond looked about ready to give up. The crowd oohed and aahed. Murlin jumped to his feet.

"Objection, Your Honors! A witness can't just produce evidence that's been withheld from the court." The crowd lulled slightly, listening for Snyder's reaction.

"Objection sustained," said Snyder. Boos moaned through the crowd. "Sheriff Spriggs, what are you driving at?"

"I'm producing evidence of bloody articles found on McLeod," said the sheriff.

"This is highly irregular," said Snyder.

The crowd, convinced Snyder was preventing the sheriff from submitting what was obviously important evidence, roared into the faces of the judges.

"Fix!"

"Cheats!"

"Accept it!"

"Lynch them all!"

Snyder banged his gavel, but its sharp retort was echoed back in loud and angry threats that blew in from those lining the open windows and tree limbs outside the courthouse. Snyder huddled with the other two judges, their animated conversation a pantomime amid the commotion. Finally, Snyder banged his gavel and held up a hand for silence. He looked over at the sheriff, who shrugged at him. Snyder's gavel again beat the audience into silence.

"The court has decided that, though irregular, the sheriff may admit his evidence." Again a blast of shouting. Again Snyder's gavel. Murlin yelled his objections over the crowd.

"Murlin, sit down, or I'll hold you in contempt of this court," shouted Snyder, and the crowd applauded. "Now, let's have some order in this madhouse. Mr. LeBlond, are you finished with the witness?"

LeBlond, looking stunned at this odd turn of events, simply waved vaguely at the judge and returned to his seat.

Murlin approached the witness box. He looked dispirited. "Sheriff Spriggs, when did you inform the defendant, McLeod, of the charges against him?"

Spriggs said, "I did not tell McLeod that a girl had been murdered or anything in reference to it until we got within a half a mile of Celina, when I read the handbill offering a reward for the murderers to him. He told me that he did not hear what the crime was before that."

"No further questions, Your Honors," said Murlin, who returned to his seat.

As Sheriff Spriggs left the stand, George felt his insides drain from him. George hazarded a look over at Spriggs, who stared back at him with a "That settles that!" look. Spriggs seemed so sure of himself, so confident. What if he were right? After all, George hadn't spoken directly with McLeod more than a few minutes, all told, since they'd been arrested.

George knew *he* hadn't done anything. That much was certain. But where had McLeod and Ab been last Sunday afternoon? Why did McLeod have blood on his shirt? George was sure of what he'd seen. And what about Jake? George had no memory of seeing any of the three before dinner. Why should George risk his own life to protect those doing nothing to defend themselves?

George tentatively raised a hand. It took a moment for Snyder to see him. Immediately on the judge gesturing to him with his gavel, George stood up, and the audience exclaimed loudly. Snyder held up a finger for George to wait, and George stood nervously as the judge gaveled and shouted for quiet and order. Finally, after Snyder yet again threatened to clear the court, the people quieted.

Snyder asked George to speak.

"Please, sir, I'd like to speak about my testimony."

"You mean that you want to add to your testimony or that you want to recant your testimony?"

"What's *recant*, sir?"

"To take back." There was a pause. "Well, speak up; we're not as young as when we started."

"I object, Your Honor!" It was Murlin, who had leapt to his feet and shouted out his objection. "My client is acting without counsel!"

"Your Honor, we must hear this boy out," said an equally loud LeBlond. He waved in the direction of the crowd. "The people demand the truth." A rumble ran through the room at this.

"I object, Your Honor!" said Murlin. "The prosecution is trying to incite the crowd." With this, the air around George whipped up into conversation, and the smell of violence came strong to his nose.

It took Snyder a full five minutes of gavel-banging, two conferences with the attorneys, and another threat to clear the court before the roar calmed into whispering, which scuttled along the outside walls like scraps of paper blown about by stray breaths of air.

The judge asked George to proceed to the stand and then speak.

George walked to the stand. His stomach heaved a bit as he realized that the entire audience was staring quietly at him. He tried not to look in the direction of Absalom, Jake, and McLeod. And he studiously avoided the back of the courtroom, where he knew his parents were watching and waiting. Instead, George looked over at Andy, who gave him a slight nod.

"On Sunday, June 23, at about three o'clock in the afternoon, McLeod told me that he struck and killed the girl; that he first had all the fun he wanted." Somehow, Snyder managed to bang the shouting and hooting into decorum.

George hesitated a second and then rushed through the rest. "Ab was with McLeod. There was blood on McLeod's shirt, and he washed it off at the pump."

Murlin was called to the stand to cross-examine George, and he immediately seized on the time issue. "Where were you when you had this alleged conversation? And at what time did it take place? Careful now—the truth is always easier to maintain than a lie."

"McLeod told me these things when he and I were trading watch chains," said George. "We were upstairs on a bed. It was after dinner."

Murlin tried to look friendly, but it was a tepid smile, almost a grimace. "Why would you find it necessary to change your testimony? Don't you know that perjury is a crime?"

"Perjury?" asked George.

"Perjury is lying to the court. You could go to jail for that."

George looked over at the judges. Snyder nodded, then added, "Just tell the truth, and there'll be no jail time. Go ahead."

"The reason I told a different story when I was first examined was because you lawyers," and here George pointed to Murlin and the defense team, "told me to go back on what I had told Johnson and Spriggs." Once more, Snyder hammered back the gale of objections blowing from the onlookers in the trees and the lawn surrounding the courthouse, through the windows and doors, and onto the suspects and lawyers.

Now Callen, Murlin, and Loughridge each took a turn on the stand. According to the defense lawyers, George had freely and clearly told them he had made false declarations to Spriggs and Johnson, and with that understanding they had advised him not to repeat his statements under oath but to tell the exact truth.

It was now eleven thirty. The defense team declined to introduce any evidence. The judges ordered Absalom and McLeod returned to prison to await the regular Circuit Court in November. Jake's hearing was delayed until after the Fourth of July holiday. He followed the others from the courtroom and across the street to the county jail.

George walked into the hot midnight a free man.

2

UNDERSTANDING

Tiffin, Ohio—June 23, 2017

David Kimmel

The subject of lynching dominated conversations throughout the week and through the Independence Day holiday. By the time Jacob Kimmel appeared before the court for his hearing at 9:00 a.m. on Friday, July 5, the audience crowded the courtroom in search of evidence to support a verdict and the sentence already settled in their minds. They very nearly carried out that sentence at the end of Jacob's hearing, when the prosecutors announced that Jacob wished to make an announcement regarding the case. Once again blindsided by one of their own clients, the defense attorneys jumped to their feet and objected to Jacob speaking to the court except through them. The crowd, thinking the lawyers were blocking Jacob from making any statement at all, exploded. While forty to fifty men rushed from the courthouse to the jail with the intent of removing McLeod and Absalom, the remainder surged toward the defense and their clients, demanding that Jacob be allowed to speak. Finally—and it was a near miss—the audience calmed down when the defense attorneys diplomatically suggested that Jacob should have his say.[1]

The crowd hushed as Jacob took the stand. His statement attempted to lay sole blame for the rape and murder on McLeod: "This feller told me at noon to-day that he had murdered the girl; that Absalom did not want to go with him, but he compelled him to go. He said Absalom did not lay hands on the girl. He also told me that he himself caught the girl and dragged or carried her into the woods."[2] With this testimony, Jacob was released and returned home on a $1500 recognizance for the Court of Common Pleas when it met in November.[3] Jacob's release brought the total to three suspects who had secured their release by testifying against McLeod.

Curiously, and though no physical evidence directly linked him to the crime, Absalom remained in jail. He had, it was true, offered up a confession to the prosecution before his own hearing on the previous Sunday, but that confession had been thrown out of court. Perhaps the authorities hoped further jail time would induce Absalom to repeat his confession. They got their wish at 11:00 p.m. on Sunday, July 7, when Absalom confessed before one of the judges, the sheriff, and the sheriff's son.[4] Longer and more detailed than any of the other testimony, Absalom's confession claimed that he and Jacob had assisted McLeod in raping Mary Secaur, but that McLeod alone had killed the girl. Because his confession is so important, it is worth quoting it all:

I, ABSALOM KIMMEL, of my own free will, do make the following confession, to-wit: While we were going through the woods on Sunday, June 23, 1872, from church, Mr. McLeod said: "Let us go a squirrel hunting." I told him we had no caps, that John Rieker lost them all on Saturday. Nothing more said until Jacob Kimmel came home, then McLeod asked Jake if any girls went [W]est, and Jake told him that several went, and McLeod said: We will go out there." We then ran the greater part of the way. When we got to the spot where the murder was committed, she, Mary Secaur, was within one hundred yards or more of us; and when she came up even with the place, he, McLeod, stepped out and said, "hold on;" when she ran to the south side of the road, and hollowed, "let me loose," in a loud tone of voice. He then grabbed her by the throat and right arm, and took her behind the bushes and threw her down. We, Jacob and myself, were off about two rods when McLeod called for us to come there. We did not go until he called us the second time; we then went to him and Jake stood at the roadside to watch, and I at the north of the girl and McLeod, when McLeod told me to take hold of her arm, which I did. At that time McLeod was holding both of the girl's hands in his mouth—the palm of hands together—holding to her throat. He then had connection with her. I then watched until Jake had connection with her also and then Jake watched until I did the same thing; then Jake and I went off about twenty-five yards, when McLeod again had connection with her, and as soon as he was through he picked up a club and hit her on the head; the club was about four inches in diameter and three feet long. I saw her throw up her hands and quiver when he struck her. He then came running up to us, and said that he had knocked her in the head. We then ran home. I saw blood on his right wristband and also on the bosom of his shirt. When we got home, I ran into the barn, Jake went into the house, and McLeod washed himself at the horse trough and afterward washed at the pump, and then went into the house, and all ate dinner. About one o'clock and about six o'clock, we went to water the horses, (myself, Jake, Andy, and George,) and when we came back I met my brother Sam at the crossroads, and jumped with a lot of boys. We then went home at sun down, and a little after we ate supper. McLeod told me that he had been back there and she was not dead yet, but that he had killed her. On Monday morning, my father told me that Alex wanted me to run off, but he wanted me to stick to the clearing.[5]

Absalom's statement immediately sent the sheriff to bring Jacob back to the Celina jail to await an indictment by a grand jury.[6] Sheriff Spriggs later claimed that Alexander McLeod offered to write a confession when the sheriff returned to the jail; by morning, though, McLeod said he had no confession to give.[7]

It might prove helpful at this point to sift through the many and varied facts presented to the public through the two hearings and various confessions and testimonies in order to determine the strength of the case against McLeod, Absalom, and Jacob. The prosecution's timeline of events on June 23, provided by the prosecution's witnesses, looked like this:

9:00	*Mary Secaur leaves her house.*[8]
9:00–10:00	*Absalom and McLeod seen at Liberty Chapel.*[9]
10:00	*Mary arrives at Liberty Chapel for Sunday school.*[10]
c. 11:30	*Absalom and McLeod leave church early.*[11]
c. 11:45	*Absalom and McLeod arrive at the Kimmel homestead.*[12]
12:00	*Jacob and William Kimmel leave church with other parishioners, including Mary Secaur.*[13]
c. 12:15	*Jacob and William seen at the Kimmel homestead.*[14]
12:30–12:45	*Earliest the accused could have arrived at the murder site if they left directly upon Jacob arriving at the Kimmel homestead.*[15]
12:45–1:00	*Mary arrives at the murder site, assuming no stopping or delays.*[16]
1:00 "or after"	*McLeod returns to the Kimmel homestead.*[17]
1:00	*Absalom, Jacob, Andy, and George water horses at the Kimmel homestead.*[18]
1:30 to 2:30	*Window of time for the accused to leave the murder scene in order to be seen at the pump.*[19]
2:00	*McLeod and Absalom seen at the pump.*[20]
2:00 or 3:00	*Jacob and Absalom water horses at the Kimmel homestead.*[21]

c. 2:00	*Dinner at the Kimmel homestead.*[22]
3:00	*William Kimmel leaves for Van Wert following dinner.*[23]
3:00	*McLeod tells George he committed the murder.*[24]
6:00	*Absalom, Jacob, Andy and George water horses; Absalom meets his brother Sam at the crossroads.*[25]
8:30	*Absalom returns home at sundown and eats supper. McLeod tells him about returning to the murder site, finding the girl still alive, and finishing her murder.*[26]

The timing of the various trips to and from the murder scene is difficult to make work, and the sightings of the suspects at the Kimmel farm conflict with each other and with Absalom's confession. Still, eyewitness testimony about the times is potentially faulty—and many of the times noted were probably estimates—so the idea that Absalom, Jacob, and McLeod could have walked to the murder site, committed the crime, and returned for dinner is at least possible, if one ignores the testimony that does not fit this timeline.

The prosecution capitalized on the suspects' supposedly guilty behavior. First, witnesses reported McLeod and Absalom walking in and out of the Sunday school or church service several times and then leaving church altogether long before the service ended, although such behavior by bored young men does not seem too unusual. Second, several witnesses testified to seeing McLeod and Andrew Kimmel on the road early Monday morning, implying that the pair sought to cross the state line at first opportunity.[27] However, in the testimony, the duos seemed neither rushed nor concerned about detection. The fact that Absalom and Jake did not remain with the tin peddlers but walked home from the state line would indicate they were not concerned about being implicated in a crime.[28]

Deputy William Johnson and Sheriff Thornton Spriggs reported McLeod making statements after his arrest that implied knowledge of the crime, despite the fact that the authorities told him nothing about it and kept him isolated. However, several of McLeod's statements indicated he was unclear as to the reason for his arrest.[29] Johnson and Spriggs related McLeod's concern over the involvement of others—particularly the Kimmels—in the crime.[30] These could be the actions of a guilty man concerned about coordinating testimony with his fellow criminals, but they could just as readily be the behavior of an understandably frightened young man who was worried that he had been betrayed by the family of his work partner for a crime he did not commit. Furthermore, in his statements to Johnson about such a betrayal, McLeod consistently denied his guilt.[31] Spriggs reported that McLeod offered confused testimony as to his whereabouts on the Sunday of the murder.[32] Once again, McLeod could be read as a guilty man scrambling to keep his lies straight, or he could be seen as having trouble remembering what had happened nearly a week before under the pressure of having been arrested without charge and illegally transported across state lines by people he had never before seen.

When the posse stopped at the murder scene on the trip from Fort Wayne to Celina, Johnson and Spriggs said, McLeod acted suspiciously and fearfully, staring at the location of the murder.[33] Johnson reported, "He cried and said it was awful—that he was not guilty: *he had never committed adultery there*—it was the first time he ever saw the *bloody spot.*" He further said that "he never touched the girl."[34] Spriggs's testimony was similar. "He turned to the fence of a field nearby, crying, and said: 'I never committed adultery here or anything else; I never saw this bloody spot before.' There was no blood on the ground that could be seen."[35] If accurate, McLeod's comments about the girl are not easily dismissed. However, McLeod acting fearfully at the murder scene is understandable under the circumstances, and it would probably have been obvious from a distance that something had happened at the murder site since the ground had been tromped by numerous people after the discovery of the body. McLeod was the son of a Scottish immigrant to Canada and had grown up in a community of other Scottish immigrants, so it seems reasonable that he would have used the expression *bloody* in its British sense. Overall, the behavior of the accused, especially McLeod, is inconclusive as evidence. There are some suspicious statements and actions, particularly his murder-site comment about "the girl," but nearly all of them can be explained away unless one is dead-set on proving his guilt.

The testimony at the June 30 hearing concentrates a great deal on the blood-smeared ribbon taken from Mary Secaur's hat and reportedly tied to McLeod's horse's bridle.[36] Andy Kimmel's story about the ribbon—that Jake and McLeod stopped at the murder scene on the way to the Indiana border Monday morning, that Jake hopped off McLeod's wagon and picked up a bottle hidden under a rock marked by the bloody ribbon, and that Jake tied the ribbon to McLeod's bridle[37]—fails to explain why McLeod would tie a bloodied souvenir of a terrible crime to his own horse's bridle or why the culprits would have hidden a bottle of whiskey at the scene of the crime in the first place. It is much easier to imagine the deputies or the sheriff planting such a piece of evidence on McLeod during the arrest. The ribbon, however, is not the only piece of physical evidence; much more significant are the bloody objects linking McLeod to the case: a shirt, a boot, pants, a penknife, and a handkerchief.[38] At his prelynching speech, McLeod claimed these stains were due to nosebleeds, which seems possible; the amount of blood reported on his clothing (evidently on the level of drops and smears) does seem to better fit a nosebleed than blood pouring from a severed head. Also, Andy Kimmel, who otherwise implicates McLeod strongly in the crime, testifies that he saw no blood on McLeod's sleeve during Sunday dinner. Still, we only have McLeod's word for the bloody-nose excuse. Otherwise, the blood on his clothing makes for a definite, concrete link to the murder, one that is difficult to deny. The blood on McLeod's boot, along with the blood on the penknife, if authentic, also provides direct evidence of McLeod's involvement in the crime. That the sheriff should wait to produce this penknife until taking the stand at the hearing is troubling, as is the fact that neither the pants nor the boot were offered as evidence at the hearing. But unless we imagine a complete fabrication of evidence—which is always a possibility—the knife and the bloody shirt certainly implicate McLeod.

Finally, we have the statements and confessions from Andrew Kimmel, George Kimmel, Jacob Kimmel, and Absalom Kimmel.[39] There are many, many discrepancies between the various versions, as shown in Table 2.1:

McLeod is the only person who participates in all of the various stories, and even then his guilt ranges from waylaying the girl and asking for sex to committing both rape and murder—the entire affair on his own initiative from start to finish. It is only in Absalom's signed confession that the Kimmel boys are implicated in the rape, and they are never implicated in the murder.

Other than Absalom, the three young men who testified against McLeod were released—one assumes in return for their testimonies. The authorities never charged Andrew Kimmel with any crime, even though he could offer no alibi stronger than McLeod's. The only difference between the two young men at the time of their arrest was that Andrew seemed to have been more compliant with the authorities. George offered three versions of his testimony—first accusing McLeod, then claiming he had been coerced, and then finally recanting that correction. Once Jacob testified against McLeod, he was released. Because Absalom's first confession was thrown out of court "in consequence of inducements having been held

	Andrew Kimmel	George Kimmel	Jacob Kimmel	Absalom Kimmel
Source of information	Direct observation for ribbon story and suspicious behavior. Absalom for information about the girl, given on June 23.	Confession to George by McLeod on June 23.	Confession to Jacob by McLeod on July 5.	Confession by Absalom on June 30, dismissed by court. Confession by Absalom on July 7
Participants in Crime(s)	Absalom, McLeod	McLeod	McLeod	Absalom, McLeod (first confession); Absalom, Jacob, McLeod (second confession)
Crime(s) Committed	None. Stopped girl and asked for sex.	Rape, murder.	Murder.	Unstated (first confession); Rape by Absalom, Jacob, and McLeod (second confession); Murder by McLeod (second confession)

out to him,"[40] it was easy to suppose that similar inducements—or the types of threats reported by George—were involved in all the statements by the accused. Absalom's second confession, in particular, seems suspicious, containing specifics not seen in any other statement and a level of detail and language difficult to square with Day's characterization of the teenager as "very much below the average in intelligence."[41] At the very least, Judge Blake seems to have altered Absalom's wording, because his confession was "reduced to writing, as it fell from the lips of the accused."[42] At worst, the authorities supplied Absalom with a prepared confession that the young man marked without reading or understanding.

Reports of the lynching scene indicate that Absalom spoke to the crowd when prompted for a confession, but they are maddeningly vague and varied in their accounts of what he said. In I. F. Raudabaugh's journal, we have a first-person account of the lynching that could potentially settle the matter, but his notes from the scene are sketchy: "Abs—while we were going through woods and C. I am innocent as you will all acknowledge in time when this is papered over. Am willing to let the law have its course."[43] The range of accounts of Absalom's statements—from his articulate, lengthy, written confession to a complete denial of guilt delivered to the crowd before his death—make it difficult to establish exactly what he knew or said about the crime. The doubts the people of Mercer County had about the totality of his confession are evidenced by the fact that they allowed Elias Secaur to talk them out of lynching Jacob and also that Jacob was released by the Court of Common Pleas at the first opportunity for the case to be reviewed by a regular legal body. And if Absalom's confession—containing the only officially recorded accusations against both Jacob and him, and serving as the only eyewitness account of the actions of McLeod—was not reliable enough to convict Jacob, then it was not reliable enough to convict Absalom or McLeod. Overall, then, the testimony and confessions on which the case was largely based were woefully compromised and would not have held up in court.

So, were McLeod and Absalom guilty? The evidence is mixed. Reports of their whereabouts throughout the day of the murder make them available to have committed the crime, though only if we discount some of the testimony. The details of McLeod's supposedly guilty behavior during his arrest are inconsistent and cannot be corroborated outside the testimonies of the sheriff, his deputy, and Andrew Kimmel. The blood-stained ribbon reportedly found tied to McLeod's bridle would have been easy for the authorities to plant, and the account of how it came to be tied there makes little sense. More damning, however, are the various articles of bloody clothing and equipment found on McLeod at the time of his arrest. Although McLeod offered an explanation for the blood on his shirt—and although we have only the sheriff's word for the bloody knife and boot—the physical evidence tying McLeod to the crime is persuasive, if not definitive. The various statements and confessions are inconsistent and, at the very least, the result of deals made between the witnesses and the authorities, if not complete fabrications created by those same authorities. Unfortunately, all of the above leaves the truth muddled. On the one hand, there is evidence that ties McLeod and—less believably—Absalom to the crime. On the other hand, a convincing scenario can be created in which the testimony of the witnesses and even the physical evidence was manipulated—if not fashioned—by the authorities in order to "solve" a crime that had disturbed the tranquility of the county.

We can probably never know the truth, but there are other kinds of truth than the whodunit variety. In the remainder of this chapter, I seek to understand three topics related to the case: the structure of a post–Civil War Midwestern lynching, the identity and character of the victim, and finally, the relationship of the Kimmel family—especially Absalom—to the community around them.

⊢⋅✦⋅०⋅✦⋅⊣

"A Little Girl Murdered." *Van Wert Bulletin.* June 28, 1872

The excitement in the neighborhood is at the highest pitch and if the perpetrator of the deed should be found it is hinted that he will be lynched.

"Horrible Crime." *Cincinnati Commercial Tribune.* July 3, 1872

Andrew Kimble, who has turned State's evidence, will have a hearing on Friday, the 5th inst., and unless the persons can clear themselves of this chain of evidence that encircles them, Judge Lynch will assume jurisdiction and institute summary justice.

Celina Journal. July 4, 1872

The brutal murder of Mary B. Secour has created the most intense excitement, and lynch law is talked of for the guilty ones, if found. Though the most terrible outrage that men could be guilty of, lynching should not be resorted to; that is a bad way of righting a wrong. There are courts provided for such cases, and it is better to allow the law to take its course. The courts of justice will bring the guilty ones to trial, and, if found guilty, they will suffer the penalty according to law.

The outraged community is so incensed that it would visit summary punishment on the guilty, but the better way is to allow the courts to administer legal punishment.

"Rape, Murder, and Lynch Law." *Dayton Herald.* July 9, 1872

One of the scoundrels turned State's evidence, but his testimony was objected to by the defendants, on the ground that it was made under fear and the hope of reward, which objection was sustained by the examining Court. This so outraged the citizens, and fearing that through the technicalities of the law justice would not be meted out they concluded that the example set by their neighboring State of Indiana, in their summary lynching of the Seymour Express robbers, would have a wholesome effect.

Tiffin, Ohio—June 23, 2017

David Kimmel

In the twenty-first century, the word *lynching* calls to mind images of enraged racist mobs terrorizing African Americans in the South, but lynchings began as acts of white-on-white summary justice—which also included tarring and feathering—in frontier areas as far back as the mid-1700s.[44] Over time, *lynching* came to be associated with extra-legal hangings[45] and spread from frontier areas to settled lands in reaction to the abolitionist movement and to events such as Nat Turner's rebellion in 1831.[46] After the Civil War, lynching flourished in the Midwest and West and was employed against whites and blacks alike, though as the century wore on, the percentage of lynchings that occurred against blacks in the South continued to rise.[47]

Along with their other cultural and personal possessions, settlers in the Midwest transported the ages-old European notions of using predictable and consistent rituals to regulate the behavior of rural communities. Lynching operated in a predictable manner, with participants consciously following an orally transmitted script, and communities used the established patterns of the lynching ritual as a means of justifying and legitimizing what would otherwise be a chaotic and lawless mob action. The first requirement for a lynching was that a horrific crime had been committed—more often a crime of homicide or rape than a crime of property.[48] When in the course of a standard lynching the community crossed the requisite emotional threshold, they would form a mob and storm the local jail; the officers of the law would resist manfully but would be overwhelmed in the face of the huge crowd of enraged citizens.[49] The established protocol furthermore dictated that once the prisoners were removed from the jail, a "trial" of sorts would be held—often at the scene of the lynching. Such sham trials operated under the presumption of guilt, with little or no chance for the defendant to defend him- or herself or to call witnesses.[50] Contemporary accounts of lynchings often stressed the orderly, competent nature of the mobs, as well as the participation of citizens from across the spectrum of the community, which indicated popular support for their actions.[51] The ritual behaviors of a lynching continued beyond the actual execution. Once the accused were dead, the crowd dispersed, and it was up to the local media to report on—and often to excuse or justify—the actions of the crowd. Newspapers did not always support summary justice, even during the earlier period of the mid- to late 1800s,[52] but they often coupled general condemnations of lynching with apologies for local instances.[53] Media reports emphasized the horrific nature of the crime, the sympathetic nature of the victim or victims, the guilt of the accused, the overwhelming public support for the lynching (as indicated by the size of the crowd), and the absence of local law enforcement structures capable of handling the case;[54] but they rarely included information on prosecutions against the lynchers.[55] While local variations occurred, the fact remains that lynching participants followed a predictable script—a script that primary accounts often overtly acknowledged in describing the actions of the mob.

During the post–Civil War period, lynching served two purposes for the communities that practiced it. First, lynching provided rural communities with an opportunity to carry out what they viewed as effective justice, avoiding the types of legalistic weaknesses they saw as endemic in the official legal system. Although lynchings in frontier territories were partially caused by the lack of official courts,[56] most lynchings in the postwar period occurred in areas served by regular courts.[57] An attitude shift away from immediate, physical retribution for crimes—"rough justice"—toward the rule of law and due process began in the Northeast in the 1830s and moved westward as the century rolled along.[58] Perhaps because of its source in the educated elite of the Northeast, this attitude change encountered resistance as it made its way into the heartland of the country. Rural and working-class Americans viewed due process as a weaker, less-efficient form of justice when compared with direct, immediate physical punishment.[59] Lynching provided the type of physical punishment a regular court might not advocate[60] and prevented—in the minds of its advocates—shrewd lawyers and incompetent or corrupt juries from releasing prisoners on technicalities.[61] More subtly, lynching was an act of community building, a ritual in which a dominant group reinforced the status-quo of racial, economic, social, and gender hierarchies.[62] Leaders of lynch mobs tended to be businessmen, professionals, and large-scale farmers—the upper tier of society.[63] The greater mass of men and women carrying out the hangings were middle-level "farmers, craftsmen, tradesmen, and the less-eminent professionals;"[64] and the victims were economically and socially separated from their more established white rural neighbors,[65] who viewed them with contempt as shiftless, immoral, and lawless.[66] Lynching, then, was not a spontaneous outburst of passion. Rather, it was a carefully regulated, planned ritual that served identifiable purposes.

James H. Day. *Lynched!*

The victim of the brutal outrage, Mary Arabelle Secaur, was only in her fourteenth year, but she was large and well developed for a child of her age. Her mother died some three years ago, since which time she has been living in the family of Mr. John Citterly, of Liberty Township, Mercer County, Ohio. She was a gentle, tractable child; being dutiful and of a kind and loving disposition, she had so ingratiated herself with Mr. and Mrs. Citterly, and so won upon their affections during her stay in the family, that, having no children of their own, they had determined to adopt her and make her heir to their estate. And not only had she, by her gentle ways and winning manners, conquered for herself a place in the affections of the Citterlys, but she had by the same process secured the good will and esteem of all her acquaintances, and she was the universal favorite of all—both old and young—in the neighborhood.[67]

"A Little Girl Murdered." *Van Wert Bulletin.* June 28, 1872

The girl's mother is dead and her father lives near Lancaster. She had been placed in a family of respectability, and had a large circle of friends.

"Horrible Crime." *Cincinnati Commercial Tribune.* July 3, 1872

The murdered girl was intelligent, modest, and remarkably attractive in personal appearance, and a general favorite in the community in which she lived.

Figure 2.1. Mary Secaur's gravestone in Liberty Chapel Cemetery. The top portion (above the visible crack) has since toppled to the ground. Photograph by David Kimmel.

Tiffin, Ohio—June 23, 2017

David Kimmel

The church that stood beside the graves when I first began to come here is gone now—burned down and bulldozed under. The cemetery is fairly typical for these country church sites. The township mows between the headstones, but there is little other upkeep. The monuments tilt this way and that as the ground beneath them settles, leaning over more and more with each passing year until the moment—maybe during the night, maybe during a hard, driving rainstorm one afternoon—the stones pass the tipping point and fall unheard into the soft grass. Mary Secaur's gravestone stands alone and weathered in the northwestern corner of the old Liberty Chapel Cemetery in Mercer County. Though woods would have blocked the view in 1872, now her headstone looks out over the just-growing fields of beans at the empty space where the Kimmel homestead once stood. The gravestone of Mary's brother, Elias, stands off to her right, partly fallen. The gaps between these two headstones and between Mary's and the next stones to her left provide plenty of space for the graves of other family members, including her mother. Mary's marker has already lost its top third. Something is burrowing beneath the stones and tipping them over. It is only a matter of time until Mary's lies in the grass. The limestone has weathered to the point that just Mary's name and basic facts are visible. Acidic rain has burned away the rest of the wording. At the top of the fallen piece is a rusted stub where an ornament—an angel? a lamb?—has long ago fallen away.

In my travels and research into the case, I have located just two images of Mary. One is the terrible woodcut from the James H. Day's book *Lynched!* In that picture, Mary is middle-aged, tired, and careworn. There are dark bags under her eyes, and her cheeks are puffy. Her hair is pulled back haphazardly, presumably tied in a knot in the back. The other image is a small reproduction—only an inch or so across—of the photograph used by the ham-handed engraver as the basis for his illustration. Here Mary is young, fresh-faced, and probably close to her age at the time of her murder. Her dark eyes look directly into ours, and she maintains that serious expression required in the days of slow shutter speeds. Her hair is neat, and she's dressed in a fine fabric with a pendant and a double-strand of beads. This is the image of a girl who was loved and cared for by the foster parents who were planning to adopt her. The pendant looks to be the same gold locket currently in the possession of her great-grandniece, Karen Feasby, which contains a lock of Mary's hair—a rather morbid memento, but a very customary nineteenth-century possession following the death of a loved one. Since her remains have undoubtedly long ago become one with the soil

Figure 2.2, a–b. Comparison of the engraving of Mary Secaur from the title page of *Lynched!* against a reproduction of the original photograph. The photograph is on a very small (less than one inch in diameter) button in the possession of Mary's great-grandniece, Karen Feasby. Engraving Ohio History Connection. Photograph by David Kimmel.

Figure 2.3, a–b. Locket in the possession of Mary's great-grandniece, Karen Feasby, containing a lock of Mary Secaur's hair. Photographs by David Kimmel.

beneath her gravestone, this curled strand of faded hair may well be the sole remaining physical manifestation of this young girl. As far as I know, she left no diary, no letters, no legal documents signed in her hand. And her murderer (or murderers) certainly left her no opportunity to speak for herself.

This is not to say that no one spoke for her. The male authors who reported the crime established for her an identity as much the product of conflicted Victorian attitudes about gender roles as anyone flesh and blood. On the one hand, Mary is a "child,"[68] a "little girl,"[69] a respectable, popular orphan whose goodness and obedience led her foster parents to seek permanent adoption.[70] At the same time, Mary is a sexual being, "remarkably attractive in personal appearance,"[71] "large and well developed for a child of her age,"[72] and "well-proportioned and quite womanly."[73] Though young, she's mature; though innocent, she's womanly. There were even early rumors that Mary had been involved with an adult neighbor, Charles Anselman, "who proved a satisfactory *alibi*, and was honorably acquitted."[74] In the minds of these male authors, Mary is the virgin *and* the whore. From the start, accounts of the murder sensationalized both the sexual nature of the crime and the destruction of her body. There is a near-pornographic quality to the descriptions, which reduce the girl to an object, to a collection of pieces. Mary Secaur is less a person than a symbol of innocence and cruelty. Her body, spread over the killing ground, is worthy of revenge.

I find it difficult to leave Mary to these men. She deserves better than these descriptions that use her more than portray her, but what can I offer in opposition to the caricatures offered by these male sources? After all, the source is key in purely historical writing, and I do not hold anything of substance that can counter these male versions of Mary. Here is where slipping toward the fictional offers a chance for an alternative. I may not be able to provide proof of a different Mary, but I can provide a vision of that other person. Of course, I am immediately suspect as a male writing about a teenage girl—and there will be those who will deny my imagination the right even to attempt to provide her with a voice. But I have listened to my relations and friends, and I have read the voices of many women and girls. And I have my own life, which, though not a woman's life, is a human life nonetheless. Like any author of fictions, I create characters who are a blending of what I have lived, witnessed, heard, and read. I hesitate to write directly from Mary's point of view, though, as her silencing is thematically important. So, I will get at Mary obliquely, through the eyes and words of another girl, Candace Hocker. Candace is one of the few complete fabrications in this book. I need freedom in creating her so that I can concentrate not on her authenticity so much as Mary's. Candace's story is about Mary as a person, not Mary as a victim. It is also a story about memory.

Liberty Township, June 23, 1902

Candace Hocker

Some items from our past stand before our eyes, clear as day; others are simply lost, their place in our minds a blurred erasure or a blank space. For instance, I can distinctly recall the double-wedding-ring bedspread Mary's foster mother had inherited from *her* mother. The colorful interlocking circles were appliquéd to a white background. The quilt betrayed its age through worn areas on the edges, material grown so thin that the batting poked through the gaps. Some of the rings had come loose from the bottom layer, and I would pick absentmindedly at the loose rings while sitting on the bed with Mary. When I visualize a scene with Mary in her room, I distinctly see us sitting on that bed on that quilt. Yet I'm not sure about the details, even of the quilt. Was it really a double-wedding-ring? Do I remember the truth, or have I re-created it in my head based on similar places I've been or other details I've observed since then? This uncertainty about my memory—no, not about my memory, which is sound as far as I can tell, but about memory, itself—is not just idle speculation. It's important for this story because all I have of Mary is what I can remember from that Sunday morning thirty years ago.

Because Liberty Chapel was basically just one big room, our various Sunday school classes met in different corners, clustered into small groups on the hard, backless benches, the wood worn smooth by years of use. The room was dim and cool after the bright heat of the morning, and it was pleasant to sit still after the dusty walk to church. Mary and I had just moved up from the older-children's group into the class for young adults. We were painfully aware of our youth within this group, which ranged from thirteen to twenty years of age. Our teacher was Mr. Hinton, who meant well but was deadly dull. He read us a Bible verse, then he made us each read the verse out loud back to him, then he told us what the verse meant and how it related to the whole story of the Bible and to our own lives. In my memory, I see eyes rolling back into heads and heads wobbling on flimsy stalks for necks. And I see the Kimmel boys in our group varied in their reaction to the lesson: George nodding along with the rhythms of Hinton's recitation, Jake staring sullenly at the teacher, and Absalom slouching in his chair and kicking one boot with the toe of the other. Occasionally, Ab snuck a look at Jake or at the stranger.

That one—only later would we know him as McLeod—sat quietly, surreptitiously surveying the girls in the group, and his eyes kept coming back to Mary. No surprise there. Men looked at Mary all the time. I am trying to remember McLeod. He looked the part of a tin peddler—no one knew his occupation at the time, but everyone would soon know much more. The funny thing is, I can't remember much about him other than what he wore: faded blond denim britches, a checked vest, and two shirts, a whitish-grayish collarless shirt beneath a red-and-white plaid overshirt. Beyond that, I can't visualize anything else about him. Was he tall? Was he short? What did his face look like? If I see his face at all, it's as he looked two weeks on, struggling for breath at the end . . . but I don't want to write about that. Suffice it to say, he's faded from view. The closer I get to the important details, the dimmer my memories become.

So there I was, enduring another Sunday school lesson, trying to keep my eyes open and to keep the lid on my anger as the boys in the group shot glances at Mary and the older girls. Mary, for her part, was sitting in rapt attention, hanging on Hinton's every word. I could never figure out if she was really listening, truly interested, or if she was just sitting there vacantly, prettily. She was getting good at that, looking pretty. She was always smiling and being attentive in church or in school. She helped around her house and even asked her foster mother if there was any little thing that she could do to help. Truth be told, I looked pretty bad by comparison, especially when she would lay on her charm at my house. My mother almost passed out one day when Mary asked her if she could help sweep the floor or beat the carpets or something—anything to repay my mother's kindness in allowing her to visit. Looking back, I guess that the difference between us was that I'd always had what I needed—a home, parents, food, and so forth—while Mary had lost it all. She appreciated her new opportunity and planned to make the best of it. But that's me talking to you as a forty-three-year-old grown-up. At the time, as a selfish thirteen year old, I was tired of Mary's perpetual halo of virtue.

Eventually, thankfully, the Sunday school lesson limped to a close, and our class stood and puddled into small conversation groups. I stood alone by the door. While the parishioners rearranged the benches and chairs for the service, I saw McLeod and Absalom talking in low voices before quietly slipping out of the church. Mary crossed to me and smiled her brightest aren't-I-adorable smile.

"Wasn't that a good lesson?" she asked.

I looked at her with disgust. "Oh, extremely interesting," I answered. "Five chapters from the first book of Kings, summarized by a droning old man."

"Well I happen to think Mr. Hinton does a splendid job. And I like hearing about the kings and the battles. It's all so exciting."

I knew I wasn't going to get anywhere with her. Over the past few months, she'd been developing quite an independent streak. Time was when I could pretty much tell Mary something and expect her to either agree with me or to spring into action on the basis of what I'd just told her. Now, her blossoming bodice had provided her with a mind of her own that she wasn't afraid to deploy, even if that meant stepping on some familiar toes.

Absalom and McLeod returned to the church and made their way to seats halfway up the aisle and over near the windows, McLeod staring impassively, Absalom grinning and laughing to himself. Whiskey fumes wafted over us as they passed by. Mary scrunched up her nose and turned away from the boys. I watched them a moment and then guided Mary to another pair of seats opposite the drinkers but where we could generally keep an eye on them and the rest of the room.

I'm trying to remember every detail I can, but to tell the truth, this Sunday just blurs into every other Sunday. After all, we didn't know at the time that anything particular would happen, so why should we pay attention to what was just another Sunday worship service? It ran the way they all did: the preacher led us in prayer, in song, in reading scripture, in another song, in a sermon—which was long and bone-dry, as always—and finally in another song. The preacher might've spoken about God's love for all mankind or about forgiveness of sins, but those would be awfully ironic, given what would happen that afternoon. Of course, now that I know what would happen, I can imagine a tension in the service—Mary not knowing that her fate would be decided in only a few hours. But I remember no foreshadowing of the kind.

Now, one thing that you need to know about worship in a country church is that people arrive late and leave early all the time. This is farm country, where the rhythm of the fields and animals dictates the farmers' schedules. Still, I do distinctly remember McLeod and Absalom getting up to leave the service about halfway through. They stood up and quietly—for

Absalom—made their way down the side aisle to the back door, followed by a rustling of soft commentary by the parishioners. After that, they were lost to sight and mind, and my attention was driven back to the sound of the leaves blowing high up in the trees, to the buzz of horseflies zooming in and out of the open windows, and to the drone of the preacher as he explained the finer points of salvation. The day was approaching noon, bright and sunny, with a hot breeze blowing the dust motes around in the sunshine that streamed through the windows. I watched as the sunlight on the floor slowly retreated behind me and dissolved into the wall. The air inside the church was hot and still now, the only sounds the shuffling of heavy work shoes on the wooden floor and the clearing of farmers' throats. But this description would fit any summer day at Liberty Chapel.

What I do distinctly remember is that I happened to glance over at Mary, who was sitting beside me. She was no longer raptly listening to the preacher's sermon. I followed her gaze across the aisle to where Billy Horne made eyes back at her. She alternated looking down at her lap and stealing peeks at Billy. He just stared at her, and every time she looked at him, his smile lit up. It was disgusting. I jabbed Mary in the ribs.

"Ouch! What are you doing, Candace?" Mary hissed.

"What are *you* doing?" I whispered back.

"Nothing," her soft voice sang.

"Nothing, my foot," I said, my voice rising just above a whisper.

I felt a tap on my shoulder, and then heard a woman's voice whisper in my ear. "You girls, hush now, and listen to the sermon. I'd hate to have to speak to your grandpa, Mary, or to your parents, Candace."

I immediately sat up straight on my bench and folded my hands in my lap. I could feel the blood rushing to my ears. "Yes ma'am," I said in a low voice.

I pretended to listen, but I kept darting my eyes over to see what Mary was up to. For her part, she sat demurely with her eyes focused on her lap. But on her face was a smirk. My ears still burned as I sat and stewed over this betrayal. How could she not be paying attention to me? A boy? It was inconceivable. Finally, we stood to sing, and I stumbled through "Holy, Holy, Holy," but I could hardly choke out a word. Mary warbled blithely along beside me as though nothing had happened.

James H. Day, *Lynched!*

*During the night preceding, and on the morning of the eventful Sunday of June
23, 1872, premonitions of danger seem to have shadowed the mind of
the little girl, as though her guardian angel or some kind invisible spirit of the
air was striving to whisper in her ear a warning of her impending doom; for
we have been told that on the morning in question, she seemed low spirited,
and related to her friends the particulars of a dream, wherein she saw herself
attacked by ruffians and cruelly murdered. But the cheerful sunlight and the
presence of kindly faces, soon dispelled the impressions that had been made
upon her mind by, what was then supposed to be, but the wild vagaries of a
dream, and her wanted cheerfulness soon returned. It is startling to think and
realize, upon what seeming trifles great events are hinged, and upon what an
exceedingly small pivot they sometimes turn. In this instance, had but the simple
impressions of a dream been accepted, as a warning of danger to come, and
guarded against for but a single day, how different might have been the result?
The commission of a horrible crime, and the terrible consequences that followed
and resulted from it, might have been averted. Mary Arabelle Secaur, in her
maiden innocence and purity, would still be living to gladden the hearts of her
relatives and friends; the public would have been spared the horrible details of
her death and the commotion that ensued, and the perpetrators of the outrage
might still be in full vigorous life, with a chance of making of themselves useful
and honored members of society. But the warning was unheeded, and the great
events that were to follow commenced to unfold and develop themselves.*[75]

┝━┥◈┝━○━◈┥━┥

Tiffin, Ohio—June 23, 2017

David Kimmel

Day's account of Mary's dream and his accompanying "What if?" are
unique to his booklet, which does not necessarily rule them out of
bounds but does call to question their authenticity. More important
than the truth of Day's account is the way it illustrates the allure of
the counterfactual. In any loss, there is a layer of guilt and regret on
the part of the survivors who are left with a feeling of "What if?" One
small change could have upset the delicate alignment of coincidence. It
is easy to imagine Mary's family and friends reliving again and again

the final day of her life, endlessly rehearsing the moments where a simple alteration in the course of events would have saved her life. And this leads me to the final purpose behind my character of Candace. She represents the urge to rewrite the past. If only Candace had been less childish, Mary might have stayed over at Candace's house for the afternoon, traveling home long after her murderers had left the scene. As Candace recalls seeing her friend walk toward home, the reader knows what Candace the narrator now knows—what the Candace of her narrative could not have known—that this was the last time she would see her friend alive.

Liberty Township, June 23, 1902

Candace Hocker

The song ended and the preacher gave the benediction, which was the signal for the congregation to head for home and dinner. I gathered up my parasol and hat, but when I turned to leave, Mary was already gone. I looked back toward the church doors, and there was Mary, side-by-side with Billy Horne! I took off after them, bulling and worming my way through the crowd until I burst out into the sunshine. Where were they? I looked around frantically. Then I saw them, passing through the church gate and out onto the road. They were surrounded by a large group of others—children as well as adults—all walking west toward the crossroads. I started off after them. As I squeezed through the bottleneck at the gate, I bumped into an elderly gentleman and heard a familiar voice.

"Well, now, Candace, where you going in such a hurry?" It was Grandpa May. I was a little embarrassed to admit that I was chasing after his granddaughter.

"Uh, I was trying to catch up with Mary."

"Looks like she already found a walking partner," he said, gesturing up to where Mary was walking along, chatting and laughing with Billy. "Why don't we walk together?" And with that, we set off down the road. Up ahead, Mary opened her parasol, shielding herself from the sun and—I might add—from my view.

I fell into step with Mr. May. I could feel him sneaking glances at me as we walked along the road. He hazarded several attempts at small talk, but I just shuffled along quietly in the dust.

"You'll never hit them from here."

"Hit who?" My face flushed slightly as I realized that the rock skipping along the ground ahead of me had been set in motion by my foot. "Oh." We walked along for a while in silence, and I resisted the urge to kick any more rocks.

"You know, Candace, it's fine, really."

"What is?"

"You and Mary. It'll be fine."

This old man was beginning to irritate me. "I don't know what you are talking about, Mr. May."

"Oh, you don't?" Mr. May sounded far from convinced. "Candace, are you jealous of Mary's new friend, or is it something else that you're jealous about?"

I stopped in the middle of the road and faced him, hands on my hips. "Number one, I am not jealous of Mary's new friend. He's a greasy, pimply, dirty little boy. How she can be interested in such a thing is beyond me. I mean, look at him lumbering along beside her—hands in his pockets, bad posture. He's probably got worms. Number two, I have no idea what you are talking about. Jealous of what?"

Mr. May looked down at me, regarding me thoughtfully. "Maybe I was wrong. I apologize."

We resumed our walk, and I kept an eye on Mary, who was getting awfully close to Billy. "I mean, there's nothing Mary's got that I haven't got," I said aloud. Well, that wasn't exactly true. But then I realized what I really meant. "And I ain't no orphan. I live with *my* parents."

Now it was Mr. May's turn to stop. "Whoa, now, Candace. Think about what you're saying."

I looked down at my dusty shoes. I wish I could say that I underwent some transformation at that moment, that I gained a valuable insight into my soul and took another step toward growing up. Instead, I turned and walked away as fast as I could, wanting to distance myself from Mr. May.

Up ahead, Mary and her beau stopped and leaned toward each other in the middle of the road. The stream of people walking along the road broke right and left around them, heading either north or south along Erastus-Durbin Road. I reached them just as Billy turned to the group of children who were calling him from the northern side of the intersection. He looked back at her—I'll never forget that look—and waved. I stood close to Mary. She was staring at him and smiling as he walked away. Her look crippled me.

Mr. May tactfully passed by without acknowledging us. We took up with the rapidly thinning crowd, occasionally having to move to the side of the road to allow passage of a buggy or a wagon taking churchgoers home.

For her part, Mary acted as if nothing had happened. "Beautiful day, isn't it, Candace? The sun is shining, the birds are singing. It's just lovely." She slipped her arm through mine and drew me close. I stomped along, sending dust puffs billowing around my ankles.

"What do you think of him?" asked Mary.

"What do I think of who?" I replied.

"William. William. Isn't that a wonderful name?"

"William? He's Billy Horne, the same bratty kid you've known for years."

Mary tightened her grip on my arm. "Oh, no. He's not either a bratty kid. He's a young man now."

"Hardly. He still tortures turtles down at the creek, I bet."

Mary laughed indulgently. "Doesn't he have dreamy eyes?"

"I think I noticed a twitch in the left one. Do you think they are the same size?" Mary laughed some more.

"And he's so strong."

My voice continued its teasing tone. "He tell you that?"

"Oh, I just know. Do you know what he did tell me?"

"I can hardly wait to find out."

"He said that he thinks about me all week long while he's doing his chores. I think about him, too, but I didn't tell him that, of course. Can you believe it?"

Now I was mad again. She wasn't joking. "No, I can't. He's dirty, and he smells like manure. He's stupid, too."

Mary's voice lost its dreamy edge. "How can you say that? You hardly even know him."

"I know him well enough. He's just like all those other disgusting farm boys at the school. You better watch out for him."

Mary dropped my arm and walked a good step or two away from me for a minute or so. "All I wanted was to talk to you about William. You're my best friend, after all."

I hadn't wanted to get into this. I didn't even know what I wanted. "It doesn't feel that way," I heard myself say.

"What are you talking about? You're not jealous of Billy, are you?" She moved over and hugged me to her. "Don't be an old silly. You're still my bosom friend. I'd do anything for you."

"Would you give up talking to Billy?"

"Candace, there's nothing to give up. I only see him one day a week."

I considered this for a while. "But you think about him. You said so yourself."

She laughed. "Well, I can think, can't I?"

"No, you have to think about me." I realized how stupid and childish I sounded, but I couldn't get other words to form.

"But I do that, too." Her arm was back through mine, and we walked along together. I should have been content; that should have been enough for me. I wish now that it had been enough, but I was greedy.

"Not enough," I whispered.

Mary dropped my arm again. "Oh, you're being childish," she said with disgust in her voice.

"That's right. I'm just a little child—a little girl. I just fade into the wood-work while you get all the men worked up." Now it was out.

"What are you talking about?" Her voice rose. "What do you mean, 'worked up'?"

Mr. May turned and looked over his shoulder at us. "Everything all right back there?"

Mary used her pleasing-the-grown-ups voice. "Oh, fine, Grandpa. We're just having a little chat." Then, in a low voice to me, she said, "How dare you talk to me like that!"

"Well, it's nothing you don't deserve." I wish I could have stopped myself. I wish I understood after all this time why I couldn't just leave things well enough alone. It's like my voice and my mind were disconnected.

"You are just a little girl. It's infuriating!"

"And you're a big, fat boy-crazy nothing." I listened to myself with disbelief.

Mary looked crestfallen. "Candace, how can you say those hurtful things?"

"I've been watching you change for four months. It's awful what you're becoming."

"Oh!" Mary took the offensive now. "You're just jealous because I'm a woman and you're still a baby."

"You think just because you ... you know ... that you're better than me or any of the other girls, but I have news for you. We all laugh at you behind your back."

"You do not. You don't even have anyone else to laugh with, even if you wanted to. You're talking like a fool."

"You think you're pretty special, but you're the fool about Billy."

Mary gave a sniff. "You don't know what you're talking about."

"My mother told me all about these boys. They talk all nice and sweet, but all they want is to lure you out into some haystack behind a wagon.

Then you have to marry them and be miserable for the rest of your life. Is that what you want?"

"Candace, it's only William. And it's only talking."

"That's what you say, now, but what'll happen when he gets you alone? What happens when he shows up below your window at night?" I heard my mother's voice come out of my mouth.

Mary thought for a moment, then tried one last time to appease me. "I'll throw him down my hair."

"Oh, you're not taking this seriously. You think it's all a joke. Well, you'll be sorry in the end, you mark my words."

"Candace, let's not fight."

The group we were walking with had been dropping people off as we passed their houses and had thinned down to Mr. May, myself, Mary, and two little girls who lived just beyond Mr. May's house. Mr. May had stopped before my farm and waited on us.

"Well, girls, here you are. Are you two still planning on spending the night together?"

We actually had planned to do just that. We had been busily working on a little play together, and we'd been all on fire to finish it off this evening. Now, however, I just wanted to be alone. "We're doing nothing of the kind. Good-bye, Mr. May. Have a good day." I stepped over the stile and walked down my front path, my back to them both.

"Candace, wait!" Mary called after me.

I ignored her and walked straight up to the front door, lifted the latch, and entered the house, letting the door bang closed behind me. Of course, I immediately snuck over to the front window to see how Mary responded to that. Their voices were muffled through the wavy glass, but clear enough to hear their conversation.

"What was all that about?" Mr. May asked.

Mary smoothed out her dress and placed her parasol artfully on her shoulder. "Oh, I haven't any idea."

"Oh, you don't." He gave Mary a pointed look, and it was clear to me that he understood more than he was revealing. "I thought you said that the two of you were staying over together."

"Well, we've changed our minds. We can do that, can't we?"

"Sure." They began walking again in silence. Soon they covered the short distance to Mr. May's front gate. They stood before the stile, Mary avoiding her grandfather's eyes. I crept out of my front door to see if I could make out what they were saying, but the distance swallowed their words. They spoke together for a bit, while the two little girls waited for them to finish. As I watched, I inched down the path to the fence. I longed to run after them, to tell her I was sorry, but I just stood there. Finally, she kissed her grandfather on the cheek and, waving to him over her shoulder, resumed her walk with the two girls.

Mr. May stood and watched her from his stile. The two little girls stopped at their own home, which was just past the Mays' house, and Mary walked on alone. Mr. May watched his granddaughter move away from him, growing smaller and smaller until she sank into a slight depression in the road, just a few hundred yards from her own home. Mr. May looked back at me, shook his head, and walked up the path to his house.

⊷⊶⊙⊷⊶

Tiffin, Ohio—June 23, 2017

David Kimmel

While the "official" accounts of the murder and lynchings portray the Kimmel family as a degenerate and dangerous presence in their Liberty Township community, those same accounts make little mention of Mary's family. Day merely states, "Her mother died some three years ago" as the lead-in to how she came to live with her foster family, the Sitterlys.[76] Her grandparents figure prominently in Day's official account, but while Mary's brothers appear, there is no mention of her father. Day and Raudabaugh fail to mention Mary's family because of ignorance, or perhaps it is because Mary's family—and, in particular her father—present a complication in the pure, simple tale of the innocent young girl murdered by the bad seed of Henry Kimmel.

Up until the 1869 death of Mary's mother, Susannah, there was little to distinguish the Secaurs from many of their neighbors in Liberty Township. Her mother's family, the Mays, had a close relationship with Henry Hinton's family, stretching back as far as the 1830s in Colerain Township in Ross County.[77] Mary's and Henry Hinton's grandmothers were members of the Cox family,[78] whose relatives populate census entries across Colerain Township in this period. It is unclear when the Secaur family moved into the township, but the 1843 marriage of Mary's parents, Joseph W. Secaur and Susannah May, was solemnized by Justice of the Peace Elias Hinton, Henry Hinton's grandfather.[79] Mary's parents lived close by her Secaur grandparents amid her May relations until sometime between 1850 and 1856, when the families migrated to Mercer County.[80] Interestingly, Mary's Secaur grandfather seems to have been abandoned by the family; he is reported as living alone and working as a toll collector in Colerain Township in 1860.[81] Mary was the youngest of six children—and the only girl. Joseph and Susannah's first child, John L., was born in 1845,[82] followed by William (1847),[83] Elias (1853)[84] and Calvin T. (1856).[85] Mary and her twin brother, Marion Monroe, were born in 1859.[86] In the summer of 1862, about a year into the Civil War, Mary's oldest brother, John, was inducted into Company F of the Ninety-Ninth Ohio Volunteer Infantry, a unit raised in Celina that included Henry Hinton's brother, Elias, and eventually Henry himself.[87] John died early in the war around Nashville, maybe from battle wounds, but more likely from one of the diseases raging through the camps full of farm boys. There is no record of how the family reacted to John's death or if they were touched further by the war.

Sometime in 1869, Mary's mother died from smallpox.[88] Perhaps her death hit Joseph particularly hard, or perhaps it was the loss of his wife in addition to the loss of his son seven years before, but Mary's father seems to have given up on his children after Susannah died. The 1870 census shows Mary and her siblings scattered across Liberty and Black Creek Townships. Mary "Seers" lived with the "Siterly" family,[89] while brothers Elias and Calvin lived to her northeast with the Robison family in Black Creek Township.[90] Day says in *Lynched!* that Mary "was accompanied, part of the way, on her return [from church] by one or two of her brothers," and that "part of the crowd, including her brother, left, going north at the first cross roads"[91]—Erastus-Durbin Road, home of the Kimmels. This might have been Calvin and Elias, but it also might have been Marion. There is also an eleven-year-old "William M. Secort" living with the Courtemann family in Black Creek Township.[92] There is no record anywhere that Marion was ever called "William," but it is possible that the same census worker who heard "Secaur" as "Seers" heard "Marion" as the much-less-unusual "William." Perhaps the oddest location for any of the Secaur family is that of Mary's father, who is reported as Joseph "Seers," living just down the road with his in-laws, Strouse May and family.[93]

The questions are obvious: Why couldn't—or wouldn't—Joseph keep his family together? Why couldn't they all just stay with the Mays? Why split up Mary and her twin brother? It all seems like "making do" on a temporary basis, but these arrangements had been in place for years by the time of Mary's murder. In fact, from what Day reports in *Lynched!*, Mary's life with the Sitterlys was on its way to becoming a permanent adoption. And what took Joseph to Fairfield County between the census and the time of the murder? The Lancaster *Eagle* reports in its July 4, 1872, issue that "Mr. Joseph W. Secaur, of Clearport, this county, received the melancholy intelligence from his brother, C. B. Secaur, of Shanes Crossing" of his daughter's death.[94] The July 11, 1872, issue of the Celina *Journal* includes this note: "Mr. Joseph Secour, father of the murdered girl, arrived in Celina on Tuesday of this week, from Fairfield County, where he has been making his home." A generous interpretation of Joseph's behavior is that he had traveled ahead to Fairfield County to start a new life for the entire family and that he intended to send for his children once he had his feet back under him. But if that was the case, why would the Sitterlys be considering adopting Mary? And why did it take Joseph over two weeks to make his way from Fairfield County to Mercer County (which was around 150 miles) after the horrible death of his only daughter? In 1915 Levi Robison recalled that back in 1840 his family—an entire household, including two cows and three children, ages five and under—took ten days to travel to Mercer County from Ashland County, about the same distance, under much worse traveling conditions.[95] It seems more likely that Joseph had already begun his new life—one that had no place in it for his children. Following his trip to Mercer County, Joseph returned to Fairfield County, where he married twenty-five-year-old Sarah Ann O'Dell on April 10, 1873.[96] He and Sarah Ann would create a completely new family of five children before his death in 1881.[97]

It also seems likely that the family life of the real Mary Secaur—her brothers scattered, her father off 150 miles to the east, maybe already involved with a woman half his age—was too confusing and disjointed to be useful to the men writing the "official" narratives of her murder and the retribution meted out by a justifiably angry community. Better a beautiful orphan child than the abandoned daughter of a broken home.

⊷—◦—⊶

Dumontville, Fairfield County, Ohio—November 23, 1873

Joseph Secaur[98]

The baby is screaming. Sarah climbs out of our bed and goes to the cradle I fashioned, intended to keep the child out of our bed, and coos to Richard as she brings him back to our warm blankets. I roll over and try to shut out the snuffling and sucking he makes until he latches on. That shut him up. Richard was named for Sarah's father—the wagonmaker-turned-farmer-turned-wagonmaker. The next child will carry my name.

There will be more children this time. God willing, this one's womb and legs won't close up against me. I know I need to keep her full of babies so she don't look around for someone her own age. She already proved herself ready to jump in bed with her father's carpenter. Lucky for me. O'Dell made a stink about it, but I think he was glad to be rid of her. A twenty-seven-year-old single daughter's no bargain for a man with nine others crammed into a few rooms over his shop. We'll move out of here once I get a little money ahead and can strike out on my own again.

I hear long, regular breathing behind me and try to picture the baby's face, but I can't see much other than red skin and black hair. He's just another baby. Try as I might, I can't recall the others, either—even the twins. Things were never the same after they came along. Trouble just seemed to seek me out. No matter where I took that family, I just couldn't seem to make a go of it.

I lie here and listen to the two of them breathing. It's a good, positive sound. When my son John died in the war, that laid me out for a spell, and it set my first wife, Susannah, against me more than ever. It wasn't any better when William left. He never said good-bye; he was just gone one day. Then, soon as I got back on my feet, Susannah up and died on me. Four children on my hands and a black depression on my back. I worked hard to align the scraps, but I could never seem to make ends meet. It's not that I don't want to care for them, but I can't do it all.

My left side is sore where the shucks have been pressing, so I roll back to face Sarah, careful not to knock the baby. The moon has come out from behind the clouds, and in the blue light I can see the dark shapes of my wife and child. When I came back here to work with O'Dell, my plan was to make enough to bring the family back together. But then that mess with Mary happened, and I was back in a hard place. Fortunately, O'Dell took me in until I was back on my feet. And Sarah was so good at comforting me in my grief that here we are. I'm going to make it work this time.

⊷⊶⊙⊷⊶

Tiffin, Ohio—June 23, 2017

David Kimmel

I feel guilty about McLeod. He stands accused along with my relatives, and he will dangle on the end of a rope beside my great-great-great uncle. Yet I give him short-shrift in this book. Partly this is because we know so little about him. Day grants him a few lines at the end of his book: "Alexander McLeod was of Scottish extraction and was born in Canada, at or near the town of Chelsea, where his parents now reside. He was a young man about twenty-one years of age, of rather prepossessing appearance, and was possessed of an intelligence and decision of character which under different auspices would have made him a useful man; but which, directed in the channel it was, made him a reckless daredevil, capable of planning and executing the most daring and execrable acts of crime. He had regular features, florid complexion, blue eyes and brown, curly hair."[99] Countering Day's version is the positive account of McLeod provided by his employer and reported by the Indiana papers. We also have access to various versions of what he said on the back of a wagon just before he was hanged. I have searched records for additional information, but what I have found is incomplete and only tentatively connected to him because he left very little in the way of a paper trail. His entry in the jail log reads "Canada West," which, in 1872, referred to the current province of Ontario. There is no Chelsea in Ontario, but there is a "Chesley" in Bruce County, Ontario. Beyond that, though, I run into dead ends. Alexander McLeod is simply too common a name for that community. Yet, I must confess part of the problem is that he simply doesn't draw me to him. For one thing, he may very well have been a rapist and a murderer; as I have shown, the evidence, while confused and varying in quality, does not rule him out. And if he was innocent—which seems more likely to me—his role in the lynching is simple to explain. He is the outsider who drew the short straw, who was in the wrong place at the wrong time, and who teamed up with a business partner who did not hesitate to throw him to the wolves. Most importantly, though, he is not my problem. This is a family story, after all—my family. Why were the Kimmels targeted by their neighbors and the authorities? And why, in particular, Absalom? The rest of this chapter seeks to answer these questions in order to provide some understanding of my family and their relationship with their community. We begin with our fictionalized-but-real Irish neighbor, Daniel Mahoney.

⊢┤◆┤◇├┤

Liberty Township, Mercer County, Ohio—Saturday, June 23, 1877

Daniel Mahoney[100]

I tossed another forkful of hay over the door and into the stall's manger. "I told you before, I cannot say what I'll do."

"But you must help. It is your duty. We must protect our families." Hengel leaned against the stall door like he owned it.

I kept forking. "It's of no use talking it to death, Hengel. I told you I have not settled my mind. Leave off and give a man a chance to think, now."

"Actually you do not need anything more to hear, my friend. Harmon is with us, and so is Wright. Where do you stand?"

I stopped working for a moment and looked straight at Hengel. The Germans—they were about as bad as the English. "Why then, I'll tell you what, Hengel. I'll let you know my mind tomorrow. Now clear off so a man can get work done."

"All good, but time moves quickly for these devils and for those who support them." And with that, Hengel clomped out of the barn and across the road toward his own farm.

I glared at Hengel's back. Was it a threat he had delivered? I would show that German a thing or two someday. Just then, the farm bell rang from the back of the house. I hurried through feeding the horses and walked up to the house. Johanna met me at the pump with a cake of homemade soap and a towel.

"Thank you, darling." I began washing in the pump. The water smelled of the cold and of iron and, now, of the harsh soap that turned my face redder than normal.

"Just so's you're forewarned, Daniel. Me da' is on his high horse all morning."

I stopped scrubbing for a moment. "Faith, he can just keep it to himself, your da'."

"Now, don't you be saying such things. He may be the old man, but it's me own father, he is, and I'll not hear yourself speaking ill of him."

"Of course not, Johanna." I dried off my face and handed back the towel. "I wouldn't be thinking it." Johanna returned my smile and, with a swish of her skirts, covered the few steps back to the rear door of the house.

Though some of our neighbors had built frame houses to replace their original settlers' log dwellings, we still lived in the old house. It was cramped and musty and cold in the winter. The plaster finish on the inside walls was beginning to crack and, in places, fall off the walls. Still, we didn't make enough on the small farm to consider buying or building another place. I stooped a bit as I stepped into the low kitchen that some previous owner had tacked onto the back.

My father-in-law sat stiffly upright in his place at the table. "Good day, Father," I said and nodded to the older man as I pulled out a chair and sat at the table. "Sure, 'tis another parched one, I fear."

"I believe you. 'Twill be, I'm sure of it."

"It's nothing out there compared to inside that oven of a kitchen," said Johanna, who'd magically sprouted three-year-old Catharine from her hip. "Here, Daniel, take this child while I get the food on the table." She handed me our young daughter and then turned her attention to our older children. "Mary, John, Johanna, Lucy! Get yourselves in here to eat, or go hungry." I bounced Catharine on my knee as the other four scrambled into the room and settled into their places at the table.

"We're after playing pirates, Da'," said Mary. The other children joined in all at once to explain their game.

"And you should be helping your poor Mam, hadn't you?" I asked.

"Now, Daniel," said Johanna, "children need play. Besides, Mary helped me with the breakfast, and John cut the wood this morning. He's the makings of a regular man of the house," she said, stroking her son's unkempt red hair.

"Is he, now?" I gave John a mock appraising look. "Ay, he's growing like a weed, isn't he, the brave, fine old crab?" John beamed and looked smugly at his sister. "But did he remember to feed the chickens this morning?"

"No, he didn't. I did it for him, on top of my other chores," said Mary. John's pride slipped from his face.

"Well, never mind that now. Let us say grace and eat!" I said. "Father, would yourself do the honors?"

Dennis cleared his throat and launched into an elaborate grace that lasted a full ten minutes. As soon as he seemed to be winding up—over the years she had learned the signs—Johanna slipped from her chair and began dishing food out of the iron kettle in the back yard. She handed the plates to Mary, who quickly brought them to her grandfather and myself before setting them before the other children. Soon everyone was happily strapping on the feedbag, except for little Lucy, who couldn't abide cabbage—though she's been eating it nearly every day of her life—and pouted at her plate.

"It's wasting good food that child is," observed Dennis.

"Aye is it. Eat your victuals, miss," I said. "You'll want that to grow up big and strong like your sister, Mary."

Lucy merely poked at her plate.

"There, now, Lucy, you need eat, girl," said her mother.

"Nothing wrong with that colleen a good thrashing wouldn't sort out," observed Dennis.

"It's her mother and I will be the judge of that," I said.

"Troth, I'm not criticizing anyone, mind you. It's just an old man I am. I disremember my place at times."

"You're laying it on a bit thick, there, Father," I said.

"Now, Daniel," reprimanded Johanna.

"Sure, I know when I'm out of line," said Dennis. "I know when my advice isn't good enough for these American Irish. I was smart enough back in the old country, but not here, no. Here it's just an old man I am, living off the charity of me own daughter and her husband."

I rolled my eyes at Johanna and went back to my plate. I knew better than to tangle with my father-in-law. The old man would talk the teeth out of a saw.

Dennis threw his napkin down on the worn pine table. "Bah, this heat puts me off my feed. Such a God-forsaken country! It freezes a body in the winter and broils it in the summer, it does."

"Sure, it's not like the fair Eire," I said. "But at least there's food to eat."

"And no landlord," added Johanna.

"Aye, the landlords," said Dennis, thoughtfully. "It'd be heaven, Ireland would be, if it weren't for them English and no mistake. Nearly as bad as this lot around here with their so-called church. Mary, mother of God, strike me dead if I can tell what goes on in it. A lot of caterwauling and scripture-reading from what I can see. No priest or chapel closer than Celina. 'Tis shameful to be living out here in the pagan wilderness."

I laughed. "'Tis hardly the pagan wilderness is Liberty Township. Them Methodists is every bit as Christian as yourself, Father."

"Bite your tongue, boy! The Lord have mercy on your soul for entertaining the thought. Christians, indeed! Heretics and Protestants the lot of them. Next you'll be telling me Ireland be better off with them Anglicans."

"I said nothing of the kind. I only said 'tis other Christians besides the Romans in the world."

"Bah," said Dennis, returning to his meal. He chewed for a few moments and then, not able to contain himself any longer, set off again. "I suppose these fine Christians be making you feel good and safe, and yourself with the wife and daughters at home. Them Kimmels attend your church next door. A likely crowd they are, too. Who knows but they'd slit your throat as soon as look at you."

"Now, nothing's been proved about them boys, and the Kimmels ne'er did a thing to any of us," I said.

"What about Hengel last year?" asked Johanna. "Beaten near to death by that Henry."

"Hengel didn't get nearly half of what he claimed, and he didn't get the third of what he deserved, if you ask me," I said.

"It was guilty of the assault Kimmel was found," said Johanna, "and yourself testified against him."

"Oh, Kimmel larruped him, all right, but to tell God's truth, I can't say as I blame him."

"That's a fine way to talk for a Christian man, talking of the beatings and such," Dennis said. "These Americans be rubbing off on you, lad."

"No, Father, I've not changed, but 'tis no picnic living next to Hengel. That man there keeps at a body until the devil's own thoughts come to mind."

"Now, Daniel," said Johanna, "We've nothing against the Hengels. It's elegant neighbors they are, and they did nothing against us."

I muttered under my breath, "That's easy for yourself to say, being stuck around the house all day."

"Which, now?"

"Oh, nothing. I was just thinking about getting up and getting back to work."

Johanna smiled. "I thought as much. Oh, speaking of Hengel, what did he want with you just a bit ago?"

"Same as yesterday and the day before that. It's wandering the neighborhood he is, pressing right or wrong for ... well, you know what for."

"Getting the mob together and taking the law into their own hands!" said Dennis. "It's the anarchy, I tell you! These Americans! And they say things about us Irish."

"Sure, they're talking about a mob—the whole county's talking about a mob," I said.

"You don't think they'll really hang them boys, do you?" asked Johanna. "What did you tell Hengel? You'll turn the bothered ear to that request."

I sighed. "Faith, 'tis not as simple as all that. I just don't know what I think. 'Tis … 'tis just not that simple, is all."

"'Tis simple as anything," said Dennis. "When Americans get it into their heads they're right about something, nothing—law, truth, righteousness, religion—can persuade them otherwise. Troth, 'tis all or nothing with them. And if they all want to murder them boys, they'll do it, sure as anything."

"What are you going to do, Daniel?" Johanna looked at me with frightened eyes.

"I told you, I don't know, yet," I said. "I don't like the idea of the mob, but if it keeps us all safe, especially yourself and the girls … That poor girl."

"That poor girl," echoed Johanna. "She was only three years older than our Mary, she was. She walked right past here the day she died."

"Those murderers walked by here, too," said Dennis. "Don't forget that, my children. There was murder committed, the foul and horrible crime. And we mustn't shirk away from punishing the wicked and the evildoers."

"But I thought you just said you were against a mob action," I said.

"Against the mob I am, but sometimes that's all there is to keep the peace. If the law can't protect its citizens in this wilderness, then the people have the right to protect themselves."

"'Tis hardly the wilderness here," I said. "Still, I just don't know what to do."

"That poor girl," said Johanna. "I get sick just thinking about her. Have you seen her grandparents or the Sitterlys this week? This whole mess weighs on them; it's eating them away from the inside. I feel like that, too. When I watch them ride past in their carriage, I can't help but notice the empty spot where that girl should be. It leaves an empty spot in me own heart. Then my mind turns to me own little children, and I begin to feeling fear and, more frightening, hate. I know I could hate them murderers if it happened to my children. And 'tis only the small distance between there and here."

"Yerrah, do your your duty, Danny. Yourself needs get out there like the man and help with the men's work of ridding the neighborhood of that gawm," Dennis said.

"What are you talking about, Father?"

"Begad, there's danger afoot, my boy. And don't tell me you don't know of it. Skulking around the neighborhood, peeking in at the windows and threatening the womenfolk."

"He bothers me, Daniel, I must confess." Johanna was starting to clean up the dishes from the table, and she spoke to us from over her shoulder. The children, finished with helping their mother, returned to the front of their house and their pirates. "I feel better with him locked up," Johanna said.

"Faith, I'll admit Ab's a bit of a problem," I said, "but he's never really done anything to anyone. He won't do the hand's turn of work without complaining, but it's the middling worker he is, if you keep on him. Everyone around here uses all them boys on core to help with getting the harvests in."

"You knew about that boy for years, and yet what did you do about it?" asked Dennis. "Nothing. Lack of the backbone—that's what it is, if you ask me."

"Well, I don't remember asking ye, now that you mention it," I said. "What happened before's got nothing to do with that girl."

"It's got everything to do with that girl. If you hadn't neglected your duties, that girl would still be alive."

I looked hard at Dennis. "You're daft, man. We don't even know the boy killed her."

"Sure, we know, all right," he said. "If yourself looks to your conscience, you'll know it, too. *And* you'll be life do something about it."

"He's got a point, you know, Daniel," said Johanna. "Those boys do seem to be guilty. It's hard to make a case in their favor."

I looked hard at the table before me. "I just don't know." I paused for a moment. "When I hear the case against them, I feel swayed by it. Folks like Hinton himself make themselves mighty persuasive. He thinks he's the quality, but 'tis a *caubage*, he is. When I get to thinking about the evidence and about who it is coming out against the boys, 'tis the loudest ones ..."

"'Tis the loudest ones who know the Kimmels, eh?" interjected Dennis. "Them nearby to the Kimmels know what's what with the likes of them."

"Nah, Dennis, you got that wrong, is why I wonder. 'Tis the ones had some beef against the Kimmels is the loudest now. Hinton's never liked them, for whatever reason. And 'tis a grudge Hengel carries on account of his beating."

"Which yourself can't blame him for, now can you?" asked Johanna.

"No, I can't. We never had any problems with the Kimmels, save some of Absalom's foolishness. But that hardly makes him the murderer, now does it?"

Dennis lowered his voice into deep warning tones. "Begob, he's the dangerous Black Man, and no joke."

"No, I wouldn't say dangerous, Da'," said Johanna. "But he is strange and unnerving, like."

"Faith, I'll grant you 'tis the *mootch* he is, and he makes me nervous sometimes, considering all you young women around the place."

"Thank you, Daniel." Johanna laughed.

"My pleasure, dear," I said. "But making us nervous and acting oddly is not the same as violating and murdering the girl."

"How about that peddler, then—that McLeod?" asked Dennis. "Figure the Scotsman for a murderer, anytime. No one knows him, and he runs away right after the murder."

"But the other peddler, that Kimmel cousin, he came with McLeod and left with him, too, yet no one suspects him. Why is that?"

"That's bothered me, too," admitted Johanna.

"Bah!" said Dennis. "Why worry about the other Kimmel? They're frontier ruffians, they are. They'd as soon cut your heart out as look at ye."

"You and your frontier," I said. "Ye'd think we had Indians lurking behind every bush, to hear you talk. It's a way off beyond Iowa, the frontier. There's more wilderness out in the wilds of Ireland than here."

"Rubbish. We're twice the men in Ireland, and we've twice the civilization."

I thought about that a moment. "Not to hear folks like Hinton talk. To him it's wild, drunken Irish we are, ready to bring down the whole country. He only comes around to talk to us when he's wanting something."

"They want something now, that's for sure," said Johanna. "How are you going to answer them?"

"Oh, I'll put them off until I make the final decision. I just can't make up my mind."

"It wouldn't be so hard to make up your mind, as you put it, if you had any backbone," Dennis said.

"Father," cried Johanna. "That's no way to talk to Daniel!"

"Troth, it's a fine lot you all are. For the life of me, if we were in Ireland, we'd not sit around waiting for some man of us to step up and do what needs to be done. There's no room for such behavior in Eire."

"Oh, no crime in Ireland, eh?" I asked.

"Not like these vicious animals, howling in the wilderness. Their courts don't work, so they resort to mob hangings. It's barbarous!"

"But you were just pushing for me to side with the Hinton gang, weren't you?" I asked.

"Certainly not! There's a place for law and order. Of course, when you're out here in the wilderness and the courts don't work properly, sometimes the people need to take the law into their own hands."

"You're not making any sense," I said. "You're arguing with yourself."

Dennis struggled to his feet and raised himself as straight as he could manage. "I'll not sit here and be insulted. Johanna, Mr. Mahoney." Dennis bowed curtly to each of us and then shuffled out of the room, back into the cool darkness of the main house.

Johanna sighed. "I wish you wouldn't argue with him, Daniel. He's just an old man."

"An old devil, if you ask me." I noticed Johanna's pained expression and stared at the table, uncomfortable with making eye contact. "Of course, I mean to say he's just a little cantankerous, he is—that's all."

Johanna brightened. "Promise me yourself won't fight with him."

"I wasn't fighting with anyone, merely answering his ideas."

"Sure, I know he can be contrary, but 'tis my own Da', he is, and we're all he has in the world. He's just not used to keeping his opinions to himself."

"I don't begrudge him his opinions. I just wish he spoke some sense." I rose and pecked her on the cheek, and then I left the kitchen.

The heat blasted my breath away as I stepped out into the afternoon sun. Though the lack of rain that spring and early summer had dried out the fields and turned the roads into piles of dust, it was a cruel, close day. The heavy, humid air always brought down my spirits, and the lunchtime discussion with my father-in-law wasn't improving my mood. Back in the barn, the regular rhythms of the work settled my thoughts into clearer channels.

It wasn't long after I set to work that Hengel and Hinton hailed me from my open barn door. I reluctantly dropped my work and headed over to face them. I was careful to remain inside the shade while they stood in the sun.

"And what can I be doing for you gentlemen?" I asked.

Hengel spoke first. "You know why we come."

Hinton ignored his partner and spoke impatiently. "As you might guess, we're here to discuss what's to be done with the fiends who outraged and murdered poor Mary Secaur."

"'Tis arrested, they are?" I asked.

"Yes, of course."

"And the sheriff holds the keys in a nice, safe place?"

"It's not that simple," said Hinton. "In our country, especially in these troubled times, there's always the chance that outsiders will intefere with the normal course of local justice."

"And what's that mean?"

"That those murderers might be moved to another county so they can avoid trial by their peers," said Hinton. "The community feels it is important that they receive justice here in Mercer County, where the blood of that poor girl is still wet on the earth."

"Yes, and in sight of that blood," added Hengel.

"The community."

"The men and women of this township, of the countryside around us, of Celina," said Hinton. "We are all of one mind on this, Daniel."

"One mind," echoed Hengel.

"Sounds like you've made up your minds, then," I said. "What do you want with me?"

"Unity." Hinton spoke as though he enjoyed the sound of the words. "All men must unite behind this common cause."

"And everyone is behind it?" I asked.

"Pretty near. That's why we're here," said Hinton.

"Then you don't really need me, do you?" I asked.

"You're either for us or against us," said Hinton. "As our forefathers said, *E Plurbus Unum,* which is Greek for 'the people united.'"

"And what if there's a mistake?" I asked.

"A mistake?"

"What if you follow your plan and them boys is innocent?" I asked.

"Innocent?" asked Hengel. "My God, these Kimmels are not at all innocent."

"We have their confessions," said Hinton.

"Confessions? From all of them?" I asked. I had not heard tell of that.

"Oh yes, signed and witnessed. All three participated in the outrage and the killing," Hinton said. "We know they did it. We just need to make sure they pay for it."

"It's the murder you are suggesting," I said.

"It's the hand of justice," said Hinton. "Now, are you on the side of justice or the side of lawfulness and disorder?"

"I don't see it as that simple," I said.

"You're either for us or against us," said Hinton. "And the community will remember who done which."

"Oh, they will?" I asked. "Well, we'll just see about that. Good day, gentlemen."

Hinton and Hengel hesitated. "Best mind the safety of your family," said Hinton. "It's a lonely place out here in the country without your neighbors behind you. Just look at the Kimmels."

"Yerra, just look to yourselves on your way off my land," I said. I turned my back on them and disappeared into the darkness of the barn.

>-+-+>-0-<+-+-<

I. F. Raudabaugh. Journal—1872

Henry Kimmel has lived in Mercer County for 30 years or more and from the first to the last has been regarded by nearly every individual of the country as a wicked and dangerous man. He has been in the habit of drinking all his life. I have been told of a number of instances in which he deliberately struck and brutally beat parties who had no cause in the world to suspect that he ever had any intention to do so. He always did this when the parties were not in a condition to defend them selves. It has not been much more than a year since he attacked an old and helpless man, and besides other injuries gouged out one of his eyes. By action after action of this kind, he has rendered himself and [his] family the terror of the community. You may judge something of the kind of example such a man would set for a family of growing boys. Inheriting such blood would seem to be enough, but it was not. The father, besides setting such examples as these, taught his boys by word of mouth. I am creditably informed that he frequently told his boys when [they were] small to go for the girls and not be afraid for that girls liked it. This of itself would not go to show so much, if everyone who has ever been about the family did not say that the whole conversations nearly always turned upon vulgar stories and vulgar scenes. Indeed I have been creditably informed that the father has been known to take unmentionable privileges with his wife in presence of the whole family. Last winter two of the boys (one of these was hung yesterday, July 8, 1872) acted in a way in the district school certainly too disgusting to relate here in detail. In the absence of the mistress they denuded themselves and in this

*condition disfronted their bodies in the presence of the whole school—consisting
in part of girls of their own age. This case was presented to the directors of the
school and the boys were expelled, though insisting all the while, in the face of
the testimony of the whole school their innocence in the matter. Mary Bell Secaur
here gave a statement to the directors for which it has been said that the boys
declared that they would pay her back sometime.*

⊷──◦──⊶

Tiffin, Ohio—June 23, 2017

David Kimmel

Two important contemporary accounts of the Secaur-McLeod-Kimmel
case—James H. Day's *Lynched!* and I. F. Raudabaugh's unpublished
journal—are unequivocal in their criticism of Henry Kimmel and his
family. Day claims, "The Kimmels were disreputable people at best, and
were feared and disliked for their bad practices by the whole neighborhood."[101] Oddly, Day's description of the Kimmels does not appear in
his July 4 *Mercer County Standard* article that serves as the word-for-
word source for the rest of this section of his book.[102] But his phrasing
is strikingly similar to that in a July 3 story published in the *Cincinnati
Commercial Tribune*, which refers to the family as "disreputable characters";[103] this description seems to have influenced other accounts in the
Cincinnati Gazette[104] and the *Van Wert Bulletin*,[105] so it's likely that Day
drew his phrasing from the Cincinnati account. Day, Raudabaugh, and
the *Commercial Tribune* reporter could hardly have been personally familiar with the residents of an out-of-the-way corner of an unimportant
township in rural Mercer County. While it is possible that the authors
canvassed the Kimmels' neighbors and impartially pieced together their
accounts of the family from multiple local sources, opinions about the
Kimmels more likely originated in a single source—a local official who
served as the self-styled voice of the neighborhood.

That official was Henry V. Hinton, justice of the peace[106] and likely
point man for contact between the township, Celina authorities, and vis-
iting reporters. Hinton organized the original autopsy of Mary Secaur,[107]
and he probably played a large role in organizing the search party before
that. When authorities traveled to Liberty Township on Tuesday and
Wednesday to investigate the case and perform the official autopsy,

Hinton led them on their tours of the murder site.[108] At the time of the murder, Hinton lived with his wife and three children in a medium-sized plot just south of his mother's much-larger concern.[109] In his mother's household lived his brother and his sister-in-law, Lydia Hinton, who was twenty-three years old and listed as a school teacher on the 1870 census form.[110] I assume hers was the schoolhouse across the road from the Hinton's[111]—the same school Mary Secaur and the Kimmels would have attended. Raudabaugh includes an incident involving Absalom and Jacob Kimmel at the school as evidence of the family's unsavory behavior.[112] Lydia would have been the logical source for such a story, and through her relative and neighbor, Henry, the story passed on to Raudabaugh. Henry, therefore, is likely the source of the entirely negative portrait Raudabaugh paints of the Kimmels in his journal; likewise, it makes sense to consider him the source for Day's description of the family in his book.

I have no direct evidence about what Henry Hinton thought of the Kimmels, the murder, or the lynchings—no narratives, no correspondence, no diaries. I am no unbiased critic, since it is my own relatives we are talking about. My re-creation of Henry Hinton is only one of many other possible interpretations of this man, including a version in which he is simply a selfless public servant interested only in protecting the lives and property of his fellow citizens. Still, there is evidence in Hinton's life and background that points in the direction of the re-creation I am presenting here: that Henry V. Hinton was a social climber who was eager to ingratiate himself with the powerful elite of Celina. For this reason, he fed the authorities what they wanted to hear about the Kimmels. He may very well have believed what he told them, too, as the Kimmels represented to Hinton the type of old-style settler family that he wished to eliminate from the community. Now, for the evidence.

First, there is Hinton's desire for social position within his community. Though he owned only average land holdings—about one-half of the land the Kimmels owned[113]—Hinton would, over the years, serve as township clerk, trustee, and justice of the peace;[114] it was in this last capacity that he would have interacted with the Celina authorities during and after the murder investigation. While one could simply see Hinton as a good citizen eager to help his community, there is evidence of self-aggrandizement in his life: Hinton would later arrange to have a post office—named after himself—brought to his crossroads; he was one of the few local farmers to buy biographical space in the 1882 *History of Van Wert and Mercer*

Counties[115]; and, to this day, his black-granite memorial lords over other, lesser stones in the Liberty Chapel Cemetery.

Something of Henry Hinton's desire for status could stem from his family background—the Hintons were original settlers in Colerain Township in Ross County, one of the earliest white settlements in Ohio.[116] Henry's grandfather and uncle served as township trustees, and his grandfather served as justice of the peace for fifteen years[117]—he officiated at the wedding of Mary Secaur's parents. Henry would have grown up with a sense of the importance and permanence of his family. It must have been a disruption for Henry when, sometime in his late teens, his parents joined his uncle Francis's family in Hopewell Township in Mercer County, just to the east of Liberty Township.[118] Henry's trustee uncle, John, bought sixty acres south of the Kimmels along Tama Road before changing his mind and selling out to Henry's father and uncle Francis in 1859.[119] I am not sure when Henry's family moved to Liberty Township, but since Henry married his Hopewell Township neighbor, Althea Rutledge, in 1860[120] and served along with his elder brother in the Civil War, my guess is that the family waited until 1865 to restart their lives in this new place.[121]

What all these dates mean is that Henry Hinton was a latecomer to Liberty Township, most likely living there just six to seven years before the murder of Mary Secaur. This sets him and his family apart from the Kimmels, who were among the longest-tenured families in the area, having received their original land grant from the United States government in the mid-1840s.[122] Furthermore, Henry and his family most likely moved into an already existing house on an already cleared farm—again, much different from Henry and Susan Kimmel, who probably built their homestead from scratch in virgin wilderness.[123] Henry Hinton must have noted the difference between his boyhood home in Ross County and the backward nature of Mercer County, and it is easy to imagine him sharing the boosterish, expansionist mentality of his generation that, as the frontier of the United States moved further west, worked to replace the free-wheeling settler culture of their forefathers with a more progressive, "civilized" culture centered on towns and cities. This new culture focused on the rule of law and participation in the political process, education, and economic growth. Undoubtedly, he supported the proposed new railroad that would bring trade and connection to the rest of the state—and was irritated by the failure of the local farmers to vote in favor of the railroad.[124] He may have continually compared himself and his little neighborhood to the townspeople and leaders in Celina—and viewed himself as more in tune with the town than with settler families such as the Kimmels.

Adding to his desire to separate himself from illiterate settlers such as Henry and Susan Kimmel may have been a nagging sense of embarrassment about his own family. If my hypothesis is correct concerning Henry's social ambitions, he must have harbored an ambivalent attitude toward his mother, who was listed as illiterate in the 1870 census, a relative rarity in the township. The only others so listed in the immediate neighborhood were the Irishman, Daniel Mahoney, and Henry and Susan Kimmel.[125] While Henry's uncle John had established himself as a prosperous farmer back in well-settled Ross County, Henry's parents had moved at least twice before settling down for good in Liberty Township, which may have shaded Henry's view of them. And it is difficult to imagine Henry being unaware that his parents' marriage date, October 10, 1839, put his May 2, 1840, birthdate under a bit of a cloud.[126] Seven-month babies (generally full-sized and healthy) were not unusual in rural communities, where betrothal traditionally brought sexual activity, yet the social climber in Henry may have been ashamed of his tainted beginnings. It is commonplace that bigots have the strongest negative feelings about folks most similar to themselves. Because Henry could not openly be angry at or embarrassed by his own parents, it seems possible he might have displaced some of these nagging feelings of inadequacy onto the Kimmels, representatives of the kind of backwoods ruffians he was working to supplant.

Henry Hinton's Civil War service probably contributed to his social ambitions. He served in Company F of the Ninety-Ninth Ohio Volunteer Infantry from December 1863 through December 1864, and then in two other regiments as the war wound down.[127] During the last thirty-five years of the century, veterans of the Army of the Republic became the driving force in American politics and business, so it would have been likely for Henry to catch this spirit of leadership earned through service to country. Complicating (or strengthening) this sense of pride in his military service might have been an equal sense of survivor's guilt. It is unclear whether Henry volunteered or was drafted, but his service started much later than that of his younger brother, Elias, who signed up with the ninety-ninth when it formed in August 1862.[128] My guess is that Henry would have been reluctant to volunteer because he left behind a one-year-old daughter and a wife who was six-months pregnant; so there may have been a nagging sense of inferiority for the draftee joining a volunteer unit that had just seen hard fighting at Chickamauga and Lookout Mountain.[129] We know little about Elias's service record aside from the fact that he was listed on the Regimental Roll of Honor on March 6, 1863.[130] It is easy to imagine Henry's sense of loss when his brother died in action near Kennesaw Mountain, Georgia, on June 20, 1864.[131] When Henry returned home a little more than a year later, he may have felt the need to prove himself worthy of survival.

One final element of Henry Hinton's character was his role as the eldest male in his extended family. In addition to the loss of Elias, the family also suffered the death of Henry's father on July 25, 1866.[132] As the oldest son, Henry would have likely had a interest in his mother's affairs, standing in as surrogate father for his siblings—possibly to his mother's and siblings' annoyance. Only thirty-two, Henry may have struggled with this patriarchal identity. It certainly would have contributed to a sense of insecurity and a desire for control of his surroundings. Added to this would have been the death of his three-year-old daughter, Ruth, just two years before the events of our story.[133] Hinton and his wife would have known grief, but he may also have possessed that desire for security that comes with such a loss. As patriarch, Henry would also have been desirous of protecting his own siblings from harm—and from suspicion in the case of Mary Secaur. After all, three of his brothers—Jacob, Franklin, and Wilson—fit right into the age bracket of the accused Kimmels and McLeod. Separating his own family from the Kimmels would have served this purpose. And as the main source of information for town men such as Day and Raudabaugh, Henry Hinton stood to play a major role in shaping the view of the Kimmels that has been passed down to us.

But it is not the source so much as the content that makes me suspicious of Raudabaugh's portrayal. Henry Kimmel is first accused of being "in the habit of drinking all his life," a not-unlikely situation for someone of the pioneer generation—the same probably could be said of many men in the neighborhood. Henry Kimmel is then accused of "deliberately [striking] and brutally beat[ing] parties who had no cause in the world to suspect that he ever had any intention to do so." Henry, in fact, was convicted of assault against Andrew Hengel in an incident occurring September 22, 1870; there were plentiful witnesses against him among his neighbors,[134] and the case was heard in the regular courts. Whether the fight was unprovoked is less clear, but the rest of Raudabaugh's portrayal of the incident is overstated, to be generous. Raudabaugh claims Henry Kimmel "attacked an old and helpless man, and besides other injuries gouged out one of his eyes." In the first place, Andrew Hengel was around fifty-one at the time of the incident, and Henry Kimmel was at least fifty-three,[135] two years older than this "old and helpless man." No record of the exact nature of the assault has survived, but the lack of any mention of the assault or even the court case in the Celina papers lowers the likelihood that Kimmel gouged out one of Hengel's eyes—that would be exactly the type of sensational detail seized on by the papers that a year later would glory in the brutal nature of Mary Secaur's murder.

The other accusations Raudabaugh makes are of a sexual nature—that Henry advised his sons to "go for the girls," that he turned conversations to "vulgar stories and vulgar scenes," and that he took "unmentionable privileges with his wife in presence of the whole family." Drunken, violent, and over-sexed—these are the accusations traditionally made against any marginalized group, particularly by the middle classes against the lower classes. The Irish, Eastern and Southern Europeans, African Americans— every group to come along and threaten homogeneous native-born white American populations was painted with the same broad brush. The exaggerations and adherence to traditional formulas in the stories about the Kimmels make me suspicious. These are the types of stories dreamed up or elaborated on by someone like Henry Hinton to separate the civilized, upwardly mobile element of his world from backward backwoods rubes such as the Kimmels.

There is one passage from Raudabaugh's account of the Kimmels—a claim that Absalom and one of his brothers exposed themselves at school—that I am unsure about. Although the story fits in with the overall attack on the Kimmels as over-sexed ruffians, this type of event is certainly possible, as there were many examples of older teenage boys causing problems in schoolhouses across the country. Officious and discipline-minded male teachers risked having the hickory turned on themselves. The disciplinary challenges facing a young woman teaching in a multi-age classroom were legion. Teenage boys being what they are, it would not surprise me if a group of them—and there were ten or more in their mid-to-late teens in the neighborhood—goaded one another until someone did something stupid. That it was two of the Kimmels may be due to character flaws—or it may just be happenstance. However, the portion of Raudabaugh's story where the Kimmel boys threatened Mary Secaur with retribution for testifying against them seems to be fabricated—it is too convenient a connection to the murder, and it runs counter to all other testimony against McLeod, Absalom, and Jacob, which emphasizes that the young men happened on Mary by accident.

So what is accurate in Raudabaugh's (which is really Henry Hinton's) characterization of the Kimmels? Fortunately, we are not left completely at the mercies of the "official" view of the Kimmel family. Although we lack direct and reliable testimony from the family members, we can track down enough information to draw a sketch of the family's background and history. We can also draw on our imaginations to create a viable, believable version of the family, one that includes their perspective and some indication of how they interacted with their neighbors. From this exploration, perhaps we can determine how likely it was that Kimmel family members should be involved in a rape and murder.

By the time of the murder in 1872, the Kimmels had lived in America for just over one hundred years. Henry's grandparents, Johann Jacob and Hanna Margaretta, immigrated from Hesse-Darmstadt to Philadelphia in 1768,[136] lived for three years to the north of Philadelphia, and then settled among a pocket of Germans in Westmoreland County, east of Pittsburgh.[137] When the revolution broke out, Johann Jacob enlisted as a private in the Eighth Pennsylvania Regiment, which served under General Wayne through the battles of Brandywine, Paoli, and Germantown before passing the winter of 1777–1778 at Valley Forge.[138] The unit returned west that summer to protect settlers against the British and the Indians, serving at Pittsburgh, Fort McIntosh on the Ohio River, and Fort Laurens in the Ohio Country.[139] Johann Jacob rejoined his family as his enlistment ended in 1779 but served in Truby's Frontier Rangers during the Indian fighting that lasted into 1782.[140] The Kimmels' eldest son, Johann Andrew, also served in the militia, this time called out in the fall of 1794 by President Washington to reestablish order during the Whiskey Rebellion in western Pennsylvania.[141]

Whether fleeing debts, escaping neighborhood or family complications, or experiencing midlife wanderlust, sometime between 1810 and 1820— around the time Henry was born in 1817—Johann Andrew moved his family north to Blacklick Township in Indiana County.[142] Within ten years, the family would move another county westward, settling in Plumcreek Township in Armstrong County.[143] It is unclear exactly when the family moved the third time, but by 1836, when Johann Andrew died of apoplexy,[144] they had headed west to Holmes County, Ohio. As with the moves to Indiana and Armstrong Counties, Johann Andrew ended up near relatives—this time near the family of his oldest son, John Kimmel.[145] The Kimmels' time in Holmes County was short-lived. John moved to a farm on Township Line Road in the recently opened Liberty Township in Mercer County in 1840,[146] followed by brothers Abraham and Henry at least by 1843.[147] Two years on, their mother, Elizabeth Kimmel of Holmes County, bought thirty-nine acres on the west side of Erastus-Durban Road at the north edge of Liberty Township.[148] This is the western half of the land owned by Henry at the time of the murder and lynchings and the plot on which the lynchings took place.

The Kimmels continued to invest in Liberty Township when John's son John Jr. bought two lots a mile west of Henry's farm in 1848 and 1849.[149] He sold out to Mary Secaur's grandfather Straus May in 1850 and moved to Allen County.[150] Henry purchased the land across Erastus-Durban Road in 1852, the second-to-last lot sold by the federal government in Liberty Township.[151] A year later, Henry's nephew William sold John's Township Line Road farm,[152] and sometime after 1854, Henry's brother Abraham left Center Township for Indiana.[153] During this decade and a half, the Kimmels integrated themselves into the life of their part of Mercer County. Four Kimmels married into local families, including Henry's 1846 marriage to Susan Hines.[154] William is listed as clerk in the township estray book.[155] Henry Kimmel would remain in the township, raising his children and interacting with his neighbors socially, financially, and legally up until the terrible events of June and July 1872.

The Kimmels were Pennsylvania Germans, the famous Pennsylvania Dutch, and it is probable that German cultural characteristics would have persisted through the generations. By the time of the revolution, Germans made up to a third of the population of Pennsylvania,[156] primarily farmers or agriculture-related artisans who had owned property in Germany but most likely incurred debt for the trip to America.[157] They settled near Germans, married Germans, spoke German at home, read German-language newspapers, and participated in a network of correspondence between relatives and former neighbors, both in America and back home in Germany.[158] The average German immigrant only loosely committed to the Reformed or Lutheran churches to which he or she belonged,[159] and cultural reluctance to display strong emotion in public made German-Americans less susceptible to evangelical outbursts such as the Great Awakening.[160] On the whole, the educational level of the German-American community was probably equal to if not above that of the rural population as a whole. Although many German immigrants to Pennsylvania began their new lives as indentured servants, as a group, they were eager to pay off their debts and become landholders as a means of investment and economic mobility.[161] Overall, the Germans in America were noted for their economic and agricultural acumen.[162] And German-American women came in for special praise for their willingness to work in the fields alongside their husbands.[163]

How German the Kimmels were by 1872 is difficult to say. Henry's father, Johann Andrew—growing up in an isolated German settlement with immigrant parents—certainly spoke German. Johann Jacob undoubtedly learned English during his military service during the revolution, and it is likely that the son also learned English. Johann Andrew married two women with decidedly English names—Anna Elizabeth Palmer and Elizabeth Spoon—as did his son Henry. A good indicator of levels of acculturation within immigrant communities is naming conventions, and all of Henry and Susan's children—with the notable exception of Absalom—were christened with the typical Anglo-American names of their day. Most likely, the "German-ness" of the Kimmels lay in their attitudes and family customs. For the most part, however, the Kimmels would have seemed thoroughly American to onlookers, particularly next to recent German immigrants such as their neighbors, the Hengels.

More influential in shaping Henry's family than their German heritage was probably their status as settlers. Settlement of the Ohio region followed a fairly predictable pattern. First, young[164] American-born[165] pioneer settlers appeared in an area—often before land became officially available for settlement[166]—built rough, one-room cabins,[167] and cleared enough land to support a subsistence lifestyle. Because cleared land was worth up to five times its original value, these settlers often sold out and moved further west,[168] using land and the labor of their large families as the commodities for their upward mobility.[169] At some point in this process, the settler families began to be replaced by other, more settled farmers, who replaced their log cabins with log houses or even frame or brick houses[170] and cultivated a third to a half of their land.[171] Settled farmers moved beyond the basic economy of settlers into a cash-crop economy—featuring a variety of crops and livestock, particularly hogs—that used waterways and, eventually, railroads to integrate farmers with the growing cities.[172] During this period, farmers and their wives would hire help—or "hire out" their own grown children to other farms in the area.[173] Settled areas developed schools, churches, gristmills, stores, and towns,[174] all of which brought to the area a more educated group of community members who sought intellectual as well as economic improvement.[175] Although the eastern and southern sections of Ohio had moved past the frontier stage into the settled farming stage by 1830,[176] the northwestern corner of Ohio had only begun to open up at this time, and by 1872 the differences in attitudes between the "backward" settlers and the more "progressive" settled farmers caused conflict between the two groups.

Changes in American culture tended to spread from the older, established East toward the developing West, with the frontier areas often following cultural patterns and rules of previous generations. Travelers and immigrants from the East complained of the backwardness of the settler class. Manners and education were two markers of progress, and settlers were criticized on both accounts, understandably in the case of education in areas where schools met infrequently and were taught by underprepared teachers who sometimes had to physically fight the older boys in a school in order to establish their authority.[177] Living in a log house with open windows, an open fireplace, and even cohabitating animals naturally made dirt a part of life in settler houses, and newly settled areas lagged behind the East in adopting new concepts of tidiness inside and outside their dwellings.[178] Ready access to alcohol combined with a demanding lifestyle to make the frontier areas notorious for drunkenness,[179] and the growth of the temperance movement was undoubtedly driven in part by Americans whose childhoods had been damaged by abuse and neglect at the hands of alcoholic parents and relatives. Working classes and minorities are often portrayed by their social betters as overactive and undercontrolled in their sex lives, and critics during this period blamed animal urges for the high birth rate among settlers. Settlers were criticized for sleeping together in their one-room dwellings,[180] though even back East, the concept of separating sleeping and living spaces emerged only in the first three decades of the nineteenth century,[181] and even though two of the first steps taken when moving from a rude one-room cabin to a more settled state were to build a loft for the children and a separate bedroom on the ground floor for the parents. Still, frontier communities tended to adhere to the sexual and moral standards of their parents' and grandparents' generations, which were more permissive than those developing in the East.[182] One final and very real aspect of settlement culture was its

violence, brought on in part by harsh living conditions,[183] corporal punishment for children,[184] and violent pastimes such as cockfights and even
bull and bear baiting.[185] As in the other problematic aspects of frontier
life, attitudes toward violence among the general American populace were
moving; the settlers simply lagged behind the crest of this wave of change.

Though Ohio had been a state for well over thirty years and the last
native peoples—those delimiters of the boundary between wilderness and
civilization—had been pushed west over the Mississippi, the last townships opened in Mercer County were still raw frontier when Henry Kimmel's
mother purchased land from the US government.[186] What is more, Henry
was a son of a son of a settler. His grandparents would have recalled life
in a European setting where the farms seemed as old and unchanging as
the land, but Henry and his father had both spent their lives breaking new
ground. By the time Henry and Susan's farm in Mercer County was cleared
and fully functioning in the early 1850s, Henry and his people had lived
in frontier or near-frontier conditions for over eighty years. Clearing and
planting a farmstead in virgin forest required a particular type of personality, and it seems reasonable to assume that Henry and his family would have
been a little rough around the edges. It is also plausible that Henry's family
may have been hard drinkers and violent. Henry Kimmel had not one but
two charges of assault on the books, the last of which occurred in 1870 and
dragged into court a number of his neighbors. The 1852 case was quashed
when court met in May of 1853, but the 1871 jury found Henry guilty.

Henry's 1870 assault-and-battery case is worth examining in some
detail because it undoubtedly contributed to the suspicion of the Kimmels
following Mary Secaur's death. Not only did many of Henry Kimmel's
neighbors—including Henry Hinton—serve as witnesses in this case of
farmer-on-farmer violence, but serving subpoenas to those witnesses
was one of the first official actions taken by Thornton Spriggs as Sheriff
of Mercer County. And Hinton, through Raudabaugh, provides this case
as evidence of the bad character of Henry and his entire family. According to the surviving court documents, on September 22, Henry Kimmel
allegedly assaulted his neighbor Andrew Hengel.[187] It took nearly a month
for the Court of Common Pleas to convene a grand jury to review the case.
Henry was formally charged with assault and battery[188] and arrested;[189] it
is unclear whether Henry spent the next month in jail, but on November
24, he and son Samuel posted $600 bond to set him free.[190] In late January
and early February, two sets of witnesses were subpoenaed, all neighbors

except for two farm laborers probably hired to help with the harvest.[191] The first group, called for the prosecution, lived on Tama Road within a mile or so of each other—except for the two hired laborers—while the second group was spread out to the south of the crossroads. The trial in late February lasted only two days. Henry was found guilty and fined $100.[192]

The court records provide only a skeleton of the case and leave many questions unanswered. What was the context of the fight? Given the date and the lists of neighbors called as witnesses, it seems likely that the neighborhood had gathered to help each other with the fall harvest. We have to imagine some argument arising that would lead to fisticuffs. And why this particular set of witnesses, especially those for the defense? It is possible the first group were the eyewitnesses while the second group were called as character witnesses by the defense, though why Henry Kimmel would subpoena Henry Hinton and his younger brother is a mystery. It is interesting that Hengel's next-door neighbor, Joseph Wells, was not a part of the first group, though geographically he fit that grouping better than the other. From this point on the facts dissipate: we know only that Henry Kimmel fought Andrew Hengel, Kimmel evidently won handily, and the injured Hengel pressed charges. Because we can only know something of the *what* from the records, it seems reasonable to employ fictionalization to flesh out the *how* and the *why* of the case. What follows is my imagining of some of the testimony featured in the depositions and the hearing.

⊱──❖──❖──❖──⊰

Andrew Hengel, Deposition Given to Sheriff H. L. Jonson on September 23, 1870, at the Celina County Jail

So, it was yesterday afternoon at three o'clock. My son John and I helped Daniel Mahoney at the corn harvest. It's the way in this country, we help our neighbors at harvest. We had made just for the lunch break, when John came to me and told me that Absalom Kimmel threatened to beat him.

These Kimmels are a wicked clan—wild ruffians. There is inbreeding among them, and they will never go far. They have a German name, but they have no German customs. The parents cannot read and write even. The father is a liar and a drunkard. The mother is a poor, tired woman, and the children are stupid and slovenly—even the girls. They are not much better than beasts of the field.

We have lived here in the neighborhood for nine years, and in that time we have had more than our share of annoyances and frustrations with Absalom Kimmel. He is nineteen years old, but he acts like a child. A few weeks before this last incident, I worked the ground and stopped to find my wife in tears and the children frightened. This Absalom had stood in the front yard, staring at the house, and spoke indecent with my wife. I immediate rushed to the Kimmels' house and was met by the father. Although I started off dignified and polite, Henry Kimmel spoke rudely and mean. He denied my accusation against his son. He did not want to recognize my right to live in peace and security in my own country. Finally, when I threatened to sue him in court, he crashed into me and wanted to twist my neck. I fear no man, but I was worried that my sons would see me fight. I left his land and went back home.

When John told me how Absalom had threatened him, I approached his father quietly and demanded—as it was my right—that he should punish his son and keep him away from the younger boys like John so that he would not bully them. Kimmel stayed his ground and stared at me, but then a strange expression slowly came over his face. He began to threaten my family and me. We argued. He was stormy and mean, while I acted rational and calm.

I must have looked away for a moment, because I did not see the punch. Kimmel hit me direct on the left eye, and I fell to the ground. I defended myself as best I could until the neighbors around us gathered together and pulled him out of the way. My son brought me home, where my wife tended my eye. Only her care saved my sight. It had become quite swollen, which is still the case. Today, I went to Dr. Hetzler, a fellow German here in Celina.

So I tell you now the whole story. Such an unlawful attack is not fitting in a law-abiding community like ours. I know that my neighbors agree with me when I say that these Kimmels always disturb the peace and are dangerous. We want to rid ourselves of this plague. I appreciate, in particular, the assistance of my neighbor Henry Hinton in this matter. A more honest Christian man I have never met.

Report Given to Sheriff H. L. Jonson by Henry V. Hinton, Justice of the Peace, Liberty Township, Mercer County, Ohio, on September 23, 1870, at the Celina County Jail

I, Henry V. Hinton, of Liberty Township, Mercer County, Ohio, hereby set down this 23rd day of September, 1870, a full account of the assault perpetuated by Henry Kimmel of Liberty Township on Joseph Hengel, also of Liberty Township, on September 22, 1870. I confirm that every word found here is complete and correct.

This unfortunate incident was solely the fault of Henry Kimmel. Henry Kimmel has lived in Mercer County for more than thirty years, and from the first to the last has been regarded by nearly every individual of the country as a wicked and dangerous man. He has drank all his life. It is only natural that his sons are violent and dangerous, since the father is abusive—physically and verbally—toward his children, his wife, his neighbors, and his animals. One of his sons, named Absalom, regularly costs the women of the neighborhood. It is no uncommon thing for a local farmer's wife to look up from her washtub to see this man-child of Henry Kimmel staring at her from the road or the edge of their clearing. To say that this behavior upsets our virtuous women would be a gross understatement. Though the neighbors have demonstrated with Kimmel about his son's behavior, their efforts meet with vile curses and threats. The neighborhood is united in seeking a way to rid itself of this menace.

The event in question occurred on September 22, 1870, a Thursday, at approximately 1:00 p.m. in the afternoon. I was first made aware of the incident when a bloodied Andrew Hengel walked into the fields of my mother, Elizabeth Hinton, where we were harvesting her corn crop. Present was myself; my younger brothers, John, Franklin, and Wilson; George Meizner; Anthony Mertz and his son, Lafayette; Elias May and his son, Byson; and Joseph Wells and his sons, William and Wilson. Hengel told us he had been assaulted by Henry Kimmel and requested my services as justice of the peace.

I accompanied Hengel to the farm of Daniel Mahoney, where the assault took place. Kimmel and his sons were working in the fields with Mahoney, Jacob Harmon and sons, Jacob Wright and sons, and two hired hands. Kimmel behaved as cool as you please, just like nothing had happened. I took statements from each of the participants and warned Kimmel to stay away from Hengel. This morning, Friday, September 23,

1870, I drove to Celina with Hengel to make a formal report of the crime, what you are reading. While in Celina, Hengel was treated for his wounds by Dr. Hetzler, who expressed surprise that Hengel remains the use of his eye.

Here's what happened, as near as I can tell from what witnesses told me. The entire group had been shocking Mahoney's corn crop during the morning of Thursday, September 22, 1870. It was hot and dry. The group was divided into teams, some bending and twining stalks into gallus hills, the others gathering together the surrounding stalks into the shocks. The teenage boys were organized into teams headed by the younger men. The workers talked as they worked.

Over the course of the morning, Absalom Kimmel made negative remarks about women and girls in the neighborhood. As I said, he is a base individual, and anyone familiar with him and his family would not be surprised at such comments. He continued his slander during the nooning. At some point, John Hengel took offense at a remark, and him and Absalom Kimmel fell to quarrelling. So far, it was only words. Following the dinner break, John Hengel appraised his father of the matter. The elder Hengel approached Henry Kimmel, and they began arguing. Suddenly and without prevarication, Kimmel—his passions no doubt inflamed by the jug of spiked switchel passed freely among his family members during the nooning—attacked the gentle German farmer, knocking him to the ground and beating him severely—to the point where he gouged out Hengel's eye. Kimmel's sons prevented the others from coming to the rescue of Hengel. After the assault, Hengel was helped to his feet by his son and led away in search of me. The rest is as already told.

Such an unprovoked attack, coming as it did out of nowhere and resulting in the assault on a helpless old man, must not go unpunished. As this cowardly assault was carried out in broad daylight before the eyes of scores of neighbors, there should be no trouble in assessing Kimmel's guilt. We must strike a blow for justice, humanity, and gentility. If this county is ever to take its place among the civilized peoples of this globe, we need to firmly establish the rule of law over lawlessness. This deed must not go unpunished.

Jacob Harmon's Testimony at the Trial of Henry Kimmel.
Celina, Ohio, February 21, 1871

I witnessed the attack by Henry Kimmel on Andrew Hengel. We had just finished dinner, when Kimmel and Hengel commenced to arguing. I still sat in the shade of one of the shocks when I heard the shouts nearby. When I arrived at the circle surrounding the two, Hengel delivered a tongue-lashing against Kimmel, much of it in the German. I remember enough from my childhood in Alsace to tell that the basis for Hengel's argument was the behavior of Kimmel's son Absalom.

I could understand Hengel's frustration with the Kimmels. After all, Absalom had antagonized everyone in the neighborhood for the past five years or so. He wandered around the neighborhood, talked to the people, and made a nuisance of himself, generally, but since he became a young man, his thoughts had settled on one thing: women. He was always behind or watched some girl or woman in the community. Women never knew when they look up they see Absalom there, staring at them. And he always said inconvenient things to the girls at school, on the way to school, out on the roads—wherever he ran into them. My Sophronia and Lydia told us of lewd comments he'd made in their presence. However, to be fair, both Lewis and William, my two oldest boys, reported that they got along fine with Absalom—and the other Kimmel boys, for that matter. Here on the edge of the township, maybe we have less interaction with the Kimmels and fewer problems with Absalom. I know that the people at the crossroads and over by the school do not like him or his people.

My two sons had worked with the boys at the harvest of corn all morning. From what Louis and William told me, Absalom Kimmel and John Hengel had commenced to argue during the morning, and their argument ran on through dinner. My boys could not recall the subject of the dispute. At one point, Absalom threatened to beat John—not an idle threat considering the difference of age. John ran to tell his father of this threat as our groups ended the break. Hengel strode over to Henry Kimmel and took up his son's cause. Henry, not one to support such behavior, argued back, and they soon began to shout. Right after I arrived at the scene, with Hengel in midsentence, Kimmel caught his jaw with a powerful right-hand blow. Hengel staggered, and Kimmel at once jumped on him. He pounded Hengel with his fists until Hengel lay beneath him on the ground. All this happened so quickly that those of us who watched just stood for a moment in shock. When we realize what happened, we jumped into the fray and pulled the two apart. I do not think Kimmel beat Hengel severely.

Hengel's son helped him up and on his way home. Hengel called Kimmel all manner of names—in English and German—and threatened to take Kimmel to court. As you know, Hengel was as good as his word, and here we are. I'd say that the charges against Henry Kimmel will be decided in favor of Hengel. After all, Kimmel did hit him first, no matter what.

Do I have ill feelings toward the Kimmels? No, I must confess that I feel pretty neutral about them. I've had a few problems with Absalom, but everyone around here has. He's more a nuisance than a threat, if you ask me.

⊶⊷⊶⊷

Daniel Mahoney's Testimony at the Trial of Henry Kimmel. Celina, Ohio, February 21, 1871

Sure, I see the whole ruction, at least the hitting part. I couldn't say what had started the fight, though I gather it had to do with Absalom Kimmel and an argument with John Hengel. Hengel, my Dutchman neighbor from across the road, and Henry Kimmel, my neighbor just to the northwest of my own lot, was standing in the middle of a circle and arguing at the top of their lungs. To tell God's truth, Hengel was getting in far and away the most words, but the majority of it was in German. I relish the great scrap as much as the next one, you know, so I was eager to see what would happen between these two able farmers. But this was no contest. Hengel—he was ballyragging away when Kimmel clouts him. Hengel hit the ground like a sack of meal, and Kimmel on him in a flash. It took four men to pull him off, swinging and cursing like the devil. Lucky for Hengel, too, or Kimmel laid on the father of a beating.

Even had I not seen it with my own eyes, 'twouldn't be hard to believe Kimmel whipped Hengel. The Kimmels would shame a field of tinkers. Rumor is Henry stood trial for assault once before, near twenty years ago. And he has his share of the arguments with people in the neighborhood.

But mostly them problems circle around his son Absalom. Anyone around here knows about Absalom, and we've all had our share of trouble with him. He's not all there, and no lie. Always stravaging the roads. But faith, other than annoying the womenfolk, he does nothing all that bad. I hired the older Kimmel boys to help with my harvest some years, and they always did good work, even Absalom. He's a bit lazy, he is, if you don't keep right on top of him. In fact, other than chasing Absalom off my property a few times for bothering Johanna, I really never had any problem with the Kimmels.

Knowing Hengel, I wonder if their fight was all the fault of Kimmel. I been neighbor to Hengel for close to ten years, and there's no more contentious Dutchman in all Christendom. He's the nice enough fellow, on the whole, but if he feels he's been cheated or treated unfairly, just look out, is all. Once he gets the idea in his head, 'tis God's own truth he's like a dog worrying a bone. Last fall, my stoat got into his corn. I'm still hearing about it. I fetched my pig, patched the fence, paid for the damaged corn, and then listened to Hengel rant about irresponsible neighbors for over a year now. So, while I'd never hit the man just because he annoys me, I feel Kimmel's urge.

⊢·⊷·○·⊶·⊣

Joseph Wells's Testimony at the Trial of Henry Kimmel.
Celina, Ohio, February 22, 1871

I wasn't working at Mahoney's. I was over at Hinton's that day. I know it may seem odd that I wasn't right across the road helping with the harvest, but living next door to Andrew Hengel for over ten years gives me little interest in spending more time with him than I have to. Let's just leave it at that for now.

I didn't see the fight, just Hengel bustling across Elizabeth Hinton's field to complain to Hinton. For whatever reason, Henry Hinton has it in for Henry Kimmel, so he didn't take much persuading to see Hengel as the innocent victim.

Me, I'm not so sure, knowing Hengel. A typical German—he knows what's best for everyone else. He's forever telling me how to run my farm and seems to think he owns the whole crossroads. Still, he's a hard-working farmer and a good citizen. If I had to pick a neighbor, though, I'd pick the Kimmels.

I've known Henry ever since he showed up at my first wife's folks' place over in Dublin Township. The Hineses had settled the year before my mother bought the plot next door from the government and moved us all from Wood County. Mom and Sarah's mother got along right off, being widows and all. And the Hineses helped our family something considerable as we cleared the forest and set up our own farm. Let's see, that was '38, and Sarah would have been nine or ten—much too young to attract the attention of a seventeen-year-old. That changed after while, naturally, and Sarah and I married in '44. Yes, this is relevant. I'm getting to that.

The Hineses lived in two houses on their land. Sarah lived with her mother and brothers and sisters in one place, and her oldest brother, Amos, lived with his wife and family in the other. But that makes it sound simpler than it was because they were always mixed and matched at each other's houses. There was some of them I never did figure out who they belonged to. The thickest friends were Sarah and Susan, Amos's oldest child. Even though Sarah was technically Susan's aunt, she was only two years older, and they were closer to sisters than any two women I've ever known. I don't think I ever saw one apart from the other until I actually took Sarah home with me on our wedding day. Susan was at our house right off the next morning. Once me and Sarah married, it was like I married the both of them. There were days when I had to throw Susan out of the house just to spend time alone with my wife.

I *am* getting to the point. It wasn't long after I married Sarah that the Kimmels bought the first half of their land over in Liberty Township. I don't know exactly how Henry got wind of Susan, but families were few and far between back then, and his uncle had lived on the township line for close to five years by then. Anyway, Henry came sniffing around about the time Sarah and I married. Henry was twice Susan's age, but I can't really say much, since Sarah wasn't much older than Susan when we got married. Girls married a little earlier back then.

Amos didn't put up a fuss, and Ann sure didn't mind when Susan moved away. There was always some tension between Susan and her mother.

Stepmother, rather. I never learned who Susan's real mother was. Sarah said the story her mother told her was that Susan was just left on the doorstep of Amos's house—the baby in the basket. But Amos always accepted Susan as his daughter, even though Ann didn't. I guess when a stranger's daughter shows up two months into your marriage it might not start things off on the right foot.

Yes, I'm hurrying to the point. Just be patient! Course, Sarah was sad to lose Susan from next door, but we wore out the roads between our place and the Kimmel's. It's only about three miles, you know. We were having babies, and they were having babies, and the two sets were all mixed up half the time. When my Sarah died birthing little Sarah, Susan was there. I don't know what I'd have done without her those three years until I married Avilla and moved in over there on her folks' land. Oh, Sarah's folks were a big help, but they had their hands full, what with John and his two boys living there after his wife died. My three little ones spent a lot of time over at the Kimmels. I guess I owe Henry and Susan for my Avilla, since I wouldn't have met her without always traveling past on the way to the Kimmels.

Sorry. I was just wanting you to know about the Kimmels. They are rough, sure, especially Henry. But those of us who went through the sparse times setting up farms in this county are probably a little uncul-tured, if you know what I mean. Susan is a kind and sweet woman, though she's been worked near to death with all the kids to care for. And Henry's a worker. You can't deny that. He's cleared that farm and worked to feed that big family of his. And they're always there if we need them, even if they do keep to themselves anymore. I can't blame them for that, what with Ab and all. I feel a little bad for how we've drifted apart a bit over the years. It's different with Avilla and having our own family, though my older ones are still friends with Henry and Susan's.

Did Henry Kimmel do it? Probably, though I wasn't there so I couldn't say. He's got a temper, and Hengel can be provoking. I imagine the jury will find in favor of Hengel, and Henry will have to pay his fine. And then we can all forget this nonsense and get back to living our lives.

Tiffin, Ohio—June 23, 2017

David Kimmel

One of the frustrating aspects of attempting to understand the Secaur-McLeod-Kimmel case is that the principals are not able to speak for themselves. Other than the reported confessions by members of the Kimmel family—any of which could have been fabricated by the authorities—we hear nothing from them. Others speak for and about them. Part of my search for understanding involves stepping beyond the meagre facts and the handful of statements and stretching toward the past with imagination. I am fascinated by the relationship between George and Jacob. For example, the fact that George offered up his double-reverse testimony naturally draws my eye, but the idea that his actions contributed to the lynching of one brother and the near-lynching of another provides rich ground for exploring his inner life. Fiction provides me a method of exploring George's personality, of proving my reading of him, and as a way of exploring the dynamic between the brothers.

⊢•◦•⊣

Liberty Township, Mercer County, Ohio—July 5, 1872

Charlie Kimmel

George is home, but Ab and Jake are still in town. Andy went home. The other one, the Cloud Man, he's still in town with Ab and Jake. I wonder if they went to the store there, but Mary Ellen just says to hush. I want Ab to come home.

I am playing in the garden, breaking up clods with a stick, when I hear a shout from the front of the house. "Jake's home! Jake's home!" It's Jennie who's hollering. I drop my stick and run around to the front of the house. Sure enough, walking up the road toward the house, is Jake. He looks hot and dusty. His feet make clouds of dust as he walks.

I sprint to him, squeezing between the rails when I reach the fence. "Jake, Jake, Jake!" I cry. I slam into his legs and hold them tight. My brother! He stops for a moment and pats me on the head. He pries me loose and walks on to the house. I patter along beside him, my feet puffing up dust below me. Puff, puff, puff. I grab his hand. I look behind us at the two sets of feet in the dust.

"Where's Ab, Jake?" I look up at him, but he pays me no mind. That's all right, since my brother is home.

We cross the stile and walk up the packed-earth path to the house. On the porch beneath the low-sloping roof stands Mommy. Our Mommy. My Mommy. She holds out her hands for Jake, and he hugs her. They stand there for a moment. He doesn't move. Then she holds him out at arm's length and wipes a tear from her eye.

"Come on in and get a drink and some food. You must be hungry from that walk."

"Yes ma'am," says Jake.

"It's Jake," I say to Mommy. "He came home, just like George."

We walk through the front door and into the low-ceilinged sitting room. The fire is out. In the middle of the day, you don't need no fire. It's summer—and we don't need fires in the summer. I like fires in the winter. They're pretty. Like an orange.

Jake and Mother lead the way into the kitchen. There Mary Ellen is standing, waiting for Jake to come through the door. She grabs him and hugs him tight. He stands stiff. She lets him go, and he sits in a chair with a sigh.

Through the back door come the girls—first Sarah, then Alice, and then Jennie. Each is a little taller than the next. They are all taller than me except Peck. He stands at the doorway, grimy thumb in his mouth. His thumb is always in his mouth because he's still a baby. He's a little boy. I'm a big boy. Not as big as Jake, though. Or George. Or Ab. I ask Mother if Ab will be home tomorrow, but she says to hush. I hush. The girls are all over Jake, hugging him and sitting on his lap. He pretends he don't like it, but he don't shoo them away.

Peck steps aside as Daddy comes in the back door. He's sweaty and dirty from the farm. Daddy's a farmer. We're all farmers, except the girls. They help Mother in the house. I help, too—sometimes in the house, sometimes in the yard. When I'm bigger, I'll help with the animals and the fields. Maybe next week I'll be bigger. Peck don't help because he's still a baby.

Daddy comes over and shakes Jake's hand. Jake's a grown-up man. Grown-up men shake hands; boys and girls and women hug. Someday I'll be a grown-up man like Jake. Daddy sits down, and he and Jake start to talk real low. I can't hear them, so I go outside into the garden. There's a gray cat in the far corner, hunting for something. Maybe a mouse, maybe a rat. I saw a rat in the barn yesterday. I threw a rock at him and scared him away. I'm not afraid of no rat, but I am afraid of the horses. They are so big, they'll stomp the life out of a little boy. I keep Peck away from them because he don't know better. I open the gate real quiet and walk even quieter. The cat is still, facing the other way. If I'm quiet, I can grab him and pet him. Otherwise, he'll run away. When you pet a cat, it rumbles. The cat don't have a name. It don't pay to name cats on a farm because they die off so fast. Just as I'm about to grab him, I hear heavy footsteps come around the corner of the shed, and it's George. The cat is gone now. I follow George into the back of the house.

It was bright outside, but it's dark inside. When my eyes get used to the dark, then I can see again. Sometimes I stare at a candle and then look away in the dark. There's a bright blue or green or orange flame shape in the dark then, but there's no candle now. George stands there, about a foot inside the door. I have to squeeze around him to get inside. He smells like hay and sweat and dust. It's not a bad smell, just a hot smell. I move past him and over by Mommy, who is holding Peck by the shoulders. The room is quiet.

"Why's it so quiet?" I ask Mommy. She shushes me, so I shush.

George just stands there, looking at the floor. Jake and Daddy and Mommy and Mary Ellen—they all stare at George. Peck has squirmed away from Mommy and has gone out through the front door. The girls are not here. I lean into Mommy, and she runs her fingers through my hair. Even in the dark kitchen, it's hot. I want to go back outside.

George clears his throat. He sounds like Daddy when he does that. "I see you're out," he says. "I'm glad."

"No thanks to you," says Jake. There's another quiet time. Mommy grips my shoulder and pulls me close. It's hot, so I squirm. She hangs on.

"What about Ab?" asks George.

"Still locked up with McLeod," says Jake.

"I heard Ab talked," George says.

"He don't know any better," says Jake. "Unlike some people."

"They threatened me."

"You don't think they threatened all of us?" asks Jake.

"Andy said McLeod did it," says George.

"Why you think they let him go?" asks Jake. "Or you?"

"You're here, so you must've talked."

"I didn't go back on my family," says Jake, standing up quickly.

"Settle down, now," says Daddy. "There's no need for all this fuss. I got one boy left in the jail. I don't need the rest squabbling." He stands up. "We got work to finish before supper. Come along and help, you two."

Daddy walks out past George, who steps aside to let him through the doorway. He and Jake stand there staring at each other.

"You heard your Dad," says Mommy. "Just get on out in the field and finish up. There's more time for all that talking after dinner." She lets go of me and turns to the sink.

George turns and walks out back. Jake follows him, but I stand there by Mother. Outside, I hear loud voices. I run to the door and look out. There on the path sits George, holding the side of his face with both hands. Jake has his back to us and is walking to Daddy and the fields.

⊢•◦•⊣

Tiffin, Ohio—June 23, 2017

David Kimmel

One of the first fictional vignettes I wrote for this project was the imagined story of a trip to town by the three principal Kimmel brothers. I wanted to explore the relationship of the three brothers, to get a deeper feel for their personalities—particularly George's need to please (or appease) his social betters. I have no evidence for this aspect of George's personality other than his performance during the hearing and Andrew Kimmel's comment that he preferred George over Jake.[193] Because Andrew so easily turned on his partner to free himself, and since George took similar action to free himself, I see George and Andrew as a type. Absalom is the fool, a source of irritation for both brothers but a social embarrassment to George, who seeks ways to ingratiate himself with the powers in Celina. The story also expresses my reading of the family's relationship to the community, represented by actual Celina citizens. Patrick Callen, twenty-one, and with no previous grocery experience, was probably staked in his share of the business by his neighbor, the wealthy and powerful lawyer, Hiram Murlin, whose sixteen-year-old son worked at the shop as a clerk. Another neighbor, Lylla Hodder—the seventeen-year-old daughter of a German-born lawyer—enters the shop with Mattie Miller, also seventeen and the daughter of a less-successful lawyer whose boarders include twenty-six-year-old Jacob Pohlmann, the Bavarian immigrant who co-owns the shop with Callen. Callen and Pohlman will announce the dissolution of their partnership in the same issue of the *Mercer County Standard* that breaks the story of Mary Secaur's murder. Into this mixture of real citizens I insert my reconstruction of the equally real Kimmel brothers.

⊢•⊶•⊙•⊰•⊣

Celina, Mercer County, February 23, 1872

The bell atop the entryway tinkled as the boys pushed open the door and entered Callen and Pohlmann's general store. They stamped the slush off their feet onto the entryway rug and pulled off their hats and work gloves. The pale daylight—weakly filtering through the plate glass windows flanking the doorway—cast bluish shadows across the plain wooden floorboards that stretched between the parallel walls of floor-to-ceiling shelves. The owners had already lit the lamps hanging from the ceiling, and the boys—their eyes adjusting to the gloomy interior—could make out the stacks of brooms, barrels of nails, and mountains of canned food running alongside the counter.

George scanned the room, noting the two men behind the counter on his left, a group of three middle-aged-to-older loafers gathered around the potbellied stove in the back of the store, and another man staring at them from behind the dry goods counter on his right. George smiled and advanced toward the man on the right. Jake and Absalom hung back, just inside the doorway. Absalom looked around at the shelves of groceries. Jake stood with his back to the corner and stared hard at the room.

"Afternoon, Mr. Pohlmann," said George. "Afternoon, gentlemen." George looked hopefully at the two manning the other counter—one in his early twenties and the other about George's own age—who simply stared in his direction. His glance at the back of the store was met with silence.

George turned his attention back to Pohlmann. "Well, looks to be getting colder as the day wears on."

"*Ja*, it will do that in the winter," answered Pohlmann, his *w*'s pronounced as *v*'s in his thick Bavarian accent. George heard snickers from the men at the back of the store. He looked at them and then glanced back at his brothers. Jake glared at the loafers; Absalom traced with his finger the image of a salmon on a can next to him. "What you boys need?"

"Well, Mr. Pohlmann, we're glad to do business with you. Our pa sent us for a bag of three-penny nails, some stove polish, twelve feet of chicken wire—we need to fix up our pen a bit—and a can of kerosene." He paused for effect, and Pohlmann jotted down the items on a piece of scratch paper. "Our ma wants a bottle of Dr. Troutner's syrup, a box of pins, and three yards of a blue calico. Do I need to repeat any of that for you?"

"Three yards?" Pohlmann said loudly for the benefit of those across the room. "Such spending!" Chuckles and whispers radiated from the stove.

"Oh, and . . ." George fumbled in his pocket and withdrew a folded piece of paper. "She wants these groceries, too." He unfolded and held the paper out for Pohlmann, who only looked annoyed and waved him away toward the other side of the room.

"Is this the grocery side of the store? Give it to Mr. Callen! Murlin, come get this boy's goods." He held out the slip toward the teenager across the room.

George crossed the room with his note in an outstretched hand. Callen took it from him unenthusiastically. He turned his back to George and began to seek out items from the floor-to-ceiling shelves along the wall. Murlin ambled out from behind the counter and made his away across the back of the store to the dry goods side. As he passed the group by the stove, Murlin said something to the men, who laughed and looked over at the three brothers. He began filling the boys' order, while Callen did the same on the grocery side. Pohlmann remained standing still, looking the boys over.

"Yes sir, quite a cold snap coming on," George said to Callen, who was facing away from him. "Dad says we'll have to work to get ready for the return of Old Man Winter after this warm spell. Course, it only got warm enough to soften the snow and turn the road into slush." He looked at Callen's unresponsive back for a moment, hesitated, and then walked over to Pohlmann's counter. George addressed the owner and the loafers at the back of the room as he spoke. "I had a hard time keeping the team going through the mud on the pike today. Quite a responsibility I have, bringing in my brothers all the way to town. Dad says he can trust me with it, though. I've proven my responsibility to him time and again."

Callen, who had finished with the order and was leaning on his elbows on the counter, deadpanned, "Your father must be quite a judge of character." More laughter from the back of the room.

"*Achtung!* Watch out!" Pohlmann yelled.

A clatter of cans fell to the floor where Absalom had knocked over a display.

"Keep control of that *depp*!" Pohlmann shouted at George directly.

George ran over to Absalom and began putting the cans back. Absalom retreated to stand next to Jake, who remained motionless by the door. George spoke to Pohlmann over his shoulder as he restacked the cans. "Yes sir, I certainly will. I'm cleaning up the mess right now. No harm done that I can see. Just an accident, nothing to worry about." Now everyone was staring at him.

"If you can't control him," said Callen, "he'll have to wait out on the street."

"Yes, sir," George said, "He don't mean no harm."

Pohlmann puffed himself up and spoke for the benefit of the others in the store, "Why you people bring him to town? No telling what he will do." Murmurs of assent from the back of the store.

George rose from the floor, looked once at his brothers and crossed the room back to Pohlmann. "Yes, sir. I don't blame you, sir. I tell my Dad to just let me leave him at the farm. Me and Jake can handle …"

"If you cannot control him, take your business elsewhere." Pohlmann turned and snapped at Murlin, who had been watching the fun, "Fill their order so we can get them out of here."

The bell jingled as two teenage girls entered the store. The whole store turned to them as they removed their winter hats and muffs in a flurry of fuss and activity. They enjoyed the men's attention.

Pohlmann cut George and immediately turned to the girls with a beaming smile. "Hello, ladies! What a nice surprise to see you this fine afternoon, Miss Miller, Miss Hodder."

Miss Miller surveyed the room, giving Jake and Absalom a little sneer. She ignored Murlin and the men in the back who appraised her silently and nodded slightly at Callen. Then, chin raised, she proceeded grandly to Pohlmann's counter.

"What can I get for you ladies?" asked Pohlmann. "I suppose you come for your mother's package, Miss Miller?"

"Yes, please, Mr. Pohlmann," she said, using her most adult voice. "All the way from New York City." Then she added to Miss Hodder, but for the whole room to hear, "My dress."

The other girl sighed. "I just can't wait to see it, Mattie."

Pohlmann squeezed passed Murlin and the loafers and entered the store-room in the back of the store. With great dignity, Mattie Miller swept her gaze around the room.

"Just country boys, Lylla," she whispered to her friend.

George beamed at her and swept off his cap, revealing his tousled, dish-water-blond hair. Mattie turned away from him to face Lylla, making sure that Murlin had a good view of her profile.

Mattie spoke loudly to Lylla. "If it's anything like the pictures, my dress will be grand. There'll be nothing like it in town. Papa says there's nothing too good for me and my seventeenth birthday, but I don't know about that."

"You sure do well by him." Lylla's voice was tinged with envy.

"I know how to manage him," Mattie said with a smile.

George advanced toward the women, rubbing his hand through his hair. "Uh, excuse me, ladies. Good afternoon, isn't it?"

Mattie turned and regarded George as she might something repulsive forgotten in the corner of a fruit cellar. Lylla looked at him a little less dismissively.

"Picking up a dress, huh? All the way from New York."

"Yes." The two girls turned to each other, whispered, and then giggled.

"We've come all the way from Liberty Township," said George.

"Oh that *is* a long, long way," said Mattie. She looked over to where Murlin was watching her. She caught his eye and smirked. "How ever did you manage?" Murlin and the other men laughed.

"Sure, I do things like this all the time. My dad relies on me to ..."

Just then, Absalom, who to this point had been entranced by a shelf of preserves, noticed the two women. He tugged Jake's coat sleeve. "Hey, Jake, look—girls. Hey, girls!"

Mattie and Lylla took one look at Absalom and burst into giggles, holding their hands in front of their mouths and turning slightly toward each other, their heads leaning together.

Absalom stepped toward the women. "Ooh, pretty." This elicited a laugh from the men in the room. Jake looked on stonily. George placed himself between the women and Absalom. Absalom, playing to the laughter, reached toward them. "You girls want to come home with us?" The laughter took on an uncertain edge.

The women looked concerned and a little frightened. Mattie spoke to Callen. "Stop laughing. It's not funny." She turned to Murlin and said, "Arlington, help us!"

Realizing his opportunity to play the hero, Callen straightened his face and spoke to the men by the stove. "All right, you lot, let's put an end to this." Then he turned to Absalom. "You there, leave her alone. You're scaring the girls."

Absalom laughed, not realizing the joke was over. He struggled to move past George to the women, but George grabbed his coat and held him back. One of the girls yelped as Absalom lunged toward them.

Shouts erupted from the men in the room.

"Hey now, watch it!"

"Clear off!"

"Stop, you!"

Just then, Pohlmann entered the room from the back door, a large package in his arms. "Will there be anything else, Miss?" Then, sensing something wrong, he demanded, "What is going on here?"

The room quieted immediately.

Mattie pointed to Absalom, "Mr. Pohlmann, this … boy is bothering us."

Pohlmann advanced toward Absalom, who shrank back against George. "*Was machst du?*" he said. "What are you doing?"

"I have it under control, Pohlmann," said Callen.

"It's okay, Mr. Pohlmann," George said, positioning himself between Pohlmann and Absalom. "Ab don't mean no harm." George looked back at Jake, who remained scowling by the front door.

"Get out, you boys!" said Pohlmann. "This is a respectable establishment."

George's voice raised in pitch. "But what about our order? You ain't filled it yet."

"It won't do to turn away custom," said Callen.

Pohlmann drew himself up, aware that everyone's eyes were on him. "Take out that *Einfaltspinsel* before I call the sheriff!" He glanced over at the girls to judge their reaction.

Jake moved to Absalom, grabbing him by the arm. "Come on, Ab." He pulled Absalom to the front of the store and out the door.

George watched his brothers and then turned his attention back to Pohlmann. "Mr. Pohlmann, you know I ain't done nothing." He looked over at Mattie and Lylla, trying to catch their eyes. They looked instead between Pohlmann and Callen and huddled a little closer together.

"Just fill the rest of his order and get him out of here," said Callen.

Pohlmann looked from Callen to Mattie, hesitated a moment, and then spoke directly to George. "We don't need your kind coming into town and causing trouble. Get out!"

"But my ma's order! I'll fetch it when I get home if we come back without it." George looked at Pohlmann desperately, but the owner stared him down. "They're the ones to be mad at," George said, pointing at the door. "You're right to throw him out, causing a fuss."

"Out of my store," Pohlmann yelled.

George closed his mouth. He looked at the girls, at the men in the back, and at the clerks, and then he hung his head and clomped to the front of the store. The thud of his big work boots on the floor was the only sound in the room as he left.

Behind him, Callen challenged Pohlmann, "What do you mean, *your* store?"

The shop bell jingled as George opened the door. He hesitated for a moment, turning back to look at Pohlmann, who was muttering something he couldn't make out. George opened his mouth as if to speak, but then, thinking better of it, exited the shop. The door tinkled again and slammed shut.

Tiffin, Ohio—June 23, 2017

David Kimmel

I will return to George and Jacob later. Right now, though, I need to write more about Absalom because I believe he is the key to understanding why the Kimmel family was targeted by the authorities. Yes, Henry Kimmel's two assault cases and Henry Hinton's attitudes toward the family played a large role, but at the bottom of the tensions within the community lay one person: Absalom. If my notions about Absalom are correct, what follows, though fictional, may have been a typical episode in the neighborhood.

⊢·⦁⊷·○·⊶·⊣

Liberty Township, Mercer County, Ohio, June 23, 1877

Daniel Mahoney

It was the late summer, and the sweat burned my eyes as I piled the straw up onto the wagon. I wiped away the moisture with my kerchief, but doing so only left a dried crust of salt and chaff on my skin. I could see the house through the shimmering haze as I leaned on the pitchfork. There, along the woods at the edge of my lot, I could make out the figure of a man, standing stock still and looking at the house. I watched the figure for a while and then saw Johanna exit the back door. She went to the pump and worked it, but I was so far away I heard nothing of the pump's protest. The pantomime continued as Johanna straightened from the pump and turned to look at the figure by the woods. They seemed to speak to one another, and she gestured angrily at the stranger before going back into the house. I threw down my rake and strode through the stubble toward the figure, whose form was ill-defined in the heat. Long before I clambered over the stile and entered the clearing, it melted away into the woods.

Johanna stood in the doorway of the low kitchen, leaning against the doorframe.

"He was out in it, again, Daniel. Troth, he makes me nervous."

"I know it, dear. I don't know what to do about it, though. It won't do any good to talk to Kimmel. You know how touchy he is about the boy."

"I worry about him and the children, Daniel."

"Surely he's not done anything to anyone."

"Yet."

"Yet. Would you like me to trudge over there to talk with them?"

"If you could, it would ease my mind."

I set off through the woods at the north edge of our lot. I followed the path, long ago worn hard and smooth, that ran between our clearing and the road where it split Kimmel's lot. Nowadays, my family had little to do with the Kimmels, except at harvest time. It wasn't any problem between the families. We were just at different stages in our lives—we were starting out, and the Kimmels were stair-stepping from twenty-eight all the way down to newborn. It was a wonder Mrs. Kimmel could still stand up after all those children.

I enjoyed the coolness of the woods, with the smell of life and decay all around me. Birds flitted through the underbrush, and chipmunks called to one another across the forest floor. The room of the woods, with its tall, green ceiling swaying in the wind kept the air cool. Though the land on my own farm was dry and the dirt crumbled to powder or hardened into fired-clay clods, the ground beneath my feet now was fresh and moist, dappled with dim green light.

At last I emerged from the woods and set off across Kimmel's clearing toward the house he and his brothers had raised near twenty years ago. The way the cabin blended into the land rather than occupying it reminded me of turf homes back in Ireland. It had a blind window on the side facing me, a mate to the one that was filled by the shadow of a head and shoulders.

As I approached, one of the younger girls ran from the water pump into the house. By the time I was within twenty yards, Kimmel was striding out to me. Like his house, Kimmel was worn but solid. The hair jutting out from beneath his felt hat was gray, but he walked with confidence and power.

"What do you want?" he demanded, then, reconsidering, stopped before me and said, "Err ... What can I do for you, Mr. Mahoney?"

I stopped and spoke, "Good day, Mr. Kimmel. 'Tis a cruel, parched season, it is."

"Yes, hot. What brings you out on my land?"

"Well ... 'tis about your Ab. I don't mean to tell yourself how to handle your affairs, you know, but he's after standing out behind my house again, and it be bothering the missus."

"What's he done?"

"Ehhh, well, nothing, really. Just standing and staring at my wife."

"Don't sound too dangerous to me."

"Well, it unsettles her, do you know what I mean? He's a grown man, he is, near about, and it ... well, it just makes her nervous with him about. Now, I've got nothing against the lad, you see. He's worked for me and done a fine job."

Kimmel's eyes narrowed slightly and his face reddened. "So, what do you want?" Kimmel asked.

"Only that you speak to the boy and ask him not to bother my wife, is all."

"Why don't you talk to him?" asked Kimmel. I could sense a rising anger in his voice.

"That's not my place, not being his father," I said diplomatically.

"You sure are acting the part."

"Well, I'll just leave it at that, then, and be going back to the work."

"You just do that, and leave raising my family to me."

I ignored the last comment and walked back to the woods. The sun beat down, and humidity lay on me like a heavy wet blanket. I wasn't too pleased with my talk with Kimmel, and I puzzled over his hard words as I entered the path through the trees.

James H. Day. *Lynched!*

Absalom Kimmel admitted his guilt from the very beginning, and, during his entire imprisonment, constantly wept and bewailed his sad condition. His conscience seemed to goad him to desperation, and would give him no rest until he had made a full confession of the dastardly crime.[194]

Absalom Kimmel was nineteen years of age—ungainly and awkward in appearance. He was very much below the average in intelligence, and there was nothing about him or in his make-up to commend him to anyone, for any good purpose whatever. He had dull, black eyes, sallow complexion, and coarse yellow hair.[195]

⊢⋅⊕⋅○⋅⊕⋅⊣

Tiffin, Ohio—June 23, 2017

David Kimmel

Absalom Kimmel is of vital interest to anyone attempting to unravel the meaning of the Secaur-McLeod-Kimmel murders. He was an ignorant, dangerous, but ultimately responsible young man who should be held accountable for his actions. He was a cognitively impaired young man, easily led into participating in an act he failed to understand or coerced into confessing to a crime he knew nothing about. I would like to explore these different possible interpretations.

On the basis of what little evidence we have concerning Absalom Kimmel, it seems likely he suffered from an intellectual disability, which is a broad diagnosis covering a wide range of syndromes that until recently were known as "mental retardation." "Intellectual disability," according to the American Association on Intellectual and Developmental Disabilities, "is a disability characterized by significant limitations both in intellectual functioning (reasoning, learning, problem solving) and in adaptive behavior, which covers a range of everyday social and practical skills. This disability originates before the age of eighteen."[196]

I am tempted to burrow into the many details of this disability to come up with a specific diagnosis for Absalom, but there are several reasons—beyond my admitted ignorance of the field and the limitations in the body of evidence—that it would be more useful to keep my diagnosis on a general level. First, the diagnosis covers a large number of syndromes and diseases, each with a complex mix of associated behaviors. Even within a particular syndrome, not everyone displays the same behaviors.[197] Second, though the mental and physical symptoms of intellectual disabilities are very real, the disability itself is created by the experience and treatment of those who are so diagnosed[198] and by institutional structures that determine who gets diagnosed and when. Third, intellectual disabilities are a moving target. Not only are the terms used constantly in flux—one generation's *feeble-minded* being another's *mentally retarded* or today's *intellectually disabled*—but the standards for diagnosis change over time.[199] Many of those diagnosed as "feeble-minded" in the early twentieth century would not have received this diagnosis before the Civil War,[200] as society has changed what is considered "normal" and therefore what is considered to be "retarded" or "disabled."[201] The categories also reflect the purposes of those who create them.[202] Proponents of institutionalizing the "feeble-minded" in the late nineteenth century had a natural incentive to define the term in such a way as to maximize the number of those afflicted. They found what they sought. Because intellectual disability is a complex, socially constructed and historically variable phenomenon, I am much better off keeping my diagnosis as general as possible.

Naturally, I am a nonprofessional making a diagnosis nearly a century-and-a-half after the fact and based only on indirect evidence, but I think I possess enough evidence to make a broad, general diagnosis of some type of moderate intellectual disability for Absalom Kimmel. My most important written evidence comes from Day's book. The phrase "very much below the average in intelligence"[203] catches my eye immediately. Because we don't know what Day considers average, it is difficult to tell where a diagnostician working today would place Absalom. None of our sources mention that Absalom had any trouble functioning on a practical level in terms of hygiene, self-care, participation in household tasks, or basic job skills,[204] but the practical requirements for a single young man working as a farm laborer in this period would have been fairly low. Because we do not know exactly where Day would place "average" in relation to our own definitions, the important issue is that the author notes a negative difference in Absalom's capabilities: "there was nothing about him or in his make-up to commend him to any one, for any good purpose whatever."[205]

Figure 2.4, a–b. Engravings from *Lynched!* of Jacob and Absalom Kimmel (left) and Absalom (right). I assume these engravings, like that of Mary Secaur, were made from photographs, but I have not located copies of the photos. Ohio History Connection.

This sense of the difference of Absalom extends to the work of the engraver employed by A. P. Snyder to illustrate Day's book. This particular engraver clearly lacked talent, as we saw with my discussion of Mary Secaur's photograph and engraving. However, the engravings of Absalom included in Day's book show the engraver emphasizing the difference in Absalom's appearance, particularly in the dual-portrait with his brother Jake. When my wife first saw these illustrations, her reaction was, "Hey, he looks Asian!" That comment, combined with "very much below the average in intelligence" naturally made me think of individuals with Down syndrome, a condition at one time known as "Mongoloidism."

Looking at these engravings of Absalom, I have a hard time seeing his appearance as matching the distinctive facial features of an individual with Down syndrome, but that is only one of many genetically caused syndromes that match intellectual disability with distinctive physical characteristics related to the eyes.[206] Perhaps this kind of physical difference is what Day refers to when he describes Absalom as "ungainly and awkward in appearance . . . [with] dull, black eyes, sallow complexion and coarse yellow hair."[207] Without the actual photograph, it's impossible to tell exactly what the engraver was trying to show, but we do know that he was emphasizing a difference in Absalom that extends to his appearance.

Individuals with intellectual disabilities generally lag behind others their age in school subjects such as reading, writing, and mathematics.[208] Though Absalom is not registered as "idiotic" or illiterate on the 1870 census form,[209] the transcription of his confession has him approving the document with "his mark," rather than with a signature, indicating low literacy skills for someone nineteen years old who has regularly attended school. Another characteristic of those diagnosed with intellectual disability is spoken language "much less complex than that of peers."[210] Absalom's printed confession displays sophisticated syntax and diction, but it is impossible to tell how much of that complexity was added during the transcription of his statement—or, in fact, was composed entirely by the authorities. We have little in the way of directly reported speech by Absalom, but what we have suggests an ability to communicate that is not overly sophisticated. Absalom's reported behavior indicates the types of problems with interpreting social cues commonly found in those at the mild to moderate level of intellectual disability,[211] particularly the tendency to be manipulated by others.[212] Absalom's behavior after his arrest illustrates a lack of understanding as to how his behavior might influence the opinion of others: "Absalom Kimmel admitted his guilt from the very beginning, and, during his entire imprisonment, constantly wept and bewailed his sad condition."[213] And at least one—I believe both—of his confessions to the crime were coerced by the authorities, who promised him release in exchange for his testimony in what must have been a manner lacking in subtlety, since the coercion was detected, while that directed to other suspects seems to have gone unnoticed. Although each of these details individually may not prove compelling, the combination of evidence does seem to support my suggestion that Absalom experienced some sort of intellectual disability—one that left him noticeably different from those around him.

⊷⊶○⊷⊶

Liberty Township and Celina, Mercer County, Ohio, August 9, 1852

Susan sat on the wooden birthing chair, knees spread and legs trembling. She was exhausted. The strong, gentle hands of her stepmother and sisters washed and dried her. She fought to control her shaking legs when the women's hands and voices helped her to stand and make what felt like a long walk to the bed. She was raised onto the mattress, and the corn husks rustled together as they gathered her in. She lay back onto the pillows piled up against the headboard and gave into gravity entirely.

Despite the heat in the room, she trembled with cold, and she was grateful for the heavy quilt someone pulled up over her.

She listened to the buzzing and bustling of Susan Meizner, the midwife, and the other women as they cleaned blood and fluid off the screaming baby boy.

"Oh," the midwife said, almost absent-mindedly.

Susan snapped open her eyes and strained to see the baby, but the weight of her exhaustion pushed her back onto the bed.

"What is it?" Susan's voice croaked out through her dried mouth and chapped lips. She tried again to lift her head, but there was no strength in her belly. Tears ran out of the corners of her eyes from the effort. "Let me see him!" This time her voice was a little louder.

"Just a minute, love," said the midwife, who seemed to have recovered her normal tone. "I'm getting him all cleaned up for you." The other voices continued.

Susan closed her eyes against the wave of pain and nausea that swept over her. The pain passed. Susan listened to her child's screams. Then more rustling. Then some low voices.

"Here he is, Susan," said a younger voice. Susan opened her eyes to see the midwife's teenage daughter, Arvella, holding a bundle of blankets. Something in those eyes troubled Susan, and she panicked.

"Give him to me," she rasped.

"Here you are," said Arvella, who leaned down to transfer the bundle into Susan's arms. She pulled back the blanket to look at her boy, and a wave of relief and love rushed into her chest. She unwrapped the blanket and held his tiny hand between her fingers. Then the other hand. Ten. She felt toes through the blanket.

"It's ten, dear. Feed the boy," said the midwife, and Susan noticed the baby's screams again. She uncovered herself and turned the boy to her breast. He rooted and snuffled a moment, then latched on, and the golden light streamed from her nipple through her veins and filled her head.

Susan thought of the last time she'd suckled a child, and the image of another birthing scene flashed before her. She felt the black weight of depression and guilt press down upon her, and in her mind's eye, she saw the blood and mess being cleaned from Sarah's still body as it was covered by her mother and aunts.

She shook the image away and looked down at her suckling child. He snorted and breathed heavily through his nose as he learned how to nurse. His light, wet hair stuck to his scalp. His face had a yellowish tint that Susan didn't remember seeing in her other three babies.

As though listening to Susan's thoughts, the midwife spoke. "That's the jaundice," she said. "It's normal enough and will pass in a few days." There was an odd hesitation at the end of her speech, as though there were more to say.

Susan looked up at the midwife, who idly tucked a stray wisp of iron-gray hair behind her ear as she regarded the new mother. Then she noticed— her stepmother and sisters and aunts and a few neighbors were all staring silently at her.

"What is it?" asked Susan.

"Nothing, dear." The midwife paused for a second. "He seems to feed well enough. Small though, compared to your others. But he'll fill out if he eats like that. Healthy, I expect."

Susan looked back down at the boy. His eye opened and stared in her direction for a moment before it closed again. Susan hugged him to her chest. "He's perfect. I couldn't have asked for a better baby," she said, though her voice caught a little.

"That's right, of course he is," said the midwife, gesturing to Susan's husband, who had just entered the room. "And here's proud Papa."

Henry knelt beside the bed. His rough farmer's hand rested on Susan's shoulder. "Are you all right?" he asked. She nodded. "Boy, is it?" She nodded again.

The sun had sunk behind the trees long before Susan Meizner gathered her skirts about her and stepped over the stile into the road. She'd not walked more than twenty steps toward the crossroads when a shout brought her up. She turned to see Henry Kimmel stomping across the clearing toward her. She waited.

"About the boy," he said, his hands gripping the top rail of the fence standing between them.

"He'll be fine," said Susan. "And the mother, too."

Henry looked relieved. "I was just wondering. The skin."

"It's only jaundice," said Susan.

"And the eyes," said Henry.

Susan hesitated. "Nothing to worry about," she lied.

Henry mumbled thanks and turned back to the house. Susan returned to her walk.

She felt a bit of guilt over lying to him like that. The eyes were worrisome. And the cry. She'd heard of this before with the Anselmans' boy, Charles. All babies were different, she reminded herself. There was no reason to worry about this one. He was healthy, along with the mother. Susan had buried the afterbirth properly in the back yard, deep enough to keep an animal from getting it. And she'd left the packet of root tea that would help with the healing.

A fourth child, so the mother would know plenty what to do. And her own mother and sisters would stay with her in turns, so she'd get by. Still, Susan would check in for a while until she got back onto her feet. And she wanted to see the boy again. Just in case.

⊢•⊕•०•⊕•⊣

Tiffin, Ohio—June 23, 2017

David Kimmel

Just as the terms and categories for describing intellectual disability have changed over time, so too have the reactions of others to the disabled. In the mid-1900s, for example, people with intellectual disability were "out of the sight and out of mind of the general public," and little attention was given to this group in popular culture or in scientific research.[214] Schoolchildren of the period tended to reject or neglect their disabled peers socially, even more so when they interacted with them directly in the limited manner of their time.[215] But such reactions are shaped by external factors, including the labels used to describe these individuals. Since the 1950s, deinstitutionalization, inclusion, and attention to such labels have been shown to change the attitudes of schoolchildren toward their peers with intellectual disabilities because these attitudes are not natural reactions to difference but rather social constructs.

Exactly how the people of rural western Ohio would have responded to someone with an intellectual disability in 1872 is difficult to pin down, since attitudes toward such individuals were changing dramatically during this period. Before systematic scientific efforts to understand and educate individuals with intellectual disabilities began in the early nineteenth century,[216] public attitudes and understanding were conflicted. One strain of thought in the eighteenth century harkened back to the Middle Ages, when "idiocy" was often conflated with "dementia" and when disabilities were viewed as the sins of the parents being visited on their children[217] as issues of character.[218] The disabled, like the poor, were viewed as a normal and unchangeable aspect of social life.[219] At the same time, though, most children with cognitive disabilities "blended into the community" and "for all practical purposes, were not mentally retarded" because at that time, the demands for reading, writing, and technical skills were lower than the norms for today.[220] Children with intellectual disabilities were included in regular schools and, when grown, participated in the lives of their communities.[221] Americans throughout the eighteenth century noted the differences in the intellectually disabled but did not fear them.[222]

Ironically, by the mid-nineteenth century, these older attitudes were changing for the worse due to the work of the very people trying to help the "feebleminded." In the early 1800s, families held the primary responsibility of caring for the intellectually disabled; when that system failed, the community as a whole had to step in, often in the guise of the new institution of almshouses.[223] Particularly in the urbanizing East, almshouses increasingly became the destination for the intellectually disabled, and by the middle of the century, reformers were documenting the horrid conditions and even physical abuse prevalent in such facilities.[224] Reformers such as J. G. Whittier and Dorothea Lynde Dix reported not only on the failures of the almshouses but also on the deplorable living conditions of children with intellectual disabilities found living with impoverished and neglectful families.[225] Because these reformers were also attempting to justify the establishment and funding of the new asylums and schools for such children, painting the home as a place of neglect and abuse served to further the impulse to withdraw children from that bad influence and into the positive environment of these new institutions.

The rhetoric of the midcentury reform movement hinged on the notion that "idiots," who in the past were viewed as an unchangeable phenomenon of nature, could be better-integrated into their communities through education.[226] The new scientifically based asylums the reformers promoted were touted as the salvation of this population. In making their case, reformers emphasized the drastic differences between the "before" of the untrained "idiot" and the "after" of the educated member of society.[227] Compare, for example, Samuel Howe's 1848 description of those with intellectual disabilities as "idle and often mischievous ... dead weights on the material prosperity of the state ... worse than useless"[228] with his guarantee that through proper education in an asylum, "almost every one of these men and women, if not beyond middle age, may be made to observe all the decencies of life; to be tidy in their dress, cleanly in their habits, industrious at work, and even familiar with the simple elements of knowledge."[229] The unintended consequence of such statements was to fundamentally change the view of individuals with intellectual disabilities from a normal part of life to a threat to normal life. While French and American educators sought to distinguish mental illness from intellectual disability[230] and developed assessment tools and classification schema that still influence procedures used today,[231] the same experts viewed "idiots," particularly "moral idiots," as dangerous and prone to being led into crime and vice.[232] After the Civil War, reformers moved away from educating and training "idiots" for reintegration into the community to removing the "feebleminded" from the general public, blaming those with intellectual disabilities for "petty thievery, vagrancy, prostitution, and illegitimacy."[233] The result of such campaigns over the last half of the century and into the new one was to change the culture's view of people with intellectual disabilities from victims of heredity and environment, but who could be trained and educated if properly cared for in specialized institutions, into threats to the culture at large who needed to be segregated from the rest of the population.[234] In the words of two reformers of the late 1960s, the emphasis had changed from "sheltering the deviant from society" to "protection of society from the deviant."[235]

This change in society's view of those with intellectual disabilities was mirrored in a change in perceptions of their parents. Over the latter part of the century, emerging theories of heredity were employed in what amounted to the old notion of the "sins of the father" as "intemperance, poverty, consanguinity (meaning marriage between cousins), insanity, scrofula, consumption, licentious habits, failed attempts at abortion, and overwork in the quest for wealth and power" on the part of parents were viewed as causes for intellectual disability in children.[236] By the 1870s, these official attitudes had infiltrated into the popular consciousness, and parents of the deviant were increasingly held responsible for the disabilities of their children.[237]

Because the Secaur-McLeod-Kimmel case occurred during the middle of the nineteenth-century change in attitudes regarding intellectual disabilities, it is difficult to determine precisely how Absalom Kimmel's disability would have affected his relationships with his family, his neighbors, and the wider community of Mercer County. Were attitudes more like those of an earlier time, when a neighborhood "idiot" may have been a figure of fun but not generally viewed as a threat? Or were community members already thinking like late-century reformers that a "feebleminded" individual such as Absalom posed a threat if not properly supervised and separated from the general population? Historians of disabilities are naturally drawn to the cutting-edge, to the most-advanced ideas of the day. But how likely were such ideas to have filtered down to a place like Mercer County, Ohio? It is difficult to imagine the farmers in the Kimmel's neighborhood as following the latest ideas of researchers and reformers, but it is possible that the idea of the disabled as a threat may have filtered into the community's consciousness through newspapers and popular fiction. Penny Richards, for example, has demonstrated how popular women's fiction in Victorian America mirrored the change in attitudes toward the parents of those with intellectual disabilities. In the 1840s, the "poor hardworking widow with her idiot son" was portrayed with sentimental sympathy;[238] three decades later, authors portrayed such families as partial causes for such disabilities.[239] Not that the Kimmels and their neighbors necessarily read these types of periodicals; rather, the change Richards has located in the stories matches an overall shift in attitudes among the populace as a whole. After all, writers of such publications gave their audiences what they wanted, so popular fiction reflected as much as it shaped general attitudes. So it is possible, even probable, that the community in Mercer County would have absorbed some of the new ideas concerning the nature of intellectual disability.

It was not a totally new idea, after all. Difference is never easily accommodated in small, rural communities; there is a reason this part of the country supported Know-Nothingism before the Civil War and would provide thousands of recruits for the revived Ku Klux Klan after World War I. My guess—and it is only an educated guess—is that Absalom with his intellectual disability would have served as a low-grade irritant in his neighborhood, something that was "not quite right." Not that the farmers were necessarily consciously looking for a chance to rid themselves of this young man, but it is interesting that the first two people reportedly arrested for the murder of Mary Secaur were Charles Anselman—who lived at home at age thirty-six, long after the age that most of his peers had left to form their own families—and Absalom Kimmel. In both cases, it is this difference that attracted the attention of the authorities. In this vignette, I return to Henry Kimmel's legal record to explore how Absalom's difference may have accounted for something of the Kimmel family's rocky relations with their neighbors as soon as a few weeks after his birth.

<hr/>

Liberty Township and Celina, Mercer County, Ohio, August 28, 1852[240]

It was a beautiful day, and Henry enjoyed the feeling of moving behind the power of some beast of burden other than himself. Tilly wasn't much of a horse—too old and slightly sway-backed from hard use—but she knew the way to town and to the bucket of oats that awaited her when she arrived at the stables. Henry leaned back and kicked his feet up onto the wagon's dashboard. Tilly plodded on.

Normally, Susan and the kids would have piled into the wagon for the trip to town, but with the new baby only three weeks old, they'd thought it best if Henry went on alone. Susan's stepmother and sisters had returned home just two days before, and although Susan was feeling better, she didn't feel up to the bone-jarring journey in this heat.

The wood under Henry's boots was weathered and worn. This wagon had brought Henry, his brother, and his mother all the way from Holmes County to what was then a forested plain between the Saint Mary's and Wabash Rivers. Grand Lake and the canal were only just completed when they moved, and when they arrived, they had joined their neighbors in clearing the land to make way for their farms. Henry nodded and waved to the farmers and their wives and children as he passed by their log houses along the pike. It still wasn't much of a road compared to what he had known back east, but the spaces between homesteads were slowly shrinking.

Though Henry had set out early in the morning, the sun was high in the sky by the time he neared the town. The fields baked in the sunshine, and the air shimmered over the road between him and the town in the distance. Passing by the occasional stands of trees, Henry could smell their cool, dark, sweet air and hear the few birds and ground animals not hunkered down, waiting out the heat of the day. Farmers busied themselves with catching up on the repairs they had neglected during the second hay mowing in the weeks before this. The corn in the fields was taller than a man's head and was just beginning to change from green to light brown. By the end of the next month, they would all be busily harvesting—hard, dusty work for a solid month. Henry would need to join in with his neighbors to shock the corn, maybe even hire a man to help. Sam and Bill were old enough to feed chickens and help their mother in the yard, but it would be years before they could help in the fields beyond carrying water or jars of switchel to the workers.

The new baby was growing and progressing normally, save his strange appearance and the different quality of his cries. Those still bothered Susan and Henry, though they hardly spoke to each other about their worries. They'd settled on Absalom, a name picked at random from the Bible. Susan had carefully copied out the heavy letters from the large, leather-bound book that had been carried westward across an ocean and over mountains, hills, and rivers by his grandparents and his father and mother. He couldn't explain why he and Susan had felt called to use the old-fashioned naming ritual this time. Susan simply brought Henry the book, and he opened it and pointed.

At last, Henry and Tilly reached the edge of Celina. Though it had grown with the canal and the reservoir, it was still a fledgling community, with none of the large-framed houses that would flank Main Street one day. Henry picked up the reins and flicked them across Tilly's back, urging her to pick up the pace a bit and look less raggle-taggle as they headed into the downtown. Most of the stores and shops along Main Street had recently added false fronts to their hewn-log exteriors; it would be some years before they would be torn down to make way for modern frame-construction and multifloor buildings. Henry headed Tilly to the blacksmith's shop, where he left her to be reshod. He had a few more errands to run, including a quick stop in the dry-goods store that doubled as the town's post office.

Henry walked along the raised-board sidewalk that kept the spring floods and mud out of the doorways of the shops. The wood sounded beneath his boots as he clomped along the walkway. Coming to the dry-goods store, he nodded to the loafers squatting along the wall. As the shop door swung closed behind him, he heard laughter from the five or six men on the porch behind him. He greeted the shopkeeper, who hailed the man he considered a regular and a good customer.

"Hello, Mr. Kimmel. How are you today? Hot enough for you?"

"I'll say. But it's not the heat, it's the humidity." Henry wiped his forehead with his red handkerchief to emphasize his point.

"Congratulations on your new baby."

"Word travels quick around here," Henry said. He eyed the shopkeeper suspiciously, wondering what he'd heard.

"People from the country track in all kinds of stories. Last couple weeks, they been full of your son, long with that two-headed calf born over in Fort Recovery."

Henry had heard about that. Bad omen. "Don't see what a birth has to keep folks talking for three weeks."

The shopkeeper hesitated for a moment or two. "I don't know, myself, but folks been saying your new one . . ."

"He's only got one head," Henry interrupted.

The shopkeeper's laugh was short and strangled. "Nothing like that. Just some silliness of the country folk, I suspect." He let the matter drop and quickly filled out Henry's order.

Henry left the store carrying his armload of goods. The loafers perked up when he walked out the door.

"Got a load there, ain't you?" one of them said. He was a young man—old enough to know better than to sit around on the street with a bunch of layabouts. Henry recognized him, but he couldn't say from where. "Taking that all out to the farrrrm?" the young man stretched out the r sound to imitate a country accent.

Henry ignored him and walked on. He could hear the snickering group shuffling to their feet and clumping down the board sidewalk behind him.

"Hey," called the head loafer, his buddies' laughter making him bolder. "Hey, I'm talking to you!"

Henry sighed and turned. "What?" he asked, his exasperation clear on his face.

"You're the fellow with that new baby, aren't you?"

"What's that to you?"

"We hear there's something funny about that boy."

Henry's eyes narrowed, and he looked hard at the loafer. "What do you mean by that?" he asked slowly.

"Oh, nothing," said the loafer, feigning nonchalance. "We were just wondering if what we heard was true, that your boy is gonna be an idiot."

"What did you say?"

The young man puffed up a bit at the challenge. "You heard me. The boy's a dummy. It was so obvious, the midwife knew right away. You folks must be doing something mighty strange out there." The others laughed. "Maybe getting a little too friendly with the cows, if you know what I mean."

Henry set down his parcels and took a step toward the loafer. "You shut up now and take all that back."

"What part—the part about you fucking animals, or the part about your idiot kid?"

Henry heard the blood rushing up into his ears as he advanced on the loafer. "You take that back, or ..." Henry couldn't quite shape the words around his thoughts of revenge.

"Or what?" The loafer checked his options out of the corner of his eyes, then continued to play to his audience, whose laughter and smart comments drove him on. "You think I can't stand out here on a public street and say what I want, especially to the likes ..."

The punch caught the young man on the edge of his chin, the force of the blow knocking him backward. A yell rose from the others as Henry grabbed their leader by the throat. The two men fell to the boardwalk with a thud, and Henry banged the loafer's head back onto the planks. The crowd jumped into the fray and pulled Henry off, but not before he got in a few good thumps.

Shopkeepers and their patrons rushed onto the boardwalks to catch a better view. Henry was held back and jostled by the loafers, who wanted to impress the audience. He looked around for his packages, but he couldn't find them in the rapidly growing crowd. He decided to forget the packages and get back to his horse and wagon. He turned and walked away from the commotion, ignoring the yells from the loafers as he turned the corner and walked the block to the blacksmith's shop. None followed. Henry inspected the new horseshoes, paid the smithy, hitched up Tilly, and set off for home.

3
LYNCHING

Liberty Township, Mercer County, Ohio—July 8, 1872

All morning they came—the humble, honest, hard-working farmers from the countryside.[1] They came from their chores, for no farmer leaves chores undone. No cows were left in pain with full udders; no horses whinnied with empty bellies. Interrupting their harvesting, threshing, and hay-making, people traveled to town on horseback, in rude wagons, and on foot from the remotest sections of the county. By ten o'clock, the streets teamed with three thousand simple country folks. They shared a purpose; they lacked only organization and direction.

As the courthouse bell struck ten, three hundred horsemen appeared on the edge of town, the flower of the county nobility. These "knights" rode in close formation to the fairgrounds, the crowd following in their wake. Arrayed in tight battle order, the horsemen listened as their captain explained the plan—simple, direct, just, manly. A hanging committee of twenty-five of the best men was designated, a chaplain was appointed, and a wagon was produced. The captain reminded the crowd of the horrible crime committed against beauty and purity, both manifest in the body of the innocent child, Mary Secaur. He carefully reviewed the evidence against the culprits, and he explained the threat that the authorities might remove the guilty parties to another county, thus thwarting timely and local justice. The captain, steel-jawed and clear-eyed, patiently ensured that the proprieties of this organizational meeting were observed. This was no furious, passionate mob—only the hand of justice.

After an hour, the captain led the three hundred men to the jail, much as Leonidas led the Spartans to destiny at the hot gates of Thermopylae. The crowd followed in orderly procession, a host of the righteous. The horsemen and crowd surrounded the jail, and the captain stepped forward. His voice rang out clearly in the silence of the late morning. "Sheriff Spriggs! The people of Mercer County have come to see justice served. Please hand over the prisoners!"

Sheriff Spriggs, regardless of his personal feelings concerning the likely guilt of the prisoners, was determined to obey the dictates of his duty to maintain law and order. Having been forewarned of the plans to remove the prisoners from his custody, he had dispatched messages that morning to his deputies, and ten stalwart men had answered his summons. They, too, took to heart their sworn duty to uphold the law and stood bravely within the jailhouse, awaiting an assault by a group of citizens who had not merely numbers but a conviction of Right on their side.

Spriggs emerged at an upper window of the crude-but-sturdy structure. "As sheriff of this county," he said, his voice ringing out over the crowd, "I am sworn to uphold the law. I urge you to let the law take its course. Justice is inevitable. The guilty have confessed to their crimes. The proper evidence has been presented. We must allow Lady Justice to manage our affairs if we are to be the civilized, law-abiding county that is our destiny. Disperse, oh citizens of Mercer County! Go back to your farms, to your shops, to your professional offices! I recognize the faces of the finest men in the county. Smear not our county's noble name through your actions! Risk not your own individual reputations, even freedom, in hindering the operations of the law!"

The crowd applauded Spriggs's noble words. In a crowd of lesser men or in a situation where the right course of action seemed less clear before them, the sheriff's speech would have dissuaded the group from carrying out their designs. However, this was no ordinary gathering. Though Spriggs's bravery and sense of duty were admired, the crowd's noble purpose was such that nothing could stop their march of justice.

Noting an unlatched window high up on the first-floor wall in the back of the building, one man in the crowd asked two sturdy yeomen farmers to lift him to the opening. His stature on the smaller side, he wriggled through easily to the interior of the jail. He ran to the front, unlatched the door, and was lost to history—his anonymous service to his community unacknowledged but for here.

And so the fortress was breached. The fearless captain, his head erect and his shoulders firm, served as the point of the crowd's thrust as they penetrated the jail to the stairs, where the sheriff blocked further ingress. Spriggs resisted this assault on his inner sanctum. Though in his heart he shared the desire for justice that drove the crowd, his sense of duty prevailed, and it took four stout men to pin him to the ground and remove the keys from his well-guarded pocket.

"Let it be noted that I and my men succumbed only to the force of numbers and that we went down defending our sworn duties," said Spriggs.

It took only moments for the leaders of this determined group to unlock three cells and remove three cowering prisoners. The brothers, Jacob Kimmel and Absalom Kimmel, along with Alexander McCloud, were whisked out of the jail into an awaiting wagon. The previous Saturday, this sturdy vehicle had carried produce to market. Now it carried the most reprehensible of cargoes, carefully watched over by the shotguns of the twenty-five volunteer lawmen.

The captain of the volunteers sounded the command, "Forward, march!" and with that, the procession set off on its respectable and well-ordered way to the lynching site, there to carry out justice against the murderers of poor Mary Secaur. While the miscreants cringed on their platform, not a tear was shed for them among the thousands who streamed along the road after them. Had these three heeded the pleas and cries and struggles of the innocent young maiden as they ravished and cruelly murdered her beneath the sunshine of the Lord's day? No. Even the most forgiving Christian in the crowd couldn't help the hardening of his heart at the sight of these wretches on their way to their just desserts.

James H. Day. *Lynched!*

The people who were present [at Jacob Kimmel's July 5 hearing] quietly dispersed and went home, apparently satisfied; but it did not require any great degree of prescience or more than ordinary intelligence to enable the most casual observer to see that mischief was brewing, and that, unless something was speedily done to allay the excitement of the populace, the result must inevitably be a mob with all its attendant horrors and pernicious effects on society.[2]

"The Lynching in Mercer Co." *Cincinnati Gazette*. July 10, 1872

Within twenty-four hours, [on Saturday, July 6,] a vigilance committee was organized, and a patrol was detailed to see that the prisoners were not transferred to another county. Sunday was the day set apart, but through the influence of Hon. F. C. Leblond and other prominent gentlemen, the execution was delayed one day. It was all that could be done to stay the hand of a just retribution.

"Lynch Law in Mercer County." *Cincinnati Gazette*. July 9, 1872

From Mr. Perwessells, the recorder of Mercer County, we learn the following: At an early hour this morning, it was apparent that unusual excitement prevailed in the quiet and peaceful village of Celina. Country people were seen to straggle in town as early as four o'clock, and as dawn approached they came in squads—mounted, on foot, and in wagons and carriages, until, at ten o'clock, three thousand people had gathered together from all quarters of the country. This was the confirmation of the whispered threats of meting out summary justice to the inhuman fiends who were proved guilty of having outraged the person and taken the life of Miss Belle Secore.

"The Murder of Mary Secour!" *Celina Journal*. July 11, 1872

About this time, a large number of men appeared on Main Street on horseback and repaired to the fair grounds to perfect plans of action. After a lapse of probably an hour, a move was made for the jail. A large crowd assembled, and the leaders demanded the prisoners. The sheriff, (who had called in assistance,) had turned the key in the outside door and gone to an upper window, and from there warned the crowd off. But the men were determined and would listen to nothing. One man passed in through a window, unlocked the outside door, and then others rushed in and seized the sheriff and after a sharp struggle got possession of the keys. All opposition was soon overcome, and the prisoners were taken out, thrown into a wagon, and hurried away.

"Lynch Law in Mercer County." *Cincinnati Gazette.* July 9, 1872

The citizens ... moved off in procession, announcing their determination of taking the prisoners to the Kimble farm, 12 miles distant, and there, within sight of the spot where two weeks ago they committed the horrible murder, they will proceed to execute the sentence pronounced by an outraged community. The procession was quiet and orderly and moved off under the guidance of men who will not return to their homes until the base wretches who have wrought such misery and terror in the community shall have paid the penalty of their lives. Your correspondent leaves to-night for the gibbet to glean further particulars.

James H. Day. *Lynched!*

The ride to the place of execution, a distance of eleven miles, must have been a terrible one to the prisoners, surrounded, as they were, by the stern and unrelenting faces of those who they knew were to perform, for them, the office of executioners, at the end of the journey; and followed and preceded, as far as the eye could reach, either way, by a concourse of human beings, all terribly exasperated against them and clamoring for their life's blood. To the calm and unexcited looker-on, it presented a scene at once grand and cowardly. Grand, because it illustrated how and to what extent the feelings of the whole people are capable of being aroused by the perpetration of a grievous wrong; and with what unanimity, and swiftness, and power they all move together to scourge and punish the perpetrators of that wrong; and cowardly, because it was three thousand, and more, unrestrained, stalwart men, pitted against, three, poor, miserable, terrified devils in manacles and irons.[3]

Liberty Township, Mercer County, Ohio—July 8, 1872[4]

The wagon groaned as the team pulled it around the turn onto Erastus-Durbin Road.[5] Though Jake and the others faced rearward, he pictured the scene unrolling slowly before the wagon. After all, he'd ridden and walked the route from the crossroads to his family home thousands of times. He envisioned the table-flat road, bordered on both sides by woods, then the trees running up against the end of a split-rail fence, and the cleared land of his family's homestead spread outward toward the log home that his father, uncle, and cousin had built with their own hands from logs cleared of the virgin forest. For Jake, the scene was eternal. The rough logs had been covered over with whitewashed clapboard siding a decade before his own birth. The sloping roofline marked where the kitchen had been tacked onto the back of the house, and a wisp of smoke curled from the iron chimney protruding from the shingled roof. The bare ground surrounding the house was packed pavement-hard by decades of foot traffic.

As the procession passed the corner of the fence line, he heard behind him the handful of yard dogs rush up against the rails, barking ferociously. They crept up along his left until the fence and the dogs became visible. Something changed in their tone when his eyes met theirs, but they barked continuously, their voices growing hoarse with the effort as they kept pace with the wagon. He saw motion in the distance out of the corner of his eye, and he craned his neck to see a figure running from the barn off across the knee-high corn before disappearing into the woods that surrounded their clearing.

The wagon jerked to his right, and its joints screamed against one another as it dipped into the shallow ditch beside the roadway. Jake was aware they had pulled into the lot directly across from his home, and along his left, the original cabin his father used for storage crept into view. The wagon suddenly stopped moving and creaking. He looked back across the road and saw small faces through the dark glass in the front room—his mother, his sisters, his younger brothers. But where was his father? Where was George?

The crowd washed up past the wagon and into the open spaces of the settlement. The fence fell, saplings were trampled, and the yard animals—chickens, dogs, cats—scurried for cover, but not before more than a few of the chickens wound up in people's bags and beneath their coats. The horsemen had all dismounted, tying their mounts to the trees surrounding the clearing, so the small meadow was a sea of human bodies and faces ringed by horse rumps. The flicking of their tails in the hot afternoon gave the edge of the woods a twitching look.

The lynching party had already located a number of smallish trees and was busily stripping them of leaves and branches. Soon, they'd fashioned the trees into forks and used those to hoist a horizontal beam—created from one of the small trees and hooked at the other end to the crotch of a large walnut tree that forked twenty feet from the ground. They threw three ropes over the crossbeam and secured them to pegs pounded into the baked earth. At the dangling ends, ready hands tied three nooses.

Absalom spoke. "What are the ropes for, Jake?" He pointed upward with his manacled hands. "Are they going to let us go now that we're home?"

Jake looked over at his brother, who looked back imploringly. "No, I don't think they're going to let us go," he said quietly. "Those ropes are for us."

Absalom thought about this for a moment and then began to whimper. "But they told me I could go home if I said what was on the paper was true. They told me that, Jake. Maybe ..."

"Maybe there's still time to save your own bloody necks if you make them feel better about stretching mine," said McLeod.

"Shut up, McLeod," said Jake. "There's no point in bickering now." But he thought, *Maybe he's right. Maybe there is a chance.*

The driver clucked and snapped the reins, and the wagon lurched forward toward the gallows. Once the three ropes dangled over the wagon bed, the driver stopped. Jake looked up at the harsh fibers of the ropes. He wondered if they'd have the strength to lift him up, if the crossbeam would hold all their weight together. Men jumped up onto the wagon bed and pulled the boys to their feet. Jake wobbled with the difficulty of standing on the unstable wagon bed while his hands and feet were bound. The crowd began to shout at the boys.

A man climbed up onto the wagon and raised his hands, gradually quieting down the crowd. He wore a severe black suit, a white shirt, and a thin bow tie, a typical preacher's uniform, but Jake didn't recognize him. The man stood for some time with his arms stretched over the crowd until the talking petered out and the air was quiet and still. The only sounds were shuffling feet and a few hot, tired crows calling from the edge of the woods.

The man puffed himself up and began to hold forth for the benefit of the crowd. "Alexander McLeod, Absalom Kimmel, and Jacob Kimmel, you have a few moments yet to live before we execute you for the murder of Mary Secaur. Do you have anything to say or any confession to make before you are put to death?" No one moved. The crowd waited expectantly, and a nervous anticipation rustled through the clearing. After a pause, a voice called out for McLeod to make a statement. Others joined in. Someone pushed McLeod in the back.

McLeod looked around at the crowd and then stared first at Absalom and then at Jake. He waited a moment or two, but then spoke loudly to the crowd. Jake was amazed at his composure and at the volume and clarity of his voice.

"I am asked to make a confession, but I cannot condemn my conscience." He paused and cleared his throat. "I know nothing of the murder. I never saw the girl in my life to my knowledge, and I never touched her. I did not commit the murder. I am innocent of that crime and know nothing whatever about it."

The crowd stood silently, listening to McLeod. He looked directly at Jake and Absalom. "The Kimmels know I went to bed after church and slept until they called me to dinner—I went downstairs and ate a hearty dinner. I can say with a clear conscience that I am not guilty." McLeod fumbled with his jacket and pulled out a small, worn New Testament. He kissed the book and then held it aloft and addressed the crowd. "I swear before God and man that I am innocent of this crime." He looked thoughtful for a moment and then gestured again with the testament. "I have a good mother who taught me to read in this, and she taught me to read and write. She always taught me better."

The crowd rumbled at this, and shouts of "Take that Bible away from the sinner!" "You lie!" and "He's guilty!" sounded out from various spots in the mob.

McLeod looked out at the hostile faces of the crowd. His voice rose slightly in pitch as he continued. "Let the law take its course, and the guilty will have to suffer. God will not let the innocent die, and I pray God to save me, for I am innocent." McLeod again lifted the Bible above his head. "If it was the last word that passed my lips, I would say I know nothing about it."

"What about the Kimmels?" shouted a voice.

McLeod quickly glanced at Absalom and Jake. "I know nothing against Kimmels' folks but what is good. Andy and I were partners ..."

Just then a voice yelled out, "Why did you say *bloody spot*?"

"I did say *bloody spot*. It's my way of speaking. My clothes have been sent to Cincinnati to be analyzed—I admit that I had blood on them." He held out his wrists to the crowd. "I have blood on me now from my nose. It is in the habit of bleeding and has bled since I started from town." McLeod pulled at his shirtfront, and for the first time, Jake noticed flecks of red on McLeod's clothing. He again held out his wrists to the crowd, looking hopefully at them. Their faces remained impassive.

A touch of panic entered McLeod's voice. "I swear to you sincerely that I am innocent of that crime. If you want to put me to death for that crime, I will have to die; but innocent blood will flow." Again, he paused to gauge the effect of his words. "I tell you the truth. I swear before God and man that I'm innocent."

He nodded toward Jake and Absalom. "Johnson and Spriggs induced the boys to say what they did." Jake felt a horrible sensation at this. "Innocent blood will flow if I have to die."

Voices yelled out from the crowd.

"Quit your lying!

"Confess!"

"Tell the truth!"

McLeod's face fell, and he added flatly, "Now, gents, you want me to tell the truth. I have told the truth and say again I am innocent."

Having said his piece, McLeod slumped slightly and continued in a lower voice. "I'm ready to die. Oh, God, comfort my poor mother and sisters. Also, may he comfort this crowd." With that, McLeod sat down on the floor on the wagon and refused to say more. Jake looked down at McLeod, who avoided eye contact with him but stared into and through and past the crowd. Those were more words than he'd ever heard McLeod utter, and Jake marveled at the peddler's eloquence. Where had he learned to speak like that?

The crowd was shouting now, calling for the other two to confess. They stood awkwardly before the angry faces. Jake was surprised when it was Absalom who first spoke. "We was going through the woods. We saw the girl. McLeod went into the road and dragged her back to the woods. It was

McLeod who done that. He hit her with the club after he went back for her."

The crowd rumbled menacingly, and Jake realized that their patience was wearing thin. Fear gripped him. He spoke to the boards of the wagon, "Lord, God, they are going to hang me, and I am innocent!" Then he raised his eyes and addressed the crowd. "I am innocent. I did nothing to the girl. It was all McLeod and Absalom." He couldn't believe he heard himself saying this. "McLeod told me he committed the murder. Absalom had nothing to do with the murder." Jake realized that he was talking in circles, and decided he'd be best-off if he shut up and sat down.

By now, the shouts of the crowd were incessant, and they called for justice, lynching, and confessions—and even for torture to extract confessions.

The leader of the lynching party held up his hands for quiet. "If there is any torture to be used, it won't be on my authority. If a murderer won't confess, let it stand as a warning to himself and to his fellows that he may die with a lie on his lips." The crowd calmed a bit at these words. "We are not here as angels of mercy but to execute men on evidence already before us, and if they desire to die with a lie on their lips, then those are their own souls in peril." He turned and addressed the three prisoners, an arm raised above them. "Look out!"

The crowd roared at this and surged toward the wagon, which rocked as the people grabbed at its sideboards. Jake shrank down in his spot on the floor of the wagon, and Absalom let out a little moan. Suddenly, the wagon bed was full of men, and Jake and the others were grabbed and roughly pulled to their feet. Jake could again see over the carpeting of faces looking up at him, most angry and shouting. He looked up across the road to his home. He could make out faces in the windows, but he couldn't tell who was there. A hand pushed down on Jake's head, and he felt a coarse rope slip over it, scraping his ears as it was pulled down over his head and around his neck. He was yanked back up, and someone behind him straightened the noose. Jake's knees threatened to give out from under him. This was it. Absalom blubbered next to him. Jake looked over at McLeod, who stared stonily ahead.

Just then, Jake saw the crowd part for a familiar face. Elias Secaur, Mary's older brother, moved to the wagon. He showed every sign of having rushed to the scene along dusty, hot roadways. Elias pulled himself up onto the bed of the wagon, took off his hat, and wiped his brow with the sleeve of his shirt. He returned his hat and addressed the crowd. "Friends, you are about to commit a wrong. I beg you to hold off."

The crowd began to shout back, and soon it was difficult to hear Elias. "No one has the right to demand retribution more than me, but it cannot come this way. We need to wait until the proper court can review the case in the fall." The crowd responded with violent outbursts and expressions of conviction as to the guilt of the trio up on the wagon. Many in the crowd shouted out directions to the hangmen to carry out the sentence.

Elias hesitated for a moment, uncertain. "You are hanging an innocent man if you hang Jake," he shouted. "I'm not convinced of his guilt. At least let Jake return to jail until the court can handle his case. Please, at least do that."

Many in the crowd began to speak amongst themselves and to shout out conflicting directions to the ring leaders. Jake looked over at Elias, who gave him a hopeful look. A little group of leaders huddled and discussed the issue, and then the spokesman jumped up onto the wagon again. "To show that we are a just and lawful body, we will take Elias's recommendation and remit the prisoner to the jail to await the next session of the circuit court." The crowd cheered. Jake found hands pulling the rope from around his neck, and then picking him up off the wagon and setting him down on the ground.

Jake's relief was numbing. He was going to live! But then he remembered his brother. Absalom looked at Jake, his face revealing that he hadn't a clue as to what had just happened. Why was Jake down there? Why was he still up on the wagon? Hadn't he said what the sheriff and his men told him to say? Jake broke eye contact. His face burned with shame. He had mentioned his brother's name to save his own neck. He was going to live, and Absalom was clearly going to die. Jake turned and looked back to his parents' house, hoping to catch a glimpse of his mother, his father, George, anyone. But the mass of people crowding up against the wagon blocked his view. All he could see were faces—faces stacked on faces, since folks had found logs and fence rails, anything they could to boost themselves up for a better view of the proceedings. Jake felt himself jostled by strong arms. He looked around behind him and saw men pushing the crowd away from the wagon.

When there was a wide circle around the prisoners, the spokesman again addressed the crowd. "I call on the condemned to speak up about their crimes before they are executed." He waited while no one spoke. After giving Absalom and McLeod time to answer, he continued. "Now, we need five volunteers to pull the ropes and to drive the wagon out from beneath these wretches."

The clearing was silent, save for the shuffling of feet. Here on the edge of the precipice, the mob hesitated. Jake felt a surge of hope. Maybe the crowd would lose its nerve and then all three would be returned to jail. But his hopes were quickly dashed—here came one volunteer, then two, then three, then all five. The spokesman clambered down from the wagon and walked over to the little knot of conspirators.

"Three cheers for the volunteers!" shouted out a voice. The crowd joined in the cheers, and Jake felt the strength and power of the crowd arrayed against the young men on the wagon.

One of the volunteers took the reins of the wagon team and waited patiently while the other four scrambled up on the wagon and helped McLeod and Absalom to climb up on the wagon's bench. Of the five, Jake recognized only Schaadt, whose plot backed up onto Tama Road just across from the murder site. The men straightened the nooses around the pair's necks and pulled the ropes taut. Then they jumped down and backed away from the wagon until the ropes stood out from the cross-beam and two volunteers stood ready to pull each rope. The executioners looked toward the little group of leaders and waited for a signal.

McLeod stared straight ahead while Absalom's chest heaved with sobs, and Jake could hear a moan coming from his brother's lips. The leaders waved to the men at the ropes, who pulled hard at the weights tied to the other end. The loops yanked against the boys' necks, and the two stretched up on their toes to release the pressure. The men pulled and pulled until both sets of the boys' feet left the bench, and they began kicking and squirming violently. The wagon moved forward and out from under the two struggling figures. The rope-men pulled until the heads of the two victims reached the pole supporting their weights. The crowd cheered.

Jake felt bile in the back of his throat, and he wanted to collapse to his knees, turn and hide his face, run from the scene, anything. But at the moment the ropes were pulled, his arms were seized from both sides, and his captives forced him to face the execution.

"Get a good look at that," said a voice in Jake's ear. "You might have weaseled out of it this time, but you'll be up there before long."

McLeod and Absalom jerked and twitched on the end of their lines. Their violent movements set their bodies spinning, and as they rotated, their legs flailed about, searching vainly for a foothold. Jake watched as Absalom's face turned in and out of view, his panicked expression burning into Jake's mind. He'd never forget his brother's bulging eyes, how his face turned red and then purple with the exertion. As the men struggled for life, the crowd grew silent.

After what seemed like an hour, but Jake would later learn was only eight minutes, both boys slowed and then finally stopped their movements. Absalom's neck was red and raw where it had rubbed against the rope. His tongue lolled out long and horrible from his open mouth, and his eyes stared out at the crowd. The bodies still twisted in the quiet afternoon sunshine, a three-quarter turn clockwise, a stop, and a three-quarter turn counter-clockwise. Each time the boys' faces turned toward the crowd, Jake could sense the people involuntarily shrink back.

The bodies were left suspended for ten more minutes, and then the volunteers were given a command to let loose the ropes, which whirred as they slithered back over the cross-beam. Two bodies thudded to the ground. Absalom lay on his back, his right leg bent unnaturally behind him. McLeod had fallen face-first and lay motionless in the dirt. Two well-dressed gentlemen stepped forward, and Jake learned from their discussion with the leaders that they were both physicians who wished to claim the bodies. McLeod was taken to Shanes Crossing, while Absalom was carried off to Fort Recovery. Jake would never see his brother again.

The wagon rolled over to where Jake stood, and he was forced up onto it. The crowd was surging down the road ahead of the wagon as it pulled out onto the road. Jake looked over at his house and saw his mother still standing in the window. He lifted a hand to her, and she did likewise through the old, imperfect glass. All around him were footsteps, hoof-steps, but no talking. The hanging had sobered the carnival atmosphere. The wagon creaked and groaned beneath him as it headed back to the jail. As he passed a tall bush on the edge of the Kimmel plot, Jake saw George emerge from the brush and stand looking at him. Jake looked quietly at his brother, then raised his hand. George returned his salute. Jake watched him until his wagon passed back over Tama Road and George was lost from view.

4
AFTERMATH

"More Victims Wanted." *Huntington Democrat*. July 11, 1872

After the mob had executed McCloud and Kimmel, they returned to the county seat in search of Callen and Murlen, the attorneys of the supposed criminals with the intention to hang them also. What has resulted from their rash and bloody designs is not now known.

"Mob Law in Celina!" *Columbus Dispatch*. July 13, 1872

Specials from Wapakonetta, Ohio, state the country around Celina, Ohio, is in a terrible state of excitement, arising from the outrage and murder of the girl Mary Belle Secor, for which two men were hung by the mob. Two men, who were supposed to have been implicated in the outrage, have since committed suicide, and the mob have taken and hung a third man this a.m. It is not yet known who he is, but it is probably young Kimball, who was spared the other day through the intercession of Miss Secor's brother. The lawyers who defended the Kimballs in their examination trial have been forced to leave the county, the mob threatening to hang them if they did not. Reports state that the most intense excitement and disorder prevails, and that the governor has been appealed to take the necessary steps to restore law and order.

"The Governor Troubled." *Mercer County Standard.*
July 18, 1872

On the arrival of Mr. Pond, the Attorney General, some fifteen or twenty of our best citizens called on him and gave him a true statement of affairs as they stood—that there were no armed bands within the county, and further, that after the hanging was done, not even any threats had been made against any person or persons, and that the people collected together for one object alone— that of hanging the murderers, and after that was done, all dispersed peaceably and quietly to their homes, and all was as quiet now as was the people of any community. . . .

The following is the report of the Attorney General to the governor on his return to Columbus, as we find it in a Columbus special dispatch to the Enquirer of last Tuesday, which puts the lie to the dispatch above alluded to.

Governor Noyes has not been called on for a military force to quell the riot in Mercer County. Attorney General Pond, at the insistence of the governor, went to Celina on Saturday and returned today. He reports the better class of citizens indignant at the outrages. The report that Dan. Callen was driven from Celina, because he was counsel for the prisoners, is not true.—Pond saw and conversed with him. He says he has not been threatened.

<hr>

Liberty Township, Mercer County, Ohio—Saturday,
June 23, 1877

Daniel Mahoney

I stand outside, watching the sky turn orange. Inside, women bustle and fuss, and a baby—named this time for my father to assuage my pride over naming the last for hers—fills his lungs with air and his belly with milk. I suppose I should be thinking about the meaning of life or the holy responsibility presented a man in his middle years when the Lord grants him another son. Instead, as the sun touches the tops of the black trees, I think of an evil that lies beyond the woodline—an evil made manifest in the brush alongside the road, and that marched down the road toward our home and carried me along with it to witness the terrible resolution of its wickedness.

I watched the brown cloud rising up above the trees for a good two hours before it reached us. It crept along the south first and then to the west. Now it was heading up the road, straight for us, tinting the sun tilting into the trees a warm orange. Johanna and I stood in the road with arms around each other as first the cloud and then the riders appeared in the distance.

"'Tis to the Kimmels they be headed," I said. "Let's go to the crossroads."

We walked to the crossroads, accompanied by the wives and children of Harmon, Wright, and some of the farther neighbors. Across the road, Wells's family had come to the corner of their fence rail and watched the approaching beast. Wells looked back at me, catching my eyes with a direct stare. I broke eye contact immediately, turning and talking to one of my own children. When I looked back, Wells was still looking at me. What did he want? Why was he looking at me? I forced my attention away from him and onto the group streaming to the crossroads.

At the intersection, we met up with Hengel's family and Elias May's large brood. All watched down the road as the tiny riders grew larger and more defined. Now we could hear the crowd, a low rumble that slowly changed into separate voices and then into shouts and calls—human now, but still unknowable.

The first riders reached the crossroads, and the procession swung around the corner and headed north to the Kimmels' place. There were well over a hundred riders. Some were farmers I knew from the township; others were the shopkeepers and important folks I saw during my trips to Celina and Shanes Crossing. They rode with stern expressions, eyes fixed forward, conscious of the eyes on them.

What *was* Wells looking at? Why at me? I wasn't a part of all this, if that's what Wells meant. Yes, I met with the men at the crossroads on Saturday, but they were all there. Except Wells. After the first meeting, Wells kept away. And when his neighbors stood in the yard and called to him, Wells walked onto his low front porch and stared at the men. I hung back, but Wells saw me. He shook his head and walked back into his house, leaving Hinton and his neighbors all puffed up on the parched earth of his front yard.

The riders continued to flow past us, approaching and wheeling around the turn and up the road toward the Kimmels' place. I noticed more neighbors in the crowd: Hinton, of course, but then Harmon, Wright, May, Meizner—the one who found the body—as well as more from farther down the way. They all made eye contact with me as they approached and navigated the turn, and I felt drawn by their stares. I tried to remember why I was standing there and not a part of the procession. It was grand, it was grim, and it was noble. Here was justice after all, the men seemed to say to me. Creaking and banging along the rutted road, the wagon carrying the prisoners emerged from the dust. As it turned to pass me, I could see the three young men clearly on the wagon bed. The peddler called McLeod looked hard at everyone as he passed them. He appeared capable of anything. It was no wonder they suspected him from the first. I felt more confident in the prisoners' guilt until Jake caught my eye. *Terror* is the only word that could describe the look Jake gave me, and I couldn't hold his gaze for more than a few seconds. I looked at Absalom, riding along in the back of the wagon. Ab looked all about him, fascinated by the crowd, the excitement, the confusion, the dust. He looked like he was watching a circus parade.

After the wagon came a wave of citizens on foot. By that time, they'd been walking in the heat and dust for two hours, and they were a ragged-looking lot, even those—and there were many, though it was a Monday—decked out in their Sunday church clothes. Still, the excitement in the air was electrifying, and I again felt myself drawn to it. I stepped forward onto the road and looked north toward the Kimmels'. The dust obscured the view, but the vanguard should have been reaching the clearing by now. The bodies rounding the corner jostled my shoulder and nudged me northward.

"Daniel Mahoney, where does ye think yer going?" Johanna's voice came from next to my right arm, but she sounded far away. "Daniel!"

I felt myself sucked into the stillness left by the passing wagon, and I stepped into the stream of people and became part of the beast. I could barely hear Johanna calling to me from far, far away as I began my journey with the crowd. The dust was much worse on the march, and I coughed and covered my mouth with my handkerchief. My eyes stung, and I was suddenly terribly thirsty. All that in the first fifty yards or so! By the time I walked the quarter of a mile to the edge of the Kimmels' property line, I was numb to the dust, noise, crowd, even thought.

Suddenly the crowd stopped, and loud voices arose all around me. We waited in the hot sun, the dust cloud slowly settling on our shoulders, heads, and feet. Up ahead, I could just make out the wagon and its prisoners, riding above the heads of the crowd. They turned into what I knew was an open field directly across from the Kimmels' house. The wagon stopped amid a flurry of activity, but they were too far away to make out anything specific in their actions. The crowd lurched into motion, and the press of people heading for the clearing carried me with them. As we neared the Kimmels' house, I could see George and a few of the others standing at their road-side fence. Looking over at the house, I could make out four or five little faces—and one very sad adult face—at the window.

A rumor rippled through the crowd that Henry Kimmel had run pell-mell for the woods when the crowd approached his land. I doubted the story, but then, I didn't see the elder Kimmel anywhere around the farm, either. George looked at the crowd passing by with a confused expression, as though he recognized the individual parts of the scene before him but could not piece together the overall picture. I was right up by the house, and George looked directly at me. I knew I was recognized, even understood, in that moment. I avoided George's eyes and studied the crowd near the clearing.

Though the tail of the crowd still ran back down the road behind them, the mob ceased to move. Every available space in the clearing was now filled. The trees along the edge of the opening were covered with boys and young men. Over the tops of the heads directly in front of me, I could barely make out a pole raised parallel to the ground. Ropes were draped over the top and hung down like snakes. Three heads appeared above the crowd, which began to rumble and shout things. Finally, the crowd quieted and I could hear a high, faint voice above the others. The voice spoke for a bit, and then the crowd shouted back at the speaker. I tried to wriggle forward through the bodies standing between me and the wagon, but the whole mass simply clenched and moved toward the ropes and heads. We were now closer but denser, and the heat from the sun and packed bodies soaked us.

I could hear another voice now, and we moved in close enough that I could finally see it was McLeod speaking. The murmurs in the mob drowned out most of what he said, but I could make out snatches: "guilty will have to suffer" ... "innocent" ... "blood" ... "God" ... "innocent."

A man about halfway between me and McLeod yelled out, "Why did you say bloody spot?" and the crowd hummed in agreement. McLeod's answer came to us broken and useless, "way of speaking" ... "blood on me" ... "innocent blood will flow" ... "God, comfort my poor mother and sisters." McLeod's head vanished, and the crowd shouted and shouted, but he did not return. The crowd yelled on, and I found myself joining in, though I don't remember anything like words—just raw emotion spilling from our mouths.

Then all three prisoner's heads floated above us again, and a fourth head joined them and yelled out over the crowd. The crowd yelled back. More heads appeared above us, this time accompanied by hands and arms that fitted the nooses around the necks of the prisoners. Then it was just the three heads again, and the crowd quieted. We all strained forward and up onto our toes to see. The crowd let loose with a call of surprise, and a fourth head appeared alongside the others. It spoke to the crowd for a moment, and the mob loudly agreed. Word passed back to us that the girl's brother begged pardon for one of the boys. We passed the message further back and yelled our agreement along with the rest of the crowd. More heads and hands and arms appeared again, and then it was just the two prisoners standing.

The sun was a good hour farther down toward the tops of the trees, its orange deepening and darkening in the suspended dust. Then the crowd gasped and stepped back as McLeod and Absalom ascended into the air. The two stopped as their heads touched the crossbar of the gallows, and both began to wriggle and spin on the ends of their ropes. An invisible force pushed the crowd away from the heads and bodies bobbing above them. After several long minutes, the bodies hung still. We waited there in the heat, packed together, quiet, for a long time. Then the bodies dropped from view, and the tension in the crowd broke.

We turned around and began to walk back out of the clearing toward the Kimmel house. No faces showed in the front windows now as we edged out into the road. It took a good hour for the crowd to work its way to the crossroads. Once there, we separated into three streams that headed off to the east, south, and west. I followed to the east. No one stood at my own gate when I pushed through the bodies toward our stile and climbed up and over the steps into my yard. I approached the front door, then stopped about halfway as the door opened. Johanna stood there with her arms crossed, looking hard at me. I turned off the path and walked across the packed earth around the house to the barn.

The sun is long gone now, and the sky has blued so no sign of its former glory remains. As the warmth of the day radiates into the darkening sky, I recall the cold grip of death settling on me in the heart of a summer's day. I think of the infant awaiting me inside my house—our house—and I feel unworthy of the task. How can I raise up a son to know right from wrong when his father failed so? Across the road, Wells's house and barn stand in black and silent reproach. Up above, a first star has emerged. I look down and notice how a rectangle of light from my house frames me against the dark earth at my feet. I rub some heat back into my arms, turn, and walk back into life.

⊱────◦────⊰

"Recommitted." *Mercer County Standard*. July 18, 1872

Jacob Kimmel, who is charged with complicity in the murder of Mary A. B. Secaur, was brought before Squire Snyder on Friday for a hearing in his case. He, through his attorney, waived an examination, and was recommitted to await the action of the next term of the Common Pleas Court, which convenes next November.

"Jacob Kimmel, Recommitted." *Celina Journal*. July 18, 1872

Friday afternoon last Jacob Kimmel was brought before Justice Snyder, and arraigned for trial for complicity in the murder [of] Mary Belle Secour. He waived examination, and was then recommitted to jail to await the action of the grand jury at the next term of the Common Pleas Court. By confession of Absalom Kimmel, Jacob Kimmel is made equally guilty with Absalom in the outrage, though the killing of the girl was said to have been done by Alex. McLeod.

Celina Journal. October 10, 1872

Henry Kimmel sells farm and household goods at his residence in Liberty Township on the 17th of this month.

⊱────◦────⊰

Liberty Township, Mercer County, Ohio—October 9, 1872

Henry Hinton walked in through the back door and into the kitchen to get a dipper full of water—and to relay the news he'd just learned from

Hengel, who'd learned it from Mahoney. But first, the water. The iron in the water combined with the material of the ladle to give his drink a satisfying bite. He leaned back against the sink and surveyed the room. Though the house itself was old—and he would address that issue soon enough—it was filled with up-to-date conveniences and decorated tastefully. The only object in the room that didn't give him pleasure was his sister-in-law, Lydia, who was sitting at the table drinking coffee with his wife. His younger brother's wife wandered over from next door entirely too often for Henry's taste.

"Seems Kimmel is ready to move on north after all," he announced to the room. Surprised sounds came from Althea and Lydia, and Henry was pleased with the impression his news made. "He's selling off equipment and whatnot on Thursday next week. I guess they bought up north in Dublin Township. Not as far away as I'd like them, but it's a start."

"I'm surprised they're leaving so soon," said Althea.

"I'm surprised it's taken this long," said Lydia. Henry and his wife gave her a puzzled look. She was an odd bird. "Would you stay after what happened to their son?"

"Well, that's not a likely occurrence, now is it?" Henry asked, irritated. Lydia would say such queer things!

"But they don't even know what's going to happen with Jake," said Althea, and Henry was slightly put out that she hadn't acknowledged his comment. "It could be the crowd all over again next month when the court meets."

"If he's guilty, there's nothing wrong with that," he said in his best end-of-discussion voice.

"If he's guilty," said Lydia. "Like those two boys were guilty?"

"Are you saying they weren't?" he asked. How like a woman to ignore an established fact! He settled into his explaining voice. "What about that ribbon? What about the 'bloody spot'? They all confessed, Lydia. They were obviously guilty. The only reason Jake is still alive is because of the girl's brother."

"Maybe because there was doubt about whether he committed murder," said Lydia. "I'll be interested to see what a judge and jury and real courtroom make of your evidence."

Althea rose from the table and gathered together their coffee cups. "Do you think they'll do anything to those responsible for the hanging?" she asked Henry with a worried look.

Henry sighed. "What are they going to do, try two thousand people?" He puffed himself up and stepped out of Althea's way. "Citizens have the right to protect themselves from violent criminals."

"To take the law into their own hands?" asked Lydia.

"If the law won't take care of the problem, sure," said Henry. He didn't like where this was headed. Lydia had been funny ever since the hangings. He walked over and stood over her. "Lydia, we're out here on the frontier between civilization and the heathen wilderness. It's the duty of fine upstanding citizens like me and mine," and here he emphasized and paused over the last word, "to protect our community from low-lives like the Kimmels."

"But it's their community, too," she said. She looked down at the table. "At least, it used to be. They've been here since the beginning."

"That's just the problem," he said, and he knew he had her now. He launched into his public-oratory voice. "There's a certain sort our grand republic needs on the frontier. A log or sod house is plenty good enough for them, and their manners match their setting."

Lydia traced the pattern on the oilcloth with her thumbnail.

"But there comes a time when a new breed arrives on the scene, bringing civilization and progress. The frontier folk must move on further west, leaving the land to those who will act as proper stewards to what God has blessed us with." Henry let his voice ring out in the room.

"Sounds like you hung those boys because they weren't the right sort, not because they were guilty," said Lydia.

"Henry didn't hang anyone, Lydia," said Althea from over at the sink. He was glad to hear his wife defend him.

"He didn't do anything to stop it," Lydia said. Henry saw tears in her eyes. "Hanging those boys was against the law. It was murder." She slapped her hand on the table to emphasize the final word.

"Be careful what you say," Henry warned. "There's a big difference between what happened to that little girl and what happened to those responsible. One was an act of barbarism; the other was . . ."

"An act of barbarism," Lydia interrupted. She stood, leaving the table as a barrier between her and Henry. "If a mob can string up a boy in front of his family and nothing can touch them, where is your civilization?"

"Those boys confessed to their crimes," Henry said. He was irritated, and his voice betrayed his anger. Lydia had that way with her foolishness.

"You know they were beaten and pressured until they confessed," said Lydia. She looked over at Althea for support, and Henry was glad to see his wife refused eye contact. Lydia's tone softened, and she seemed to speak to herself, "I saw how scared they were up there on the wagon, especially that poor Absalom. He scarcely understood what was happening to him. Where's the civilization in that?" She aimed this last question squarely at Henry.

"That poor Absalom!" Henry said with disgust in his voice. "You've sure changed your tune about him! Weren't you the one who complained about him and said something must be done after that scene at the school?"

"I know what I said." Lydia looked down at the table that stood between them. "I've changed my mind, the more I've thought about it all."

"Come now, Lydia," said Althea. "There was something wrong with that boy. He worried all of us women."

"I know he wasn't normal," Lydia said to the table. "A nineteen-year-old who can't read is not normal. But that just adds to the problem."

"He knew enough to know what he was doing," Henry said. "And there was nothing right with McLeod even you can find. He was a stranger and a dangerous element."

"But we knew almost nothing about him," said Lydia.

"That's exactly the point," said Henry. He knew exactly where he stood on this. "We have to protect our own from strangers like him." He paused for a moment and changed into his sympathetic, caring voice. "I know it's hard to understand because you're a woman and don't have to worry like we men do."

"You don't think women worry?" He was surprised that this was Althea speaking, and her voice didn't sound sympathetic or caring.

"Not the way a man who has a wife and small children to protect does." Henry felt the justice and importance in his words. "Not to mention a widowed mother with a house full of children next door."

"Those 'children' are nearly grown up, and your mother can certainly take care of herself," said Lydia. "Besides, your brothers are the same age as the Kimmels. Did you ever think of that?"

"What do you mean?" he demanded. It was impossible to talk with someone so irrational and unpredictable.

Lydia's voice was level, and she leaned her hands on the table as she spoke. "I mean they are old enough to have attacked Mary Secaur. Along with probably twenty other young men in this neighborhood."

"Lydia, you can't really mean that!" said Althea.

"Well, why the Kimmel boys? I heard nothing in that so-called hearing that pointed to them any more than it might have pointed to any other boy—or man—in the area."

"What about the ribbon they found on McLeod's horse?" he asked. He was surprised at the stupidity of his brother's young wife. It was that way with women, though. "What about the blood on McLeod's shirt? What about his suspicious behavior?"

"That ribbon would have been easy for the sheriff to provide." Henry snorted, but she went on. "That whole thing about stopping at the murder site to pick it up on the way out of the state the next morning just doesn't make sense." She drifted away from the table and addressed the wall somewhere above and to the right of Henry's head. Then she snapped back directly at Henry. "And if they did it, why didn't the Kimmel boys leave with McLeod?"

"Like any criminals, they think they are smarter than everyone else, that no one will figure out their crime," Henry said. "I saw plenty of badness in the war, Lydia—enough to know that those committing evil don't think through their actions. Sometimes evil just takes control and things happen."

Henry remembered a door being kicked in and a press of blue-coated bodies pouring into the front hallway of a large house in northern Alabama. He saw himself running into the dining room with them, tearing open drawers and doors in search of silver. He shook himself free of what he knew happened next.

"Responsible men must take on the job of watching for evil and rubbing it out when we find it," he said with what he hoped sounded like surety.

"But what happens when responsible men make a mistake? What protects people from that?" asked Lydia.

"Right is always right, and God will guide the righteous." And with that, Henry stomped from the room and out to the barn, slamming the door as he left.

⊢⊶⊙⊷⊣

"The Liberty Township Horror!" *Mercer County Standard.* July 11, 1872

They were both undoubtedly guilty of such a heinous outrage and murder, as finds no parallel in all the annals of crime, and they richly deserved the punishment meted out to them; but who shall say that the time or manner of their punishment was either well or wisely chosen. Every good citizen must deprecate the occurrence of such scenes of unauthorized violence as took place on Monday last. But it has taken place and cannot be undone. Crimination and recrimination is now useless, but we can set our faces steadily against such things in the future, and by holding law and order as paramount, guard against their recurrence.

Celina Journal. July 18, 1872

The summary execution of Alex. McLeod and Absalom Kimmel as the perpetrators of the fiendish murder of Mary Belle Secour, is a terrible warning to evil-doers, though it was in direct violation of all law and order. If guilty, few will say the punishment they received was not deserved. But laws are provided for all cases, and men selected to execute them; and it is better to await "the law's delay" than to violate the law in administering punishment,—especially where there is a possibility of an innocent man suffering. It is to be hoped that there will never again be such a scene witnessed in this county as occurred on Monday of last week.

Mercer County Standard. July 18, 1872

A neck-tie party came off near Celina on Monday. It is said 3,000 persons were in attendance.

—Wapak Democrat.

It was, without doubt, the largest party of the kind that ever assembled in the United States, and we hope that it may never again be our fortune to attend another such a gather for a like purpose. One such party as that was, is enough for a lifetime.

—ED. STANDARD.

"The Opinions of Our Neighbors of Us."
Mercer County Standard. July 25, 1872[1]

With our deep sense of the Christian virtues—charity, forgiveness, long suffering, &c., we declare, that our neighbors of Mercer County are not only excusable, but did that which was unqualifiedly just. The judgment of the law would probably have consigned the criminals to the same fate, but then, that process would not have adequately expressed the sense of horror, abiding in the whole community at the unprecedented and almost indefinable outrage. It cannot be said the precedent will be glad, for it is impossible that this generation can be afflicted with a recurrence of an offense at all approaching the one there dealt with. The people of Mercer County have not injured their fair name— they have added merit to it. That community is safest from crimes, where each individual feels the infliction, when any one of its number has outraged. How well this was expressed in this case, may be known, that after a few days deliberation, the whole people rose up to dispose of the miscreants. They moved together quietly, soberly, orderly, without excitement, but with deliberate determination; each one of three thousand—old men, middle aged, and young— ready and willing to take the responsibility. And so they went to the work undisguised, for they were neither ashamed nor afraid of what they were to do. Not knowing of the purpose previously, we fully approve of what was done, and we have written what we have, to express it, believing it due to our neighbors that we should do so.

"The Mercer County Mob." *Mercer County Standard.* July 25, 1872[2]

We understand that the principals engaged in the late Mercer County hanging are to be prosecuted by the proper authorities. No excuses will justify the crime under the law, and we were surprised to see good men, men whose counsels should have been against such illegal proceedings, the leaders of the mob and encouraging others. The law was made to punish those who violate it, and if those who should uphold it, violate it from any cause whatever, they surely could not expect exemption from its penalties. If men are to be charged with crime and hung at the will of the mob, then no man is safe.

We understand that there were prominent men from this county who took active part in the murder of McLeod and Kimmel. Others took their families and rode thirty or forty miles thro' the broiling sun to the place of execution, thus indirectly aiding and inciting others on that occasion. Men are supreme in the control of their own families, but we feel that there is no language that we could employ that would too strongly condemn the head of a family from taking wife and children to such a scene as was recently enacted in Mercer county.

It is the first mob in which any of our citizens were active participants, and we sincerely hope it will be the last. While no excuses could justify the double crime of McLeod and Kimmel, who were promptly apprehended and in the custody of the officers of the law held to answer for their crimes; so, on the other hand, no excuses would justify a mob in taking their lives, and when that mob did take their lives, in the eye of the law they were murderers.

Mercer County Standard. August 8, 1872

Frank LeBlond is a law-abiding citizen and deprecates as much as anyone, the mode and manner of disposing of McLeod and Kimmel, but at the same time he does not propose to go to extremes in the matter, and institute proceedings to prosecute those who were engaged in the lynching, as he believes our people are now satisfied, and nothing short of what was done would have restored quiet in our midst. While we all would rather the law had been left to take its course with its criminals, we do not believe anything is now to be gained by resorting to prosecutions to avenge the wrong done.

Mercer County Standard. August 8, 1872

[Reprints a short notice of the rape of a young girl just over the border in Indiana.] If the aforementioned story is true, we should not be surprised if we had another case of lynching, in our adjoining county of Jay, in Indiana, if the wretch is again caught. No punishment is severe enough for such wretches, and we have almost come to the conclusion that extermination on sight, is the true policy to be adopted in all such cases as the above.

Celina Journal. November 28, 1872

There are fourteen persons in the prison cells of San Francisco awaiting trial for the crime of murder, and twenty-one in New York on similar charges. We will venture to say that more than one-half of them will go unhung. A vigilance *committee is strongly talked of in New York to mete out a just reward to some of the cold-blooded murderers that, by the peculiarities of the law there, go clear and as a consequence assassinations are more frequent. Come Mercer County on 'em.*

><><><

Blue Springs, Nebraska—July 8, 1912

Lydia Hinton

My purpose is to sit beneath someone else's tree and listen to the wind.

I realized my purpose today during lunch. All morning, I had this itch in the back of my mind, something unsettled and worrisome, perhaps something I was supposed to have done or something I had done that I oughtn't. Usually, given enough time, I can worm my way back through my thoughts to the source of my unease. But there it was, a worry, a feeling that something was left undone or unsaid. I've never been much of one to hide my emotions—you could have asked Jacob about that—so Lizzy kept watching me. I'd look over from peeling potatoes or trimming the pie or what-have-you, and she'd look away, reddened. I considered asking her why she kept staring. Try as I might, I just couldn't pin down the source of this feeling, so as I sat there in Lizzy's kitchen eating the soup we'd made for the men who came steaming into the close room—Lizzy's Daryl and my own boys, Cleveland and Dean—my mind wandered about, looking for this rumor of a thought. I doubt anything particular was said that caught my attention—after all, I have been sitting in kitchens listening to men have the same conversation about chores and crops and weather for all my life. But something nudged my mind to consider the date, and I heard myself gasp. All the eyes at the table, big and little, turned to me. I don't know what they thought they'd heard. Maybe that I was choking. And maybe I was, but it was on an image, not the soup or bread. I dropped my spoon and ran from the house—or limped as fast as my hip would permit. Lizzy has a bench set up here beneath the only tree on their land worthy of the name. I waved away my children's concern with an excuse about the heat, and they trooped back inside, though Lizzy looked back at me before she disappeared back into the darkness.

And now I sit beneath her tree and listen to the wind and repeat over and over in my mind one surety: forty years ago today, I participated in the killing of two men just younger than the men back in that kitchen.

I condoned the execution of those who murdered Mary Secaur. A beautiful, bright, wonderful girl was robbed of her virtue, future, and life by savages whose actions were an affront to civilization. We women knew our vulnerability out there in the countryside with few neighbors and the law a dozen miles away. We all felt uneasy until the men settled on their suspects and arrested the Kimmels and McLeod. If it could happen to Mary, it could happen to any of the least of us. A community cannot survive if its men refuse to protect the virtue and safety of its women. If hanging those murderers made this a safer place, then so be it. And the three were clearly guilty. Anyone who had heard or read the evidence agreed on that. One of the three, the feeble-minded one, Absalom, had even confessed. So, we the people were justified in seeing punishment meted out. We wanted justice and we wanted it now. We would not hazard the chance that a legal technicality, some trick of a clever lawyer, might deprive us of justice. No, it was better, we knew, to take matters into our own hands. And it was a communal decision, a spontaneous expression of local sovereignty. Those, anyway, were my thoughts before. Now I remember just how unprepared I was for what would happen.

I remember how hot it was that day. The dust roiled up from the road and choked us. It stuck in our hair, in our nostrils, in the deepest folds of our clothing. Every house along the path taken by the mob was coated in a thin layer of dust for weeks following the lynching. That dust sifted through the cracks in windows and beneath doors, and it powdered everything in our houses. I didn't think much of it at the time, beyond it being a nuisance, but now I see it as a sign of our collective responsibility, if not guilt, for what happened. We could see the dust long before we heard the crowd, and we heard the crowd long before we saw it. We watched the wagon pass us, and then my whole family, without any prior discussion or planning, joined the throng. The crowd was orderly enough, but there was a Sunday picnic air to the event. It was exciting; we were participating in history. Like the others, I was caught up in the crowd, marching and yelling with them, subsuming my identity into that of the greater good.

When we arrived at the Kimmel homestead, the crowd surged in to fill the open area. People stood on the rail fence before the house until it collapsed beneath their weight. They climbed trees; they set their children on their shoulders. I was too far back to hear much of the proceedings, but I shouted along with the crowd when they shouted, and I strained my neck to catch a glimpse of the action. I wish I could dignify my participation in the event by reporting that I was praying for the salvation of the murderers or that I was reflecting on the wonderful power of the citizenry to take the law into their own hands. But to tell the truth, as I stood shoulder to shoulder with the others and the sun beat down on our heads, I simply hoped it would all finish soon so I could return home and slake my thirst with a drink from the pump. Though my view was partially blocked, I could see the gallows and below where men pulled the three criminals to their feet on the bed of the wagon. I watched but could not hear Elias Secaur, the murdered girl's brother, climb up and address the crowd. Word passed from person to person of his noble request that Jacob Kimmel be returned to the prison to await a proper trial. I cheered along with the rest of them when Jacob was taken down from the wagon, and I gloried in the surge of self-satisfaction that swept through the crowd at our nobility and justice.

Then everything changed. I saw the two boys jerked up by the ropes and the wagon pulled out from beneath their feet. I had read about hangings, and they always seemed to me a clean, tidy affair. This was anything but clean and tidy. The older one, McLeod, struggled very little, but Absalom jerked and swayed on the end of his rope in a manner terrible to behold. I know not what possessed me, but something compelled me to watch that boy die, and he died slowly and violently. He gasped for air, he strained to break free from his bonds, and then finally—after minutes of this torture—he slumped into stillness, his tongue lolling out of his mouth like a long pink snake. I was amazed at its length. Living on a farm, death is a constant companion, but I had never witnessed a murder. A healthy young man's desire to live is a terrible thing to see wrenched from him.

So I sit here in the thin shade of a tree planted by the hopeful soul who broke the prairie sod and built this house, now wind-scoured to a bright gray. The wind hisses high up in the tree's leaves, and I realize my purpose is to remember. I remember how the people headed for home, quickly and quietly, feeling anything but justified and self-satisfied. We had just watched two young men murdered before our eyes.

I know we could deflect our guilt by calling it an "execution," but the mob murdered those boys who now rock in the wind high above my head. I wonder how many of the crowd remain on this earth, and how many of them are right now sitting beneath a tree and remembering. Something in the wind brings to my mind the image of my brother-in-law, Henry. I haven't seen him or thought of him in close to thirty years. But the thought of those boys swinging in the wind pushes forward Henry's solid, sure face. He was a man who had no doubts. He knew things. He knew the Kimmels were bad folks, and he knew the crowd had acted justly.

———◇———

Mercer County Standard. July 18, 1872

Over two hundred extra copies of the STANDARD were sold last Wednesday and Thursday, and calls for more were made, but could not be supplied.

Announcement

On or about the 25th of the present month, we will issue from this office in pamphlet form, a full and complete history of the outrage and murder of the little girl, Mary Belle Secaur, on the 23d of June, 1872, together with a correct account of the subsequent swift vengeance inflicted on two of the supposed murderers by an infuriated populace. The pamphlet will be neatly printed on a superior-quality of paper, and will be embellished with several fine engravings of the principal actors in the drama. The retail price will be twenty-five cents per copy. A liberal discount will be made to wholesale purchasers. Orders should be sent in at once.

Address,
A. P. J. SNYDER,
Celina, Mercer Co., O.

Mercer County Standard. July 25, 1872

The first order for the little book about the murder of Mary Secaur called for 1,000 copies. . . .

Buy a copy of the little book about the murder of Mary Belle Secaur. It will be printed at this office, and will be out in a few days. Illustrated. Price, only 25 cents.

Mercer County Standard. August 1, 1872

To the Public

Our pamphlet containing the history of the late murder of Mary Secaur, will be ready for sale and delivery at noon on Friday next, August 2d. This will be the only complete and reliable history published and no one should fail to procure a copy. . . .

News dealers all over the country can now send in their orders for the pamphlet about the murder of Mary A. Secaur. The delay in not getting it out sooner was caused by the material not arriving. Will be ready this week.

Any relic of the parties who were lynched in this county few days since is now sought after with avidity and secured if possible; therefore, as a token of remembrance, everybody should have a picture of the criminals, which will be for sale at this office the last of this week. Price, single photograph, 15 cents; photograph of each person, three separate pictures, 35 cents.

Mercer County Standard. August 8, 1872

Special Notice to the Public

I have disposed of the right to sell the pamphlet, entitled "Lynched," to Spriggs & Co., to whom all orders should be addressed in future. All orders I have received will be filled by me as soon as I can do so. Having the misfortune to "pi" a greater portion of the matter after it was set up is the cause of the delay in getting out the work, but I hope to be able by next week to fill all the orders that may be sent to Spriggs & Co., as I am to do the printing for them.

A. P. J. SNYDER

Price List of *Lynched!*

Retail, per copy, 30 cents; wholesale, 33 1/3 per cent. discount from the above.—100 copies considered wholesaling. Jobbing prices 40 per cent. discount from retail price—500 copies considered jobbing.

SPRIGGS & CO.

Tiffin, Ohio—June 23, 2017

David Kimmel

The lynchings of McLeod and Absalom Kimmel shook the community, and the effects on individual participants must have lingered for years. In the three preceding vignettes, I presented varied perspectives on the event. Daniel Mahoney stands at the crossroads as an individual, a collection of personal history, motivations, character traits, and relationships. When he steps into the current heading north to the Kimmel farm, Daniel abandons his identity and agency to the mob. He is guilty of no wrongdoing in the deaths of the two young men, but he shares the communal guilt of the mob—his presence is his approval is his guilt. Standing at the crossroads is Joseph Wells, representing the citizens—there must have been some—who stood against their neighbors in favor of rational thought and due process. And yet is Wells all that much superior to Daniel? Is it enough merely to disapprove of the mob and its intent without openly trying to stop it? For every Schindler, there are thousands on thousands of Schmidts filing past the bodies, holding handkerchiefs to noses and repeating, "We did not know." I like to imagine myself resisting if I were in Daniel's place, but would I? I have my share of independence of thought and mouth, often to the chagrin of my sensible self. But the stakes are nothing like those facing Daniel and his neighbors. Fear of retaliation was both real and realistic. Stepping out into the road in the face of hundreds, possibly thousands of enraged citizens would have required courage, conviction, and a certain lack of sense. Still, not defying the crowd is not the same as participating in the lynching, and between those two extremes lie gradations—from acquiescence to observation to encouragement.

Though I have no solid evidence that Henry Hinton joined the lynch mob, it is difficult for me to imagine him not joining or approving of the work of the crowd. He represents the apologists, those who either lacked any sense of guilt or who papered it over with sureties of justice and the will of the people. Opposing him is a real woman—his sister-in-law Lydia—whom I have enlisted to represent those who followed along with the mob but who rejected the easy platitudes of the Henry Hintons. The difference lies not just in Lydia's doubts contrasted against Henry's surety about the justice of the lynchings—and the guilt of the lynchers. It lies in their very minds. Lydia feels and thinks and reflects and frets over her participation in the lynching, her mind searching for answers, unsettled by the fact that she contributed to the murder of two boys. Henry has none of Lydia's problems. He possesses the ability to rationalize his actions and the actions of the crowd, smother all doubt beneath a layer of fine-sounding language and abstractions.

<hr/>

Celina Journal. November 14, 1872

Mercer County Common Pleas Court is in session this week, bringing here several lawyers from a distance; also, many people from the country who cannot get along without lawing.

The Court of Common Pleas for this county, convened on Monday last, Phelps on the bench. This being the first term held in this county since the terrible tragedies of June and July last, great anxiety was felt by all to ascertain just what action was likely to be taken by the authorities in reference to the leaders and participators in the mob. Strong fears were entertained by many that a vindictive policy would be pursued and that something rash and impolitic might be done which would have a tendency to aggravate and make matters worse instead of better. But such fears are no longer entertained. We are glad to be able to say that Judge Phelps, in his charge to the grand jury, took a proper view of the condition of affairs and faced the situation squarely, and by his moderation and good sense, done very much toward allaying the feeling of uneasiness that existed among portions of our people and at the same time inculcated and begat a higher regard for law and order.

We thank Judge Phelps for his charge to the grand jury and assure him that he has, by it, if it were possible, raised himself in the esteem of the better portion of our people.

Today (Wednesday) the grand jury reported to the court that they were unable to find an indictment against Jacob Kimmel, the last the party accused of the murder of Mary Secaur, and an order was immediately granted for his release from confinement in jail.[3]

Tiffin, Ohio—June 23, 2017

David Kimmel

Then there are my own people, the Kimmels. The murder, the arrests, the hearings, the lynchings—all of these events hit this family right between the eyes. We know an outline of the family's life following the murder of their son and brother. Jake was returned to the Celina jail where he remained until the circuit court convened in November; he was released almost immediately. Meanwhile, his parents sold off the land they'd cleared and farmed for twenty-seven years, where they'd spent their entire married life together, and moved three miles north to a place on Township Line Road. There the family restarted its life, integrating into the community around it, some of whom—Chivingtons and Testers— were already relations, and others of whom—Felvers and Chivingtons and Testers—became relatives. Their descendants still reside in the area. The details of life following the lynching of their son and brother are limited to land deeds, census entries, death certificates, and obituaries. These family members call out to me to make an attempt at a deeper understanding of their experiences. In the following vignettes, I explore beyond the facts to imagine something of the ways the Kimmels coped with the shock and rage and guilt they carried with them into their new life. I begin with a voice I have used before—five-year-old Charlie Kimmel.

Dublin Township, Mercer County, Ohio—November 3, 1872

Charlie Kimmel

We heard them before we saw them. It was a long, long wait. They sounded like thunder before they sounded like voices. And they were voices a long time before they were people. When the people come, it's best to hide. Next time, I'll hide, and I'll take Ab and Jake with me. Jake got down off that wagon, but Ab and the Cloud Man stayed up there. I called to Ab, but Mommy said shush, so I tried. The people smashed our fence and trampled the clearing flat. You can still see across the road where they all stood. You can still see the wagon tracks. Ab and the Cloud Man stood on the wagon. Then Ab wriggled and danced on the end of the rope. The Cloud Man did too. I laughed, but Mommy shook me, so I stopped. Jake went away on the wagon. We're waiting for Jake to come home. It's been so long. I keep running out to the road to see. Ab won't come home; he's gone to a better place. If I find out where they took him, I'll bring him home. We'll be together again. I miss Ab. I miss Jake. Jake will come home. Ab won't.

I help Daddy with Jake and Ab's chores now that we live on a new farm. They still haven't come home. Jake's coming home someday. I ran down to the crossroads this morning to see if he was on his way. I waited a terrible long time in the road in front of Bill's place, but I didn't see Jake. Mary Ellen says I shouldn't wait like that. Jake will be home, but it takes a while. It must be a long walk. I'll try again tomorrow. He might not know we moved, and he'll walk on past if I don't watch for him. Ab's not coming home any more. I miss Ab. I miss Jake.

Mommy is quiet. She keeps hugging me and Peck. I don't like it; I'm a big boy. I don't need hugs. Peck's a little boy, so he likes it. Yesterday, Peck found some kittens. A tom had gotten at them. There was blood. Peck cried and cried. I didn't cry because I'm a big boy. It did make me feel funny to look at them, though. Mary Ellen helped us to bury the kittens. There were two black ones, one orange, and one striped. We buried them out behind the corn crib. Once, Jennie locked me in the crib. I wasn't scared of losing my air, but I was scared of the shadows. Somewhere, Ab is in a box like that. In the crib, I hollered and hollered so's Jennie would let me go, but she never did. Finally, Mary Ellen found me and let me go.

When we go in to lunch, Mommy and Daddy don't talk. Just us kids. That's OK because they are all worn out. That's what Mary Ellen says. Daddy looks sad. Mommy just looks blank. I try to make everyone laugh, but they tell me to shush. I try.

▷─◆─○─◈─◁

Tiffin, Ohio—June 23, 2017

David Kimmel

I now return to George Kimmel, whose point of view I have borrowed again and again in this book. George was certainly innocent of any participation in the attack on Mary Secaur, and he was technically innocent of contributing to the lynching of his brother and McLeod. But his dramatic double-reverse testimony at the June 30 hearing did nothing to help and certainly complicated matters for the accused. I have already re-created one reunion between George and Jacob, along with an earlier imaginary trip into Celina. I complete my treatment of the brothers with one final vignette—a mid-November walk in the woods, a meeting with a fictional seer, and a confrontation.

▷─◆─○─◈─◁

Liberty Township, November 13, 1872

The wind stung George's face as he stumbled over the stubble along the edge of the wood. The slate sky was no longer spitting snow, but he was darned if it felt any warmer. He'd only been hunting for an hour, and already he was chilled to the bone. He stopped for a moment, gun barrel resting on his shoulder. He hadn't seen a thing since he left the farm. Why had his father sent him out here tramping around hard-rutted fields? George wasn't the hunter in the family. He could shoot straight enough, but it was Jake who could find the game. He was cold, hungry, and bored. The land was played out, anyway. He bet there wasn't more than a rabbit or two in the whole township.

He shrugged down into his jacket and started walking along the wood line again. His father would expect him home no earlier than dinner time, which was still hours from now, so it really didn't matter where he walked. Not that they were keeping track of his whereabouts. They didn't care about where he was or what he did or what he thought. They'd never even talked to him about it at all. That's what got to him the most—their silence. That and his mother avoiding his eyes. She seemed to be some-place else, hardly speaking to anyone. And his father just took it qui-etly ... at least toward her. With George, he was curt and hard. Do this, do that. We're short-handed. With George's mother he was docile, observant. Guilty. George pictured the family at the front windows, watching the crowd coming up the road toward them. Then his father was no longer with them. Then the crowd swept into the empty lot across the road.

George found himself standing still, staring vacantly at a woodchuck hole at the base of an ancient oak tree. He resumed his walk and his pitiful search for game. Inside the woods to his left, chipmunks chirped to track his progress. Otherwise, there was nothing. No, not nothing. He shook off the image of his brother the last time he'd seen him, raised high above the crowd, side-by-side with McLeod. Best not think about all that. Keep the mind empty. Pretend to hunt.

He walked for a while with his eyes on the edge of the woods, scanning the brush for any sign of movement. Nothing but the brown lines of black raspberry canes against the lighter brown of the leaves covering the earth. Why wouldn't his mother talk to him? What happened to Ab wasn't his doing. He only said what was true. And nothing more than what Andy said. Or Jake. It wasn't his fault that Ab signed that paper. All Ab had to do was to keep quiet and let McLeod take the blame. There was nothing on Ab. So why did George look away anytime his mother turned her empty gaze in his direction?

George noticed that he'd wandered into the woods again. He looked up at the pale sun through the bare, black branches. Well, why not? Maybe he'd scare up something in the woods. He sure wasn't finding anything out in the open. Of course, Jake wouldn't do it this way. He'd complain about how George didn't know nothing about hunting. Well, George knew plenty—and plenty that Jake would never know. Anyway, he was a better hunter than Ab, who made such a racket it was a wonder they ever shot anything. And you sure didn't want to walk out in front of him with a loaded gun in his hands.

George stopped. In his mind flashed the image of Ab rotating slowly at the end of a rope. He set off quickly, trying to outwalk the picture, but the faster he walked, the more he was pursued by the crowd, the wagon, the ropes, his brother kicking. It was bad enough at night. It wasn't fair; he hadn't done anything. He hadn't been with McLeod. Wasn't he the one who warned the others about the trader? Stick with Andy, he said. McLeod—there was something not to be trusted about him. And who was right? Of course it was George—he was the one to listen to. He did nothing but tell the truth.

A branch whipped across George's face. Ah! He pressed the heel of his hand against his eye. It figured. It just figured. He was now deeper into the woods, a section of the old forest that had never been cleared. Towering above him, oaks spread their long arms against the gray sky. He dabbed his eye with the cuff of his jacket. He walked again.

The truth. George told the truth. McLeod *had* talked to him about the girl. They *had* been with McLeod. It was only a matter of adding two and two together. The sheriff said so himself. The justices had all praised him. They knew he was speaking the truth; George hadn't gone back on anybody. He wouldn't go back on his brothers. He only told what he knew about McLeod. The truth. And what he said wasn't what put McLeod on that wagon. What about the ribbon? What about the blood at the pump? He saw that with his own eyes. McLeod had blood on his shirt that night at dinner. George saw it. And McLeod was all on fire to get moving the next morning. What'd he want to leave so soon for if he hadn't done it? What were Jake and Ab doing with McLeod in the first place? They should've listened to George. Andy didn't do that to the girl; Andy knew right from wrong. It was McLeod. Who was he, anyway, coming around here and causing a ruckus? It wasn't George's fault. He tried to warn them. He tried to watch out for them, for Ab especially. It wasn't his fault—it was Jake. Ab always listened to Jake. He should've listened to George, not to Jake. Jake didn't know. Jake followed McLeod. Jake probably did it, too. Ab said he did. Ab said they both did. Why would he lie? The sheriff said McLeod told him. It was in the newspaper. Ab told them, and they wrote it down. Ab wouldn't lie. He didn't know how. If what Ab said was true, then what he'd said must be true. It was true. McLeod had told him. They were sitting on the bed. McLeod had told him about the girl. The other two were with McLeod. There was nothing he could do—McLeod did it. And Ab confessed. The sheriff said so. There was nothing to feel guilty about.

George stepped through light brush and onto the road. How'd he get all the way down here? He must've walked longer or faster than he realized. He looked off the road toward the spot. The *bloody spot*, McLeod had said. He admitted to that, even on the wagon.

A man coughed and stood up from the dried weeds beside the road. A small, grizzled man, he wore a filthy hat along with a patched and faded jacket far too light for this weather. He sucked on a pipe and blew a cloud of blue smoke toward George. The man gestured toward the spot.

"Say it happened right over there."

"What?"

"I don't know myself, weren't there, but that's what they tell me. Say it was a Sunday afternoon in June."

"I don't know what you're talking about." George turned to head the other way. The man jumped toward George and grabbed his arm. George jerked his arm free and snapped his gun around.

"Easy, brother," said the man. "Put that thing down before you hurt someone, namely me. I got a mighty aversion to being shot. Had enough of that during the war."

George lowered the gun. "Well, don't go jumping out of the woods and grabbing people, then."

The man laughed. "Fair enough." He paused for a moment, then leaned confidentially toward George. "Want to see it? The spot?"

"No. What are you talking about?"

The man held out his hand. "Name's Sayer. I'm from Iowa, but my people was from Indiana. Enlisted in '62 and been marching ever since." George ignored his outstretched hand. Sayer laughed a few times and looked off into the trees.

George wondered how he could get away from this tramp. Who knew what kind of devilment this old vet might be up to? "I got to go. It's getting late, and I need to be home for chores." George set off down the road away from the spot.

"Hey, slow down, there, brother." Sayer hobbled up along beside George, who begrudgingly slowed for his unwanted partner.

Sayer pulled a small bottle from inside his jacket. "Want a snort?" He held it out to George, who shook his head. "Don't mind if I do." Sayer laughed at his joke and pulled the cork from the bottle. "Here's to easy work and easier women." George and Sayer stopped while the tramp tilted his head back and took a large swallow. He exhaled and smacked his lips. "Good for what ails ya."

George started to walk again, Sayer keeping pace with him. The pair walked along for a while in silence. George wondered how long he'd be stuck with the man. Sayer breathed loudly through his nose as he struggled to keep even with George. He had an odd lilt to his gait, and George looked down to see the cause.

"Caught a ball at Vicksburg, right in my calf. The doctors—those bastards— they wanted to take my leg, but I fought 'em off. I walked right out of there. I says, 'Doc, I only got two, and I won't have you hacking away at one of 'em.' He hollered something fierce when I walked out, but I won't hear none of it. I been walking ever since. Walked up north, walked east, walked west, walked back down south, all the way to N'Orleans. They got some hot times down there, let me tell you. Course, you're too young for that."

"I ain't all that young."

"Course not. I can see that." The two walked along in silence for a few minutes. "I near 'bout lost my leg, walking around with a ball in it. My calf swole up to the size of my thigh, turned red, got hot to the touch. Kept walking, though. Finally it settled down, pretty much. They say there was three of them done it."

"Three of what?" George looked out of the corner of his eye at the man bobbing up and down beside him.

"Say she weren't found 'til the next day. Hogs ate her. Some kinda waste, if you ask me." George fixed his eyes ahead of him on the road. "Hogs ate her brains. I seen that during the war. The battlefields were just a hog's paradise. Free meat, just laying around. Wonder why they go for the brains? Ooh ... the smell, though. Bet that girl smelled. Hot day and all. Head about cut off. You probably wonder how come I know so much about it, huh? I read it in the paper—more than one paper, matter fact." The man reached inside his jacket and pulled out a fistful of newspapers. "I read all the time. Papers everywhere. People just leave them lay when they're done with them. When I seen this story, I knew I had to come. Just like with the other ones."

"What other ones?"

"Oh, I follow them all over. I read about them, and I have to go see for myself. Slow as I travel, I don't have much chance of getting there until it's all over. Like now. Couldn't see nothing back there where it happened, and people here 'bouts don't have too much to say. I ain't been out to where they strung them up, yet. Know where it is?"

"No."

"You live around here, don't you? There had to been talk, even if you don't read. You got to know something about the biggest story in these parts in years." George sped up a bit, and the tramp hobbled along beside him. "Shoot, I know all about it, and I only read about it. I'd a give anything to seen them string up those boys. I seen plenty of bodies hanging from trees, but I never been there when they was still alive. Something about the life at the end of a line. You know you're alive on the end of that rope, I bet. You ever seen anyone lynched?"

George looked down at his hands. "No, I never ..."

"I hear the body dances sometimes. Sure be a sight to see. I seen lots of bodies. None of them dancing. That girl sure got it. Them three boys had their fun with her, the way I hear it. Did you know the girl? Was she pretty as the papers said? Thirteen, that's the best. Hard to get with a musket ball in your pants. They got lucky. Like a Sunday miracle. She just walked up to them. It just don't happen like that. You know, you could slow down a bit. It'd help with the leg and all."

George increased his speed. "I need to get home and do my chores."

"Oh, chores never helped nobody. They'll wait. Hell, I have chores back home been waiting for me for ten years." He laughed a phlegmy laugh that slid into a coughing fit.

George noticed they'd come to the crossroads by Straus May's place. The girl had walked right past here that day. He glanced guiltily at May's house. A horse stood in the lot out by the barn, harnessed and saddled and awaiting a rider with its head down and rear facing the wind.

"How'd they get caught, I like to know. I hear their own family turn them in." Sayer cleared his throat and spit a large brown-and-red hawk onto the dirt. "How can you turn on your own flesh and blood? Must be some kind of family do that."

"They're not bad," George said quietly.

"Three of them lynched, turned in by their own kin. I'd say there's something wrong with a family do that."

George fixed his eyes on his feet as they passed May's house. "Nobody turned anybody in."

"That's not what the paper said. Said one brother stood up in court and went back on them. Said that's what put the crowd over, and they rushed to the jail and did it right then."

"That's not true. It didn't happen like that."

"Were you there or not?"

"I was there."

"Oh ho! Now we're getting somewhere! Did they do it? Who was it turned them in? Why'd their brother turn on them?

"No one turned on anyone."

Sayer laughed. "That's not what I heard. Five arrested and three kept in jail. Seems to me someone got off somehow. And there ain't no surer way to get off than to blame someone else. I'd be strung up myself if that wasn't true. Make the sheriff's job easy, that's my motto. I follow these cases all over this country. It's all the same. Somebody murders or rapes; somebody gets lynched. So long as the figures add up, no one worries about who plays what part. Best to play the safest part if you got the choice—though I suppose you already know that, being so grown up and all."

George stopped and looked at Sayer. "What do you mean by that?" he asked slowly. He lowered his gun from his shoulder and held it across his body, a waist-high barrier between him and Sayer. "I think it's time we parted company. I don't know what you're trying to suggest, but I don't like it. I don't like you much, either." George gestured with the gun barrel. "You go on back the way we came or wherever you want. Just quit following me."

Sayer smiled, revealing a row of brownish, decayed teeth. "Sure. You just get on home. It ain't like I never talked to a guilty boy before." And with that he turned and hobbled away from George, who watched him for a moment and then turned himself and headed toward his own crossroad and home.

The afternoon had gotten along, and the gray light had dimmed considerably, taking the temperature down with it. As George walked the road toward his house, the wind blew steadily from the north into his face. Since he'd left Sayer, his mind had gone around and around on the same track. What had Sayer meant by "guilty boy"? George wasn't guilty of anything. He didn't need some old tramp coming along and accusing him, either. Five were arrested and three were kept in jail! Five were arrested and three were guilty, more like. A thought gripped him at the base of his skull, but he shook it away. There was nothing he could have done for any of them.

George clambered over the rails of the fence and stomped on through the field toward the barn. Since he was early, he'd check in with his father to see if there were any more chores to be done before dinner. He pulled the gun down off his shoulder. He'd hear about it for not finding anything to shoot. But he had tried, hadn't he? He'd walked all over the county, not to mention meeting that strange tramp.

George rounded the corner into the barn and stopped short. There looking at him were his father and Jake. The latter's face was red and raw from the wind and what looked like an inexpert recent shave.

"Hi."

His father and brother nodded. Then his father crossed over to him and took the gun from George's hands.

"I'll leave you two," he said and left the barn.

George and Jake stood awkwardly. Jake looked tired, thin, drawn out. His clothes were wrinkled but clean. Next to his muddy shoes lay a cloth bag George knew held the change of clothing his mother had taken Jake on her visit two days before.

"You're home," said George.

"Yeah."

"I'm glad."

Jake looked down at the floor and scraped at a piece of dried mud or manure with the toe of his worn shoe. A horse clomped heavily in its stall over in the north pen.

"Was it hard?" George asked.

Jake considered with his shoe for a moment. "What do you think? Just one day after another, staring at them walls."

"It hasn't been easy on anyone." George couldn't think of what to do with his hands. They just hung there at his sides.

"Yeah, I bet," said Jake. His arms were crossed before him, and his chin was jutted out, as if in an accusation.

In the relative warmth of the animal-heated barn, George suddenly felt the weariness of his long walk in the cold. He walked over to the stall gate and stared a moment at the rounded mass of the horse. Its tail swished. George turned back to face Jake and leaned against a post. "Thank God for Elias," he said.

Jake had walked farther into the barn. He picked at a harness hanging from one of the log walls of the pen across from George. "I was glad for that." Jake had a faraway look on his face for a moment, but then he looked right into George's eyes. "Shouldn't have had to do that, though, if people had kept their mouths shut."

Now it was out. "Hey, I didn't say nothing that wasn't true," said George. Jake gave George a thin-lipped, narrow-eyed look. "I did talk to McLeod. He did tell me about the girl."

"Oh, and when was that?" asked Jake. He'd taken a few steps toward George. There was a sarcastic tang to his voice.

"Before dinner," said George. He tried to picture the scene. There was McLeod, sitting across from him on Ab's bed. He saw that clearly. "No, it was after."

"You don't know, do you?" Jake had closed the space between them by another step or two.

"Give me a second," said George. He held a hand out toward Jake for silence. A low humming had started up in George's head. He took a step along the wall to his right. "It's hard to remember that far back."

"It's hard to remember because it's a lie." Jake had shifted his motion to his own right, and the two had begun a slow spiral.

"You can't call me a liar," said George, his voice slightly louder to cover the humming.

"I can when you are." There was a definite edge to Jake's speech. Their spiraling tightened slightly.

"And who are you to talk about the truth?" asked George. "I didn't say nothing that you didn't say, too." Their orbits sped up and closed in.

"You said Ab done it," said Jake, voice flat and clipped.

"I said McLeod told me that," said George. He was shouting now.

"Same thing," said Jake. "And just as much a lie."

They were now a step away from each other, slowly revolving in the large open center of the barn, tensed and ready to strike.

"You take that back," said George. The humming in his head was louder and louder.

"You know it's true," said Jake. "You're a liar."

George lunged toward his brother. Jake sidestepped him, and George fell past him. Jake's fist connected just behind his left ear, and he hit the floor hard. George lay in the straw and mud and shit that covered the puncheons of the floor. The back of his head rang, and his chin stung from slamming into the ground. He half-rolled onto his side. Jake stood a handful of steps away, staring down at George, his fists still clenched, ready to strike again. George clambered to his feet and rubbed the back of his head. His stomach felt queasy.

"Look," said Jake. "I didn't come back here to fight you."

George stood and squinted at his brother in hatred. His thoughts were an angry, incoherent jumble. "If I'm a liar, so are you," he said. "You went back on McLeod just as much as me."

Jake looked thoughtful. He lowered his arms and unclenched his fists. "Yeah. It seemed like the way out. You, Andy, then me." Jake drifted back over to the harnesses and ran his hand over the smooth leather.

"What about Ab and what he said?"

Jake shook his head. "Ab nearly got me killed." He thought for a moment. "He definitely got himself killed."

"And you didn't help any?" asked George. He was back at the stall gate. He felt sick.

"What's that supposed to mean?" The edge had returned to Jake's voice.

George thought. What did he mean? Then he knew. "Well, was his confession . . .?"

"True? What do you think?" asked Jake.

"That's what I'm asking. Did you all do what Absalom said you did?"

"I can't believe you're asking me that." Jake was back walking again, circling round toward the open double barn doors.

"Well?"

Jake stood silhouetted against what was left of the late-afternoon daylight. "No."

"What about Ab and McLeod?"

"No." Jake's outline was silent for a moment. "I don't think so." Another pause. "I don't know."

Back in the south pen somewhere, a cow lowed. The horse in the stall behind George stomped and blew air out its nose. The room smelled of hay and manure and animals and life.

"Ab wouldn't do that," said George.

"I don't know," said Jake. He was now walking back toward the harnesses. "They wasn't there when I came home from church. They was gone long enough to do it."

"McLeod was gone after dinner," said George. "And he had blood on his shirt."

"He had blood on his shirt," Jake said, more to the air than to George. He stopped at the harnesses. "But his nose bled. I seen it."

"He had blood on his shirt, and he told me what he did," said George, taking a step toward Jake.

"No, he didn't," said Jake, heading toward the open doorway. George wanted to grab his brother and hold him still. The back of his head throbbed.

"Yes, he told me upstairs." George tried to picture the scene. "We were sitting on the beds upstairs after dinner, and he told me what he done. We was swapping watch chains, and he told me."

"No, he never told you that. He never told you nothing like it." Jake was back in the doorway.

"We was sitting on the beds upstairs. I can picture it clear as day," said George. And he did. He saw McLeod right there on Ab's bed.

"No, McLeod never talked to you," said Jake. He hesitated. "And he never told me nothing in the jail," said Jake.

George was silent. Jake stood still in the fading light.

"You know we just said those things so's they'd let us go, same as Andy," said Jake.

"There was blood on his shirt," said George. He heard his voice rise in pitch. "They had it in the hearing."

"That blood don't prove nothing," said Jake.

Now it was George who was moving, fading across the open room toward Jake's harnesses. "What about the bloody ribbon?" asked George.

Jake laughed. "That ribbon almost got us all killed. But the sheriff coulda put that on McLeod's bridle just as easy as anyone."

George stopped and looked puzzled at his brother. "You didn't stop and pick it up on the way to the state line?"

Jake made a disgusted noise. "That's the stupidest thing I ever heard. If we did commit murder, why would we do something that dumb? That hearing was the first time any of us ever seen that ribbon." Jake had taken a few steps toward George.

"But the sheriff said . . ."

"The sheriff lied," said Jake. "Look, they threatened you if you didn't say those things about McLeod, didn't they? They threatened all of us if we didn't go back on McLeod. I ain't proud of what I said, but it was my only chance." He paused for a moment in the middle of the room. "Our only chance."

"I never went back on anyone. I'm no liar." George was shaking his head.

"Face it, you sold McLeod just like I did," said Jake. He shook his finger at George. Then his face got an awful look on it. "And Ab."

"No, we never said anything about Ab," said George.

"You did," said Jake. And he was moving again to his right. "You said McLeod told you Ab was with him."

Jake stopped and reversed direction. He was talking to the room in general now. "And I did, too. Or just the same as saying it." He stopped and turned to George. "They were out for Ab and McLeod, don't you see? Whatever we said they used as a reason to go for them."

George kept shaking away this idea. "But it was Ab who said it. He almost got you killed, too."

"It wouldn't have stuck if we hadn't gone back on McLeod. What we said backed up Ab." Jake's face had an odd smile. "And we don't have the excuse of being idiots. We knew what we was doing."

"But I only told the truth," said George, vaguely.

"You lied just like I lied, George. You and me and Andy killed McLeod just as much as that mob did." He looked off. "And Ab, too."

George looked out past his brother through the open doors. His eyes focused on something out beyond the woods in the distance. "Five was arrested and three came home," he said to no one in particular.

"What's that?" asked Jake.

George thought back to that afternoon in June. McLeod had blood on his shirt sleeve at dinner. McLeod never sat across from George on Ab's bed. He never told him anything about the girl or him or Ab. McLeod hardly ever even talked to George; that's what had made it possible. The horse banged a heavy hoof on the floor. George saw the woods and the deputies. He saw the crowded courtroom. He saw himself standing up before the crowd. He saw himself standing up a second time. He saw himself watching his brother raised up above the crowd. And he felt the tears sliding down his cheeks.

George's brother was blurry through the water. His breath caught. "What did we do, Jake?"

"What we needed to stay alive," said Jake.

The cow lowed again, and the other animals shifted in their stalls. It was nearly dark, now, and they sensed dinner time was approaching.

"What do we do now?" asked George.

"We keep on living."

The two stood silently, listening to the darkness fall. Then they set to work feeding and watering the animals.

Tiffin, Ohio—June 23, 2017

David Kimmel

The Kimmel sons conducted a slow-motion dispersal following the lynching of their brother. Samuel, who was already married to Sarah

Tester and with a small daughter at the time of the murder, had six children before they all moved to Harper County in Kansas sometime in 1883. Samuel and Sarah overcame the hardships that sent many pioneers of the Great Plains to early graves or back east in defeat. By the next century, Samuel was considered a major cattle rancher in his section of Kansas.[4] My great-great grandfather, William, married Lydia Tester, a cousin of Sarah's, six years after the murder.[5] William eventually took over his parents' farm in Dublin Township, where he and Lydia raised three boys to adulthood.[6] Jacob married Mary Elizabeth Chivington the same year as William's marriage,[7] and the couple soon after moved to Kansas, where they are found in the 1880 census.[8] By 1884, Jacob and Mary moved across the border to Kansas City, where they remained until at least 1891.[9] In 1900, the family lived back in Mercer County.[10] Jacob and company later moved to Hartford City, Indiana, where he remained until his death in 1927.[11] George still lived at home with his mother and younger siblings in 1880.[12] From there he is difficult to trace, but I believe he's the "George Kimball/Kimble" who lived in Rockford in 1900, Dayton in 1910, and Celina in 1920.[13] Charlie followed his brothers to Kansas sometime in the 1880s, but he died of pneumonia in November of 1886 in Kansas City at the age of nineteen.[14] My assumption—based on information in his death record along with a plain hunch—is that he lived with or near Jacob at the time of his death. Though I have found few details of his life between 1880 and 1900, John Andrew Kimmel, known as "Peck," seems to have joined the migration to Kansas after reaching maturity. In 1905, he married Alvena Derr,[15] herself born in Kansas in 1888 of German immigrant parents.[16] Peck and Alvina moved along with her parents to Memphis at least by 1908, when their first daughter was born.[17] Their second-youngest daughter was born in Tennessee around 1913, and their youngest in Ohio in 1926,[18] so sometime between those dates their family moved to Rockford, where John Andrew and Alvina were buried in Riverside Cemetery on the edge of town in 1957 and 1958.[19]

That the Kimmel boys should move west is not surprising. The settling of the Great Plains was the project of their generation. Nearly every person born before 1840 in Liberty Township had come from somewhere to the east, and their paternal grandmother had lived in at least five counties across two states. In fact, Henry and Susan Kimmel were unusual for settling in so solidly in their Liberty Township homestead. Of the boys who followed the flow west, only Samuel remained. The rest either died (Charlie) or trickled back toward their original home.

The conflict and diaspora of the young men in the Kimmel family is the complete opposite of the experiences of their sisters, who lived out most of their lives within seven miles of the house where they were born and whose graves cluster around one another along the edge of Riverside Cemetery. Mary Ellen was twenty-two when she watched the crowd kill her brother.[20] A little over a year later, she married Clark Felver, a young widower living between his parents and her brother William and almost directly across Township Line Road from her parent's new farm. In 1880, she and Clark lived on that same farm with three sons, the oldest, George, from Clark's first marriage.[21] Clark and Mary Ellen moved to Dublin Township by 1900,[22] where they lived until Clark died in 1904 and Mary Ellen in 1934.[23]

Sarah Anna is a cypher. First, her name. She's listed as "Eve," in the 1860 census; in 1870 she's "Sarah," and in 1880, she's "Sarah A."[24] In her brother William's obituary (1923), she's listed as "Anna McKay."[25] It is that name that appears on her headstone in Riverside Cemetery, buried alongside her husband, David, but it is unclear when she switched from Sarah to Anna. Working backward, we find her widowed in Rockford in 1930, living with David in Rockford in 1920, and living with him on the Upper Peninsula of Michigan in 1910, the couple having married some-time around 1908.[26] For David, Anna is a second wife, since he is listed in the same spot in the 1900 census, living with his wife of twenty-one years, Elizabeth, and their two daughters, ages fifteen and six.[27] Where Elizabeth and the two girls had gone in 1910 is as big a mystery as what a girl from Mercer County was doing in the far north of Michigan. To add to the muddle, David and Anna do not seem to have had any chil-dren, but Anna's 1910 listing reports her as the mother of one. A possible candidate for this honor is sixteen-year-old Belle D., who lived with her grandmother, Susan, in 1900.[28] I cannot find Anna in 1900, but the 1930 census lists her "age at first marriage" as twenty-five, which would have been 1884, the same year Belle D. was born.

Compared to Anna, Alice is a walk in the park. Married to Samuel's brother-in-law Wilson Tester in 1882, Alice had five children—three of whom were alive in 1900.[29] The couple lived in Rockford in 1910 and 1920, at the latter date being listed on the same page as her brother William and his half-his-age wife, Ida S.[30] Alice is listed as dying in 1927 on her headstone in Riverside Cemetery. The youngest sister, Jennie, married

William Atkinson around 1904, and the couple seem to have lived out their lives in rural Dublin Township, close by William in 1910 and his son Ferdellus, my great-grandfather, in 1930.[31] The 1910 census lists the couple as living with a six-year-old daughter, Helen, who seems to have been adopted, as her birthplace and those of her parents are listed as Indiana and Jennie is listed in 1910 as having given birth to no children.[32] Jennie died in 1945 and is buried near her sisters in Riverside Cemetery.[33]

The closeness of the Kimmel sisters contrasts with the tensions among the brothers—those I can document and those I have imagined. Earlier, I sent the oldest sister, Mary Ellen, down to the crossroads to gather information about the murder of their young neighbor. In the next vignette, I recruit Mary Ellen to explore the effects of the murder and lynchings on the women in the Kimmel family a year out from the drama of 1872. The focus here is on relationships—past, present, and future.

⊢⊣⊹⊙⊱⊢⊣

Dublin Township, Mercer County, Ohio July 15, 1873

Mary Ellen Kimmel

The sheet floated above the bed, the air catching beneath it for a moment before spilling out, letting the sheet collapse. Mary Ellen tucked it in around the mattress and moved on to the next pallet. She moved calmly and purposefully; the faster the job was through, the sooner they could get out of this furnace. The air was still and stifling—mid-July muggy. Any small breeze that blew through the trees outside was blocked by the log walls, and the thin planks of the roof simply radiated heat. The only sounds were the whoosh of the sheets, the creaking of the floorboards, and the soft chatting of her younger sisters in the other room.

It was a bother to wash the sheets once a week, but it was proper, even if they did live in a house made of logs. She missed their old house. It was made of logs, too, but it had been finished inside and out, and that had made all the difference. Her uncle, cousin, and father had raised it with their own hands, and her parents had lived there for most of their married lives, over twenty years.

"All done, Mary Ellen," Sarah called from next door. "Let's get out of this bake oven!"

Mary Ellen looked in at the girls' work and nodded her approval—though it was hardly up to her standards of neatness. Her sisters were just too young and full of life, and it was just too hot up here to worry about details. She followed the girls down the corner staircase to the main room, the temperature dropping by a third as they descended. Unlike the old house with its tacked-on rear kitchen, this one was still just one common room and a bedroom set off by a thin partition. Her mother and little Jennie worked at the table in the main room. At least the family had been able to bring along their furnishings when they left the old place—and the table, the wash basin, the hutch for their dishes, and the iron stove made a world of difference. Mary Ellen looked at the mantel and shuddered at the thought of women cooking over an open fire in that fireplace.

"Mary Ellen, take Sarah and Alice outside and weed until lunch. Jennie can stay here with me." Her mother didn't even look up as she gave directions, working intently on crimping the crusts of the three apple pies the family would make short work of at lunchtime. She looked haggard, her mother did. Mary Ellen didn't ever want to be that old—forty-five—and yet she knew her sisters thought the same about her. Twenty-three and still stuck at home. Of course, what would she be doing any different if she were married and on her own?

The three were out in the kitchen garden now, bending over in the hot sun. Though she'd put on a wide-brimmed hat, Mary Ellen could feel the heat on her back and head; the straw of the hat crackled in the heat. She stood and flapped her dress a bit to cool off.

"I hate weeding," Alice whined.

Mary Ellen smiled. "Well, it's not my favorite, either, but it's got to be done."

"It's so pointless," said Alice. She held up a dandelion and examined its long, white root. "They're just going to grow back again." She pitched the plant over the low garden fence.

"Don't be a baby," said Sarah. "Just do your work and keep still!"

"Keep still, yourself, bossy!"

"Let's just work and not fuss," said Mary Ellen.

They worked for a while, their hoes snicking into the soil. The ground was rock-hard between the rows, even with straw laid down to keep in the moisture. The weeds seemed to pull back when they yanked on them.

"Ow, stupid thistle!" Alice threw down her hoe and stood sucking urgently at her palm.

"Oh, did baby hurt herself?"

"Shut up, Sarah! And who's the baby? I'm not the one crying all night."

Mary Ellen sighed. "Will both of you just stop? You're acting like children."

They worked in silence for another ten minutes or so. Mary Ellen could sense her sisters continuing the fight in their heads. The heat made her despair.

"I do not cry at night. Do I, Mary?"

Mary Ellen thought for a moment. "Well, lately you've been a little emotional, Sarah. It happens." She gave Alice a warning look. "And it doesn't mean she's a baby. What seems to be the problem?"

"I don't know. I'm just down a lot lately." Sarah continued to hoe, striking at the hard earth. "Maybe it's the heat, maybe … I don't know. I really miss Ab."

"Yeah," said Mary Ellen. She thought of her brother for a moment. It was hard to believe it had been a year. She could see his face before her with that sheepish smile of his. Then she saw him the other way. "It's hard on everyone."

"I miss him, too," said Alice, a note of pleading in her voice.

"I know you do, darling," said Mary Ellen.

"He was fun and nice to me," said Alice. "Unlike some people."

"What's that supposed to mean?" asked Sarah, raising her voice. "You're always doing that, turning everything into an attack on me. I'm sick of it."

"What's going on out there?" It was their mother. "You girls working or playing?"

"Working, Mother," called Mary Ellen. She lowered her voice. "You two, keep it down. You want her to hear you? You know how she's been."

"Sorry," said Alice.

"Sorry," said Sarah. "But it's not like we didn't lose him, too."

"It's not the same," said Mary Ellen. "It's different for mothers."

She thought of herself as a mother, of little Georgie, of Clark's question. A five year old. Nearly as old as Peck. That was stepping in it, wasn't it?

They worked longer. "What was it like?" asked Sarah. She stopped hoeing, and her voice took on a wondering quality.

"What was what like?" asked Mary Ellen, continuing along her row.

"For Mary."

"Oh," said Mary Ellen. An image appeared before her, but she blinked it away. "Just put it out of your head."

"I try," said Sarah. "She was my friend."

"Oh, it's different for you. You're *older.*" Alice placed a snide emphasis on the last word. "Well, she was my friend, too."

"You don't even know what we're talking about," said Sarah.

"I do too. You're talking about Mary and how she was ... *murdered.*" Alice said the word in a way that indicated the special mystery and significance of the term.

"No, stupid. I'm talking about what happened before she was killed," said Sarah.

"What? Walking home from church?" asked Alice.

"This is not something to talk about," said Mary Ellen.

But Sarah ran right over the end of Mary Ellen's speech. "See? She doesn't know. It's the worst thing that can happen, but little Alice is just a child."

"That's enough, Sarah." Mary Ellen looked over at Alice, whose face was balled up with injustice. "You and I can talk later."

"What? I'm old enough. Tell me what you're talking about!" Alice looked ready to stamp a petulant foot.

"They say it happens lots more than people let on." Sarah said this softly to the distant woods.

"People don't end up eaten by hogs all the time," said Alice.

"No, the other thing," Sarah said, her voice low. "You know, boys are always after it, and we're all out here in the country. They all want to."

"All of them?" asked Alice. "Want to what? Kill us?"

"Don't be silly," said Mary Ellen. "It's not like that. Now hush, Sarah; you're scaring your sister." Still, Mary Ellen knew. She'd heard the stories. Boyfriends, strangers, brothers, uncles, fathers. Men took what they wanted. And they protected each other.

"It's too horrible to think about," said Sarah. "Just awful. And it could've been any of us. Just think of it. Awful." She trailed off, gazing vacantly at something just above the woodline.

"Just quit thinking *and talking* about it," said Mary Ellen. She sliced a stalk of Queen Anne's lace with her hoe blade.

They worked in silence a while, the sun bearing down on their backs and shoulders, no sound but the wind in the trees and the chinking of the hoes in the ground.

Sarah's hoe halted. "Do you think they did it?"

"Who did what?" asked Mary Ellen. "No, of course not. Don't be stupid."

"Where were they in the afternoon that day?"

"How should I know? I don't keep track of my brothers all day." Mary Ellen waved vaguely at the air before her. "Just because I don't know where they were don't mean they'd do something like that."

"They all want to," ventured Sarah.

"Kill us? Even our brothers?" Alice screwed up her face.

"Don't be silly." Mary Ellen's voice grew stern, grown-up. "That's not anything to talk about. No one in our family would, and that's all there is to say about it." She watched her hoe chop at the weeds, but then looked up and saw Sarah staring at her. "They didn't do anything," she said, crisply. "How can you think Ab would ..."

"Well, McLeod, then. We don't know nothing about him."

"He always looked at me funny," added Alice.

"Funny how?" asked Mary Ellen.

"Like a ... like a murderer. He was scary." Alice's words were teetering on the fulcrum between knowledge and an immature terror of the boogeyman.

"That don't mean he did ... that he'd ... that they'd ..."

"It don't mean that they didn't, neither," said Sarah. "Look, he was right here in our house. He spent the night in our house after he done it. He slept up there with just a thin wall between him and us. It could've been one of us."

"Nonsense. It don't bear thinking on," said Mary Ellen. She smacked at the earth, but it was clear in the silence that followed along what row all their thoughts ran.

"He said he done it," said Sarah.

"What are you talking about?" asked Mary Ellen.

"You know ... *Ab*."

"Not Ab," said Mary Ellen.

"He confessed," said Sarah.

"You don't know what they done to him before he signed that confession." Mary Ellen thought a moment. "He couldn't hardly read. What they printed didn't sound like Ab, did it?"

"No, it didn't," ventured Alice.

"You don't know anything about it. You're too young!" yelled Sarah.

"There's no reason to yell at her," said Mary Ellen. She looked up at the yellow disk in the sky, directly overhead. "Let's just forget the whole thing and go in to lunch."

Just then George came around the house, followed by their father and then by Jake. They were tired and sweaty, their hats, clothes, and faces covered with the fine yellow dust of the wheat chaff.

"Dinner's almost ready," Mary Ellen told them. "Better wash up."

The men halted and did an about-face, trudging back to the barn lot. Why was it that men forgot to do the simplest things?

Was Clark like that? She honestly didn't know that much about him. He'd noticed her since the day they moved in, he said. He couldn't stop thinking about her, he said. And he strongly hinted that he'd have a certain question for her when they met again this evening. She knew the question, but she wondered about her answer.

She stood, and the movement plus the heat caused her head to fill with a red hum and the land to tilt. Eyes closed, she waited for the vertigo to pass.

She knew the sensible answer—the one she should make. Of course, Clark would make a good match. He already had a house, he was a good farmer, he was connected in the neighborhood, and he seemed genuinely interested in her. But there was Georgie, Clark's son. His wife had only passed away two years before. Was Clark really interested in her—or only in a housekeeper? And how would Georgie take to her? The five-year-old seemed friendly enough whenever they met, but step-relations could be delicate.

Mary Ellen guessed that Clark's Georgie wouldn't be the happy little boy he seemed to be if Clark weren't a good man. And he certainly had nothing to do with his wife's death. Word was she died of pleurisy and that Clark had stayed a dutiful husband until the end, standing watch all night long at her bedside. He certainly seemed stable enough.

Mary Ellen's father and brothers returned from the pump, wiping their hands on their trouser legs. While she'd like to have them actually wash the dust off their hands and faces, she knew it was a losing battle. She and her sisters gathered up their tools and followed the men through the back door.

With a family this size, it was only possible to eat in shifts. First, the men. They worked hard, and they deserved to eat hot food and as much as they wanted. Henry pulled out a chair and sat down. Jake and George sat opposite and as far apart as possible, though George had sidled up to the right hand of his father. Charlie and little Peck had joined them, filling in empty seats around their older brothers. Her father mumbled something over the food, and then he and the other four dug in. They ate like machines, not speaking, hardly chewing, grabbing food from the platters and stuffing it in their mouths. The only noises were their smacking and munching and the background noises of their mother preparing even greater quantities of food. The temperature, already high with the heat of cooking, soared as the males brought their heat-soaked clothing, along with their fervent feeding, into the large, dim room.

"Alice, go fetch me a pitcher of water," said her mother.

"I'll get it!" said Mary Ellen, taking the pitcher and escaping into the relative cool of the midday sun. Crossing the bare ground on the way to the pump, she slowed her pace—and her thoughts. Clark Felver. Mary Ellen Felver. That didn't sound too bad. Of course, he hadn't asked, but it was coming. She'd make him wait a day or so before she'd answer. It would be one of the few times in her life when she'd have some control.

She thought then of her mother, of her tired, tired face. Her vacant eyes. When Mary Ellen looked at her mother, she saw someone who was exhausted, someone who managed only by continuing her movement. If she ever stopped, Mary Ellen knew her mother would lay herself down and quit. Would Mary Ellen's own life end like that?

The pump squeaked as she pulled up and pushed down on the long iron handle. After a few pumps, the water glugged theatrically. Mary Ellen held the pitcher up under the spout, and the water poured forth.

What was her mother like when she first married her father? It seemed an impossible question. She had always been the same matronly force, holding the family together through sheer willpower. When they'd been visited by the small pox, her mother stood firm, nursing each of them through the illness—all the while ignoring her own symptoms. Mary Ellen recalled seeing her mother once peeling apples from the fruit cellar for a pie. Though breath fogged before her face—even in the kitchen—she stood at the table, bending over the apples, paring knife in hand. Drops of perspiration formed on her forehead, trickled down her face, gathered on the end of her nose, before plopping off and landing in the bowl of apples.

Mary Ellen set the full pitcher on the ground away from the mud and cupped her hands beneath the flow. She splashed her face, then pulled down on the pump handle.

Her mother had grown up on a farm in the just-broken woods, so she had gone into marriage and the Kimmels' homestead with few illusions. Hard work was just what needed done, she always said. That was why Mary Ellen was so surprised at her mother's reaction to Ab's death. Though her mother had been around death before—and who hadn't in this country?—though she'd bounced back from adversity before, she simply had collapsed in on herself.

She felt the tightness in her lower back as she straightened, pitcher in hand, and looked off through the shimmering heat at the house and barn across the road. Clark's house and barn.

Had Clark or any of his family or any of their new neighbors been in the mob that day? It didn't seem likely. But then, who would have thought that the same people who waved as they passed by on the road—the same people who walked with them to church, the same people whose children played with, fought with, and surreptitiously courted her own siblings—that those same neighbors would roar up the road, tear down their split-rail fence, and string up her brother?

Mary Ellen entered the back door. Dinner was fast-disappearing, and her father and brothers were making get-back-to-the-fields noises. She set the pitcher down on the work table and stood with her back to the wall, watching her family. Her mother worked in the background, fixing their own lunch. The boys, fed and rested, were gearing themselves up for another trip outside. As if by some unseen signal, all five pushed back their chairs with heavy scraping and stood up. They, of course, didn't carry any of their dishes as they stomped back out of the house, little Peck taking up the tail-end of the procession. Mary Ellen's father called back something about suppertime as he passed through the doorway.

Mary Ellen and her sisters set new places for the girls. They all sat down, said a quick grace, and tucked into their lunches. While they ate, Mary Ellen stole a look at her mother. She ate silently, staring ahead at a spot on the table as she mechanically moved the fork from her plate to her mouth, then chewed. Mary Ellen ignored the chatter of her three sisters and focused in on her mother. She felt a heavy sadness settle on her as she watched her mother eat. She longed to rush around the table and throw her arms around her mother's neck, but she knew what that would get her.

This woman, who was always full of love and life and cheerfulness, who whistled as she washed and cooked, who was the solid and dependable rock on which the family rested, had simply quit.

Was it inevitable? Was Ab's death the straw that broke her mother's back?

How heavy a straw was her father's reaction? One minute he was with them as they sprang from their dinner to check on the commotion coming up the road, but the next moment he was missing. And he hadn't returned to the house until the bodies were cut down and the crowd had dispersed. He still tried to make it all work. He toiled just as hard on the farm as ever before. He spoke to his family with the same gentleness that she'd known all her life.

But it was clear to Mary Ellen that something irrevocable had stepped between him and his wife. He spoke, she listened, and she might even answer, but there was nothing communicated beyond simply living, simply breathing, eating, drinking. Before all this, her mother would smile at her father across the table. Mary Ellen would secretly observe them, hearing their coded phrases, couched in the double terms required by life in a large family. Now, though, there was nothing. They woke up, performed their duties, went to bed. Nothing.

Did all couples reach this point? Would she and Clark end in such a state? Mary Ellen had hired out to help Clark's mother with housework from time to time, so she'd been able to see his parents at home. They seemed truly happy with one another. Would she and Clark be like them? Or would something wash out their love?

Clark hadn't even spoken much to her—much less propose—and here she was, trying to predict the end of their lives together. And did she want a life together? When she married—if she married—she'd be losing her own identity, becoming someone else. She guessed that was why women changed their names. It reflected their new status as part of the husband's life. If she married Clark, she'd move across the road to his house. It would mark the first time she'd be away from her parents overnight. All those little details of living with a family—all the adjustments made to each others' whims and fancies and biases and rebellions—would have to be remade in her new place, in her new life. What if Clark didn't like how she kept house? What if he didn't like her cooking?

Then there was that other thing, the physical thing. Years before—it seemed like centuries before—her mother had given her a basic overview of the facts of life. Mary Ellen knew what happened on a wedding night and also what would happen because of that night. He'd already been married, so there was no mystery for him. But Mary Ellen had little practical knowledge—and the unknown was a terrifying place. Would it hurt? Would she be brave enough?

They rose from the table at once and cleared it of the dishes. Their mother sent all but Mary Ellen out to the garden to finish the weeding. Mary Ellen and her mother set to work cleaning the dishes and storing them away in the hutch for the next meal. The dishes clinked together and rapped against the wood as they were set down. Otherwise, the room was quiet except for the two women's breathing and the regular ticking of the clock. It took quite a while before Mary Ellen worked up the nerve to speak. Even then, her voice was tentative, uncertain. "Mother … do you think we could talk?"

Her mother turned and bored her black eyes into Mary Ellen, one last cup poised in mid-drying. Then she sighed, walked to the hutch, set the cup down, and pulled two chairs out from the table. "Of course, dear. Now what is it?"

Mary Ellen took a chair. The two regarded one another in silence. Again, Mary Ellen noticed the clock ticking and tried to regulate her breathing against that rhythm. She plunged in.

"Mother, I need to talk to you about two things." She hesitated. "They're not really related. Well, yes, I guess they are. Oh, it's confusing."

"Come on, don't dawdle. There's work to be done."

"I know. I'm sorry. It's just that, well, I've been worried about you. You don't seem yourself since … you know."

Her mother looked fixedly at her for a long time, her face a mask. Mary Ellen was just about to break the silence when her mother spoke.

"What do you expect?"

"I know, I know. It's been terrible. But it's a whole year," Mary Ellen said.

"A whole year ain't near enough to forget." Her voice, flat and drained, matched her eyes.

"I didn't mean that." Mary Ellen hesitated. "I mean, isn't it time to try to come to grips with it?" She rushed through the rest. "I'll never forget. I don't want to. And I don't want you to, either. But a person can't just stop living."

Her mother set her jaw, and Mary Ellen braced herself for her response. "Have you missed any meals? Has anyone missed clean clothes or a clean house?"

"I'm not talking about us. I'm talking about you." Mary Ellen paused. "No, it is about us, too. You just can't go off and leave us. You're here, but you're not here at the same time. Not the way you used to be."

Her mother sat staring at her. The clock ticked, the only sound in the room. "A body can only give so much."

Mary Ellen reached across the table, but her mother ignored the gesture. "Just think about your babies. I'm grown, ready to leave home. But you have Alice and Sarah and Charlie and Peck. They need their mother."

"They got their mother. I'm here, ain't I?"

"Not the way you used to be."

"The world ain't the way it used to be."

The clock continued its methodical beat. Her mother looked down at her hand on the table. Idly, she traced the path of the grain on the table.

"I knew right off something was different," she said. "No, I knew even before he was born. He rode different—lower, somehow—than you or Sam or Bill. When he looked up at me, though, I melted. I loved all you children, but Ab took my heart. It might have been his eyes; they were so different. Of course, it didn't take long before we got the visits from the neighbors. Made me mad the way they edged in here to see him. There was something behind their visits and whispers. And as he grew, the complaints grew right along with him."

"I know. We all dealt with that."

Mary Ellen's mother exhaled dismissively. "You don't know the half of it. The comments, the visits, the staring at church. The more time went on, the less I could abide by it. We finally left off going to church, and there went another link to the neighbors. That's one thing I miss the most out here . . . the neighbors. That and my house. We lived there since this was raw forest, since before almost any of those people came to the county. And they drove us out." She paused. Her face blushed, and her eyes welled. "And they killed my baby."

Mary Ellen reached across the table and took her mother's hand. She could feel it tremble. Mary Ellen felt hot tears stream down her own face and drip onto the table. She absently wiped at them with her sleeve, but the fabric merely smeared them across the wood. The image of her brother hanging above the heads of the crowd was clear before her now. She heard the crowd shout and then the silence, saw his body—and McLeod's— rotating slowly at the end of the ropes.

Susan sniffed loudly, and her voice quavered, "They didn't even let me hold him. Didn't let us bury him. They just cut the rope and threw him away." Mary Ellen squeezed her hand, and she squeezed back, hard. "And that man left me alone. Left me alone with six children and a mob in the road. Didn't say nothing. Just gone. I can't forget that. I'll never forget that."

Mary Ellen wiped her nose with her free arm. "He's suffered, too, Mother."

Susan stared straight at her. "Don't tell me what he's suffered." Her voice was low, precise, clipped. "My child was killed, and he did nothing. Nothing to prevent it. He can't suffer enough for that."

"What could he have done?" asked Mary Ellen. "He thought they came for him, too. Lord knows they were looking for a reason." She thought of the other time, when the sheriff had led her father away in cuffs to the jailhouse. She remembered seeing him stand before the court to receive his verdict and fine. He'd been drinking when he hit Hengel, but he could always control his drinking. It had to have been something Hengel did to deserve it.

"For twenty-seven years, I covered for that man. I worked like a dog while he lay drunk as a hog on that bed."

"No, Mother. He's been sick. He suffers from the pleurisy."

"He suffers from the bottle, and you know it. You're old enough to stop fooling yourself, Mary Ellen."

Mary Ellen knew her father was good. She knew he was misunderstood. He worked hard. He was a good man.

Then she saw him standing in the doorway, leaning against the doorframe, a bottle in one hand. The other hand gestured wildly, backlit by the lamp in the kitchen. Mary Ellen was small, and her brothers crowded around her. They all watched the man in the doorway, and her mother held them close to her on the bed.

Again, she saw her brothers dragging him into the lot, Sam holding him under his arms and Bill carrying his feet. They dropped him in the trough and pumped cold water down on his head. He spluttered and shook his head, rubbed the water out of his eyes, cursed them, and fell back into the trough.

"He's my dad," was all Mary Ellen could think to say.

"Yes he is. Yes he is."

They sat quietly for a while, listening to the clock.

"What are you going to do?" Mary Ellen's voice was soft.

Susan sat still for a while, considering. "I just want to lie down and rest. Let the world get on without me. I done enough. What more can they expect?"

"You have children."

"Yes."

"And a husband."

Nothing. Then, "Yes." Susan listened to the clock. "When I first met your father, I thought, 'Now there's a man.' I thought we were so in love that our love would last forever. What a little fool I was! Didn't know nothing about nothing."

Something told Mary Ellen to wait, to avoid jumping in.

"Still, it was good at first. I'd be lying to say we wasn't happy. We worked hard together, building our farm, raising you children. Then Absalom came along. I noticed a change. There was a distance. Maybe it was just the bottle. Still, there was good times. It took time to get to where we are now. There was good times. And you children." Susan stared off at a point somewhere past Mary Ellen's left shoulder. "I still have you children. And I suppose after twenty-seven years, there ain't nothing that should surprise me. I suppose it's time to get back to living."

"I think so, Mother. It's time. Ab wouldn't want . . ."

"Ab wouldn't notice."

"Ab would notice the change in you. He'd be bothered."

Another pause while the clock ticked away. "He would."

"We need you back. The kids need you back."

"And what about you?"

Mary Ellen looked up. "What do you mean?"

"Don't tell me you don't know what I'm talking about. I may be fagged out and rundown, but I ain't asleep. I see how Clark Felver looks across the road every time he visits his folks. He ain't looking at our crops."

Mary Ellen blushed. "It's that obvious?"

Susan patted her hand. "Darling, a mother notices. Has he asked you?"

"Tonight. Probably."

"And what are you going to tell him?"

Mary Ellen considered for a while. "I just don't know, Mother. What do you think?"

"I can't answer that one for you. Only you know what you feel. Do you love him?"

"Does it matter?"

"Sometimes it helps."

"Seems like we both need to have a conversation this evening, then."

⊢•⊷•⊶•⊣

Tiffin, Ohio—June 23, 2017

David Kimmel

A single-voiced, straightforward fictional narrative such as Mary Ellen's presents readers with just one path through the garden of storytelling options. My portrayal of Mary Ellen and her sisters is based on facts; it is not fact itself. Yet the story implies an inevitability to their character and actions. How much more does this phenomenon impact our view of Susan and Henry! My narrator presents just one Susan, one Henry, out of myriad potential Susans and Henrys.

It seems fitting, therefore, to give the Kimmel parents the last word at this point in the book. Here at the ends of their lives, they have the opportunity to look back. The odd thing about endings is that they are also beginnings. Beginning-middle-end only exists in narrative. Life is not like that. Life's river flows on and on, one moment after another, after another. Only from some vantage point can we see the shape of the river. In the middle of the current, we know we don't want to drown. Or we wish we already had. By the time we sit on the shore, it may be too late.

⊢•⊷•⊶•⊣

Liberty Township, Mercer County, Ohio—August 30, 1878

Henry Kimmel

The bed pushes up against my back, my head, my limbs. I'm unable to move under the weight of actions and inactions piled on my chest, towering above me, swaying in the slight breeze caused by the speech of those gathered around me. I turn my head and see my own face looking down at me again and again. Lips move, but I hear nothing. The stack shifts, and my ribs creak with the pressure. I try to tell the others to take care not to jostle me or the whole thing will fall down. But my mouth won't work. For some reason, the pile must not fall over. I look through my mind, but

I can't find the reason. I just know that buried in the stack is something that will burn me if exposed to the air.

The room is close and thick with the bodies and clothes packed in here. I try to tell them to open the window, to give me some air, that my breath catches in my throat, but again, I cannot speak. Outside, the leaves ripple against the bright-blue sky. I try to remember what I am to do today, but nothing comes to mind. Something about trees.

The wall glows orange. More and more faces peer down at me—always at my face—except one. I just can't place her. There's something I am supposed to tell her, and in my excitement I begin to cough. The coughing lasts a lifetime. I feel I'm drowning. Maybe it's water that is pressing down on me. The room shimmers as I look up through the water.

The face I can't remember is looking down at me, lit from one side by an oil lamp in this dark room. She smiles slightly when she sees my eyes open. She moves her lips, but the sound is muffled, suppressed by the water weighing down on us. I want to tell her to leave, to get some air, to get out of the water, but I am too tired. Then I remember what it was I needed to tell her. But my eyes close, and the darkness presses down on me.

⊢⊢•─◦─⊸⊣⊣

Dublin Township, Mercer County, Ohio—June 23, 1909

Susan Kimmel

I sit here in the shade of the great oak tree whose roots reach deep into the earth, pulling out moisture long gone from the upper levels of the soil. A slight breeze rustles the leaves high up in the branches, but down here on the ground, where the heat of the new summer has already begun to bake the soil like a kiln, all is still, save the *peenk* of the blackbirds.

It's been thirty-nine years since my womb was filled with anything but air, but now the doctor says it's filling with death. I can tell from the way he avoids my eyes when he talks that he's only pretending to treat me, so I'm only pretending to take the quack medicines he gives me.

I sit here under this tree and think about how my roots spread deep and wide into the soil of this land—deeper than anyone knows, if the secret my father told me on his deathbed was true. But if families are trees, we are more cottonwoods than oaks. Our seeds float on the wind, which blows our children where it will. At one time my parents, their parents, my cousins, my sisters, my Sarah were all clustered together. Then, as though spring had come, we floated away from our tree. The same has happened with my children, who have scattered to Kansas, Missouri, Tennessee, Michigan, and Indiana. I have grandchildren I've never set eyes on but for photos.

This isn't the tree I thought I'd be sitting under at this age. Henry and his brothers left a few of the great trees on each of their farms when they cleared the forest so long ago. I would sit under Old Mother and snap beans while watching my babies crawl on the quilt my mother—or, rather, my father's wife—had given me when I married Henry. But my time under that tree ended when they marched up the road and tore down our fences, trampled our plants into the dust, and pulled the wagon out from under my baby—my special one. And then they stole him away. I never even had the chance to say good-bye, to cry over his body, to prepare him for burial, to visit his grave. But I'll soon be joining him in the soil. We'll be a part of this land that turned against us.

⊢·⊣·⊙·⊢·⊣

Tiffin, Ohio—June 23, 2017

David Kimmel

I lied. My discussion of the aftermath of the Secaur-McLeod-Kimmel murders can only end with the strange tale of Thomas Bradwell Douglass.

On March 26, 1874, the case burst back into the public consciousness through a dramatic story appearing in the *Mercer County Standard* and other area papers, which the *Standard* claims originated in the *Illustrated Police News*.[34] According to the *Standard* story, Thomas Bradwell Douglass, a man in the tuberculosis ward of the Denver city hospital, summoned a priest a half an hour before his death on January 10, 1874, in order to confess to the murder of Mary Secaur.[35] In a separate story in the same issue, the *Standard* reported, "the Hon. D. J. Callen, who was one of the attorneys for the accused parties, intends to make such an investigation into the matter as to satisfy the public as to whether the parties hung by the mob—McLeod and Kimmel—were really the guilty parties or not."[36] The *Standard* professed "no hesitancy in saying that we do not believe one word of the story," but the *Van Wert Bulletin* wrote in a column following the revelations of Douglass's supposed confession, "From evidence in our possession, we advise Hon. D. J. Callen to keep out of the 'investigation' business. What he knows about the Thomas Bradwell Douglass confession might be very damaging if allowed to go before the public."[37] Callen apparently contacted authorities in Denver because the April 9 edition of the *Standard* reprinted an article from the *Denver Daily Times* in which "Father Quigley," a Catholic priest, reported having investigated the Douglass confession at the request of Callen. Quigley "failed to find any trace of 'Thomas Bradwell Douglass,' and is certain that no confession as aforementioned was ever confided to any priest in Colorado."[38] Around the same time, the *Delphos Herald* reprinted a letter from Denver reporting on further efforts to track down the truth behind the Douglass confession. Unless the communications from Denver are forgeries—and this seems unlikely as they originate from two different sources in Ohio—it would seem that there is little to support the authenticity of the Douglass confession. I have conducted my own search for Douglass. I cannot find anyone of that name in the 1870 census living in Mercer County—or even in Colorado. Of course, Thomas Douglass (with one or two final consonants) is a fairly common name, and the clues are scarce. Death records for Colorado at this time do not help to locate him, either. The record in this far-off territory is incomplete, so there still is a chance that he lived, he died, and he confessed as recorded in the newspaper. Who would foist such a hoax on the public remains unclear.

As though Douglass's 1874 confession weren't strange enough, the story took an even odder turn in March 1926 when a nearly identical story appeared in newspapers—presented as though the deathbed confession had just happened, fifty-two years after the original appearance of the same story. Perhaps someone found a clipping and mailed it to the newspaper in good conscience, and the story took a life from there. Perhaps people sympathetic to the Kimmels or McLeod submitted the story in an effort to exonerate their family names. It seems odd that no one in 1926 remembered the 1874 version of the same story, though that may be explained by the length of time between the events. At any rate, this second "confession" does nothing to strengthen the authenticity of Thomas Bradwell Douglass's 1874 confession. If anything, the repetition makes the confession even more suspicious. In all, it is difficult to view this confession seriously. There may have been a Thomas Bradwell Douglass, but the believability of his confession is weak.

5

GRIEVING

Tiffin, Ohio—June 23, 2017

David Kimmel

We drove through the evening and the night to pick up my mother and take her to my father at the hospital, across the breadth of the state from Columbus to Akron to Van Wert. It was well past midnight by the time we arrived in my grandmother Kimmel's room. I know that I should remember the details like it was yesterday, but it was over thirty years ago, and I remember almost nothing of the room, the hospital, or our visit that night. My grandmother was sleeping, painkillers separating her consciousness from the cancer eating away at her womb. I do not even remember if we spent the night at the hospital or at her apartment thirteen miles south in Rockford. What I do remember is that close to daybreak, I sat on an uncomfortable plastic-and-steel waiting room chair and held my father as he unexpectedly sobbed into my shoulder. Here was this enormous, strong preacher man, for whom a handshake was an extravagant display of affection, and then there was skinny me with my arms around him. All that careful German-American control of emotion had just let loose in a surge of grief that lasted a good five minutes. Then it was over, and we patted and separated and were back to ourselves again.

Twelve years later, I was back on the road. I drove the thirty-five miles of two-lane state highway from Tiffin to Port Clinton in twenty-five minutes. Still, my mother must have been alone in the emergency waiting room for fifteen minutes or so before I arrived, alone with the knowledge that they had failed to save my father after his massive heart attack. I rushed into the room, sat down beside her, and felt her grief and anger and terror wash over me. There was nothing to do but wrap her in my arms, cry along with her, and try to absorb as much of her pain as I could. It soaked through my shirt and welled up in me and poured out my eyes. I am not sure how long this lasted, and I am not sure whether this was the worst—or if the worst was standing by the gurney in the darkened emergency room and straining to hold her up as she cried and talked to his yellowed, already waxen face, petting his hair.

I know that grief differs for each of us. Even for a single individual, it morphs itself into alternate forms over time. It sinks into our bones and never really leaves us. All we can do is to negotiate a space for it and focus on the rest of life. I have watched family and friends grieve in as many ways as there are people. Some of them have been noble, and some have been hysterical. But for me, the two times I held my parents are the two most pure, mystifying, and terrible experiences I have survived. And what is truly terrifying is that I know they will not be the last or even the worst.

Liberty Township, Mercer County, Ohio—May 12, 1875[1]

Strouse May

I guide Rufus out the drive to the road and head east. A good horse knows the way, so I am free to enjoy the day. Rufus is one reason I can still ride out on my own at seventy-four years of age. Harvey has to help me lift the saddle now, but otherwise I can ready a horse and ride it. Normally, Rufus is a calm, even-tempered horse, but today he seems to feel the springtime in his bones as he trots along. Isabella wouldn't like to see her father riding this fast, but then, she's getting to be an old maid and worries too much. So long as Harvey is able to help manage the farm, we'll be in fine shape.

I pull Rufus into the chapel lot and leave him to graze alongside the road. Polly's stone is a tall, white limestone obelisk standing on a granite base. There's an identical marker standing in the back of the stonecutter's shop, awaiting my days. I pass my fingers over hers: "69 y. 7 m. & 22 d." It hardly seems a fitting summary for an entire life of love and work and heartache. I pull a few weeds from around the base and then just stand there before her, thinking about how if only Mary had stayed for dinner with us that day, as she had so many other Sundays, she'd still be alive, and so would my Polly. My love just folded in on herself and was gone within two months of her granddaughter.

I walk back to Mary's stone, topped by its guardian angel. If only we'd been able to guard her better. Beside Mary stands her mother. Susannah's death begat Mary's, which begat Polly's. And here I am without any of them.

If only we had taken in Mary and the other children, instead of allowing their father to scatter them all over the county. But Polly and I had neither the room nor energy for all five of them, plus Joseph—or so it seemed. Or was it that Joseph had already stepped out on the road to Lancaster and that girl with the child on the way? For him, it's as though none of this happened. For me it's as though it will never end.

<hr />

Liberty Township, Mercer County, Ohio—July 9, 1872

Sarah Sitterly

In my dreams, Mary walks through our front door, sets her parasol and testament on the chair where I've told her again and again not to, trips into the kitchen where I am preparing Sunday dinner, and hugs me hard, telling me she loves me. I'm surprised by this show of emotion. She's been getting too old for such things lately, her mind on boys, school, and who knows what all. I return her hug and stroke her soft hair, still warm from the afternoon sunshine.

In my dreams, Mary walks through our front door two hours late. She calls to us from the front room, where she's dropped her parasol and testament on the chair. She joins us at the table, laughing and smiling and full of life. She'd stopped to visit her grandmother on the way home from church. Yes, they are both fine. She just had a feeling she should see her, is all. I rise and fix her a plate while an unbroken stream of words rolls from her mouth to fill our home with life and youth.

In my dreams, Mary walks through our front door early Monday morning. She leaves her parasol and testament in the front room where she knows she's not supposed to and rushes into the kitchen where John has just sat down to his breakfast, chores all finished. She runs to him and hugs him, but then sits and tells us how she'd spent the night with her grandparents and her cousins, and how even her brother Marion was there. She picks at a knot in the table when she says that, and my heart hurts to know that she misses him, her other half. I look at John, who gives me a tight-lipped smile. We've been through this again and again. One is enough. We just cannot take on both twins right now, no matter how much we'd like to. Mary's thoughtfulness only lasts a few seconds, and then she is off on an explanation of Candace's new dress, on how Elias is crawling and even pulling himself up, and he's so smart and strong and beautiful. I set the food before her, and our lives are full.

In my dreams, I call John in from the fields when Mary hasn't returned by mid-morning. The dew is long-gone, and John's footsteps raise puffs of dust as he strides across the field to me. I tell him Mary is still not home, that even if she had stopped over with her grandparents or with Candace, it's not like her to be so late. John looks back at his plow horse, waiting patiently in the field. He sighs so I can hear it, which irritates me. I tell him the plowing can wait, that he needs to find out what's become of Mary. Just then we hear a shout, and Mary comes tromping through the weeds around the side of the house. She laughs and apologizes for being so late. Her grandmother's hip was hurting, and she'd stayed over after breakfast to help her to read-up. I snap at her about remembering our feelings, too, off all day without a word. She says she's sorry, and I know I can't stay mad at her for long. John's back grows smaller as he walks across the rows to his waiting horse.

In my dreams, I sit in the closed parlor, staring out the front window, hoping for a sign of John and Mary. The clock measures out the movement of the sun along the floor, my fears growing with the length of the shadows. The road glows against the dark of the woods, rippled in the glass. I touch one of the bubbles, but the surface is smooth. Then, past my finger I see them—John and Mary, walking toward me, hand in hand. I can see her chatting with him as they pass through our iron gate and walk up the path to the front door. I am standing before the stairs as the door opens, my mouth open with the scolding I've been planning all afternoon. But something in her eyes tells me it's enough that's she's coming through the door. She comes to me and hugs me. I am surprised at this intimacy; lately she's grown too old for me. She says she's sorry, that she'd spent the night with her grandparents and then stopped at Candace's and simply forgot the time. I know I won't be angry with her anymore.

In my dreams, John runs into the parlor where I lie prostrate on the camel-back sofa in the room dimmed by pulled shades. It's all a mistake, he says. Meizner was wrong. It was just her parasol and testament they found in the brush. Mary was at her grandparents' all along. Here she is. Mary rushes into the room and falls on my neck. We both have a good cry, and I cannot remember whatever I was upset about.

In my dreams, Mary lies on the sofa in our dim parlor. Her face is ashen, her lips thin and set. She is not breathing. I scream when I see her, and the sound makes her jump. Her eyes open, and she looks at me startled, uncomprehending. The room fills with neighbors who shout with joy at this miracle I've wrought. Mary looks around in wonder at the life and love around her.

In my dreams, Mary's body is not torn, and her blood does not seep into the pattern of our parlor carpet. Her head is not smashed and connected to her almost-nude body by a thin strip of meat. I do not scream and fall to the floor when I see her.

In my dreams, I force myself to look into the rough pine box where they've placed my Mary. Her face is perfect; her body is whole and beautiful. I bend to kiss her cheek, and her eyes flutter open. She calls me Mother and throws her arms around my neck. The room gasps at the miracle.

In my dreams, Mary and Marion walk through the front door, shouting to us as they drop their testaments, Mary's parasol, and Marion's jacket there on the floor in the parlor where I've told them not to. They tell us of the adventure they've just had—of how they thought they saw figures in the woods just off the road. Marion had yelled, and the figures disappeared into the darkness. John and I tell them they probably imagined it, that it was the heat and light playing tricks on them. They laugh and argue about it, refusing to let go of this silly fantasy. I set plates full of food before my children and feel a wave of happiness bring tears to my eyes.

In my dreams, Mr. May looks relieved as he tells us about how his daughter has recovered from the consumption and how she was down one day and up the next morning, fixing breakfast for her husband and her houseful of children. I smile vaguely. I am happy for him, but in my heart there is an emptiness that I can't quite place as I turn back to our lonely house. That evening I tell John about my desire for a child, and we talk about how we might adopt some day.

In my dreams, my first child is perfect, her body whole and her heart beating. She cries as the midwife places her on my chest, and I weep with joy. Her body pulses with life, and I think about our long lives to come.

In my dreams, I don't wake screaming into the darkness that envelops my soul.

⊢⊣◆○◆⊢⊣

Liberty Township, Mercer County, Ohio—July 9, 1872

Marion Secaur

We lie here in the hot woods. The sunshine on both sides of the road is filled with the cries of the insects. There is sunshine around us, and the air is filled with rustling and digging. The sunshine is filled with our screams.

Outside, insects sing into the blackness. Inside, there is no sound but the other boarder's soft snoring. Sweat clings to my body in the still air, unmoved even by the open window at the end of the small room. I try to block from my mind the sound of the hogs that surrounded us, the sight of the trees that waved in the sunlight.

We are too small to know time. We have always been here in the soft blankets. The sun has always warmed our faces. We reach toward it. One of us is hungry. We cry. The face appears and smiles and coos and is beautiful. It has always been here for us. It will always smile down at us and gather us into arms that love us.

I lie staring up at the boards that form both the ceiling and roof. The darkness is incomplete. Lines regular and dark mark off the space from peak to eaves.

We lie staring up at the leaves rippling in the breeze against a flawless, deep-blue sky. The air is heavy here in this brushy edge of the woods, but that doesn't affect our breathing. There is no breathing. Our heart lies still in our chest, the blood it pumped having soaked into the humus behind our neck. The searing pain in our head is long gone, as is the numbness and blackness that followed.

We are together as we have been together since before there was a now. The shade is chilled, but the sunshine is still warm. We laugh as he covers us in the dried leaves. Then the leaves block the light, their dry smell fills our nostrils, and we cry. He pulls away the leaves, and we laugh together. It has always been like this. It will always be like this.

Our dress is bunched up around our waist—at least, that which has not been torn from us. The blood down there moistens the soil beneath us. In the trees around us we hear the hissing of the leaves and an occasional chirp from a bird not stunned to silence from the heat. In the brush and leaves are rustling and rooting and snorting sounds.

I sit up on my cot, pull on some pants, a shirt, and my shoes. I move carefully and quietly, trying to avoid waking the other boarder as I lift the latch on the door and slip out into the night. The air is much cooler out here than where we sleep in the shed tacked onto the back of the house. The moonlight dapples the ground beneath the enormous oak left standing by those who built the house.

We run in the dark, chasing the lights. We catch them, and the light leaks from between our fingers. We peek into the dark cave of our hands. Dark. Light. We giggle. She laughs over there in the darkness as we throw the lights into the air and shout with life.

We lie in the bright, hot, close room—a room that is filled with sobbing. Low voices murmur comforts to one another. They have carefully pieced us back together, but it's no good. We are separated.

A black shape detaches itself from the larger shape of the house and moves to me. A wet nose nudges my hand, and I absently pat the head that bumps against my leg. The dog and I walk along the road, a light line between two black borders in the darkness, baked hard by the sun and churned to powder by hooves and feet and wheels.

We are riding to another new home. The trees pass too slowly, so we scramble about on the furniture and trunks piled up high in the wagon. She tells us to settle down, to stop jumping from the bureau onto the pile of bedding. We scramble down from the wagon and run along beside the horses. Our feet make puffs in the dust on the road.

I settle into the regular rhythm of my walking. The moon grows orange as it disappears down among the black shapes of the trees on my right. The dog walks beside me, rushes off into the black, returns, repeats. The night is darker now. We pass an occasional farm, and the dogs rush out to the fences barking, sniffing, then wagging their tails.

The insects scream in the trees across the road from the churchyard, and the sun bears down on our bare head, our black shoulders. The crowd smells of hot wool and sweat. A voice drones on for a long, long time about sorrow and salvation. We cannot make out the words through the heated pine that's just inches from our face. The air inside will last us forever.

We stand in the cemetery with our arms around each other, the rain wetting us through despite the umbrella I hold above our heads. Her box sits next to the open mouth of the grave. Our hearts are torn apart by this loss, but the fear is worse. What will happen to us after they put her in the ground and shovel that mound of dirt on top of her? We look at our father, standing across from us, staring uncomprehendingly at the grave.

The rows of gravestones glow against the black grass. The crickets mark my progress between the stones with a silence that accompanies me. I stop at the last stone, a mound of bare earth before it. The white limestone stands straight and definitive. It's too dark to make out the words, but my fingers trace the letters of her name.

The earth drums against the wood—slowly at first, then gathering in rhythm. The sound is muffled, then grows quieter and quieter until there is nothing.

Though we are miles apart, I can feel our presence. As we lie here in this strange bed in this strange room, we know I'm awake, too. I'm also staring at the ceiling, thinking of us. Our breathing is synchronized. Her bed is softer, prettier, newer than the pallet and straw ticking I lie on, but neither one is ours. We've been equally abandoned. We wish I could come stealthily to our bed as I've done so many times before. We could sleep then.

The dog emerges from the blackness as I step back onto the road. The dome of the sky, sprinkled with white lights, has tilted while I've walked. I continue along, down to the crossroads and right toward their farm. Here, the road is wooded and dark on both sides, the old-growth trees towering above us, blocking out all but the strip of lights leading us straight ahead.

We stand together in the crowd, watching the scene before us. We keep well back, out of the limelight. Even when Elias steps forth to rescue Jake, we don't say anything.

The dog and I stand still between the two halves of their farm. Behind us is the new house, the barn, the farm animals, and the family, still breathing and living. Before us is the clearing with the tumble-down old house, now a shed. And the tree. For some reason, their dogs stay quiet and in the darkness behind us.

When the wagon is pulled away and the boys dance on the end of their ropes, we shudder and hug close, but I stand there impassively, no emotion betrayed on my face. They ask me if this is worth it, if I feel vindicated, if we're avenged. We feel a sob deep down inside, but there's no sign of it on my face. As they cut down the bodies, we walk away, feeling empty and separate. We look again for our father, but he's nowhere to be seen. We blend into the crowd, washed away by its force in the ebb tide that carries us back down the road.

⊢+⊹⊱–○–⊰⊹+⊣

Liberty Township, Mercer County, Ohio—July 9, 1872

Henry Kimmel

When a mare foals, the wet, shaky newborn struggles up onto its spindly legs, his future set. There's a smell of life in the stall that lingers with the hay and manure and blood. The foal doesn't know or worry, and neither does the mare. They are animals. They endure.

When I enter the kitchen, she hides in plain sight, her back iron, rigid, set against me. She brings food to the table, but she's not really there.

She doesn't say grace—just sets the food on the table and sits. She eats nothing but stares at something on the wall just above the children's heads. They chatter and quarrel and vie for attention. She ignores them. The children and I are a job, a chore to finish up, not a real part of her or her life.

When you first hold a newborn baby, it seems impossible that anything this small could ever survive, let alone grow into a man or a woman. Every time, it's that same feeling: a tingling all over, and your breath is short like you just ran in from the rain—or when you get too hot in the sun and have to sit in the shade. You're outside yourself, standing there watching you holding that tiny child, that little part of you. You feel you are the largest, strongest, most important person in the world. But you know the truth, and that fear grabs ahold of you and squeezes the breath out of you. No matter how tight the hand is that has reached into your chest, you just have to keep going. There are others looking to you. You must provide. You must keep on. It's hard, but you're a man, and a man endures things.

When I speak directly to her, she responds simply with no extra words, no connection to what she's saying. Her only reaction is a slight cringe at the sound of my voice, so I stop trying to talk beyond asking for the salt. What's left unsaid inside me churns and bubbles as it rots and festers. I can feel its stink as it expands inside me. Sometime it'll burst, and I won't be able to keep the evil gasses inside any longer.

When I saw the wagon pulling into our lot before a flood of angry faces, I fought down the urge to fight, to rush out into that swirl and grab my boys off the wagon before the whirlpool took them under. I knew I'd never be able to swim that far against the current; I'd simply be swallowed up and would never be seen again, which would do my other children no good. So I stayed on the shore and watched. But now I think, maybe I drowned after all.

When a mare foals, the horse doesn't worry about the future. It just lives. Whatever comes along, the horse simply endures. Maybe that's how we're different. A man knows he's there, knows what might happen, knows what has already happened, good and bad. A man endures anyway, but it's hard.

⊢⊷⊶⊙⊷⊶⊣

Liberty Township, Mercer County, Ohio—July 9, 1872

Susan Kimmel

The yeast is beginning to bubble and froth in the water, so I stir in the flour. Gradually, stirring with my wooden spoon as I go, I mix more and more flour into the mixture, which grows increasingly stiff. Outside, the leaves ripple high in the air, and through the open door, I can see patches of blue as the leaves flip from green to white and back.

I withdraw the spoon, gather the dough together with my hands, form it into a ball, and drop it onto the flour-dusted kitchen table. My hands know what to do. The hiss of the wind seems calming, restful. Outside, two figures hang still from the crossbeam above a silent wall of bodies. One figure rotates on the end of its rope, its face turning slowly toward me.

I fold the dough in half, give it a quarter turn, and flatten it with the heels of both hands. I lean into my work, trying to beat back the images in my mind. If I could only stay busy. Beneath the window, there is the sound of voices and the *shick, shick, shick* of a hoe as it strikes the earth. My daughters' voices. One, lower and older, speaks first; then another, higher and younger, answers. Their words are too soft for me to make out the sense, but I understand the cadence.

Again and again I fold the dough, turning and flattening it as I work. It gradually smooths into an elastic mass, the individual ingredients blending into a single identity. A long snake of anger and hatred slithers up the road, led by "heroes" on horseback and a wagon that carries my life in it. First, there is just a murmur, but then there is the low rumble of hoofbeats beneath the hum of the crowd. I lean on the heels of my hands; the harder I press, the better. A laugh drifts through the window, answered by two more laughs.

At last the dough is ready: smooth, pliant, and springing back to the touch, tiny pockets of air breaking the surface when I fold it one last time. The snake slithers up the road toward us. My husband and son stand beside me. Riders emerge from the mass, pulling the snake behind them up the road and through the gap in the fence into the clearing. My son stands beside me.

I scoop up the dough, shape it in my hands, and return it to the bowl. I cover the bowl with a clean towel and set it on the table to rest. I am so tired. Kneading the dough had been a matter of inertia—once started, the process perpetuated itself. Now I sit with my hands over my face, my elbows on the tabletop. My eyes are closed, and I need the support of my hands to keep my face from smashing into the tabletop.

The crowd shimmers, ripples, and bubbles in the glass. I hold my breath as my body vibrates with the hum of the crowd that laps against the door and walls. I absently stroke little Peck's hair. Ties from the rail fence along the road lie strewn about both the yard and the far lot. I count my children, touching each one as they huddle around me.

I open my eyes and stare down between my hands at the table. The grain runs across my line of vision. I follow the curve of a line down the length of its board. These once were rings. I sit up and feel the worn wood of the table top, the almost imperceptible changes in the surface. I carefully count out nineteen lines of grain, each one different yet somehow the same. If they cut me open in nineteen years, would there be rings outside this one? I doubt it. I imagine the outer rings fusing into a black mass, growing but never differentiating from one another.

A roar breaks on the house as the dark mass ebbs toward the clearing. Dark lines of poles wriggle above the crowd. Three ropes leap over the cross-beam. I watch George watch the spectacle. His eyes notice mine, and his expression slips from fascinated to worried to chastened before he turns back to the window.

I force my mind up out of the grooves in the table and look at the sky through the trees outside my window. This window faces the woods, away from that other side of the house, away from the clearing across the road, where every weed is now smashed and ground into the hard dirt by hundreds, maybe thousands of feet. My body feels the imprint of every one of those feet. My eyes droop again, and my head weighs hundreds of pounds, threatening to topple off my neck. I cradle my head in my arms on the table for just a moment. Just to rest. Just for a moment.

In the dark gray rectangle, bare trees wave frantically. The back door blows inward against my hand when I release the lock. Low gray clouds scud across the sky. I draw my shawl up around my neck and shoulders.

The gate to the kitchen garden bangs open and then closed according to the whims of the wind. Behind the low fence, the garden lies fallow, dried weeds and dead plant matter choking the spaces between rusted corn stalks and blasted, rotting pumpkins and gourds. The air is still with chill.

There is a rippling sound in the oak tree across the road. Hundreds of crows crowd its bare branches, silent but for a nervous shuffling and ruffling. A large crow glides from the tree to perch on the fence just ten feet away. It regards me calmly, its black feathers iridescent in the dim light. The bird stalks along the fence in one direction, then heads back in the other. The crow lets out three shrill caws. Rippling turns to thunder. I hunch my head down between my shoulders at the sound. Cawing loudly, the black mass streams from the tree, flying low over my head and then over the roof of the house. I can feel the pulses of air from the birds' wings.

From the thick branch suspended between two forks, two ropes dangle, their ends looped and knotted. I wrap my hand around a knot and feel the stiff fibers on my palm. With both hands, I pull down on the rope, which slithers easily over the cross beam. Hand over hand, I pull. The end flips up and out from the beam, and the entire length lies jumbled at my feet.

A low moan rises from the scrubby brush at the edge of the clearing. I kneel beside the prone figure lying face-down on the cold, leaf-strewn ground. I hesitate, afraid to touch the man, but then reach out to gently roll him over onto his back. I want to scream, but no sound comes out. I cradle Absalom's head in my lap as he stirs and whimpers, his eyes closed. I brush the broken leaves and loose dirt from his face and straighten his hair with my fingers. His lashes flicker slightly and his lids shift as the eyes move below them. I stroke his pale cheek. It is cold to the touch—or my hands are too cold; I can't decide. I touch his dark lips and pull his shirt open to reveal the deep red abrasions on his neck, just beginning to turn purple and spread into bruises. I stroke his cheek and smooth his hair again. Closing my eyes, I hum to my son. His low moan changes into a high-pitched wail, and I open my eyes again.

In my lap, where Absalom's head had been, a tiny baby—red, wet, and steaming in the cold air—now screams and flails his arms and legs in the air. He screws up his face in fury as he screeches. The thick, bluish umbilical cord runs from his fat belly across my lap and up under my dress. I pull off my shawl and wrap the little boy in the fabric. I must get him inside and warm.

The baby's face turns purple with the effort of his screams. I snuggle him tighter to me as I walk back to the house. Across the road, my family stands in the front window: Sarah clings to Mary Ellen, and George stands next to Susan—next to me. I yell to myself, but my voice is lost in the wind. They turn suddenly and disappear into the blackness of the house.

I am running. I am standing at the crossroads. The houses, farms, and woodlots have all vanished. The lone object on the plain is a little church building. I turn and run down Tama Road. Snow blows uninterrupted across unbroken fields until it drifts on itself in the roadway. The snow slows me to a walk, but I trudge on, the baby held close to my chest. I am walking toward a slight depression in the road nearly two miles off.

My arms cramped and feet numb, I finally reach the declivity and see a house just beyond it, standing forlorn in an empty lot, surrounded by a large, empty field. I come to a stop before the house, gulping huge gasps of air. Behind me, the church and my own house sit alone on the flat, white plain.

The two-story frame house regards me through its two ground-floor windows and open front door. One window is free of glass; the other's panes are cracked and jagged. A front porch, added long after the house was originally built, now lies collapsed into a jumble of boards and brush, revealing the original façade, wind-blasted to a pale gray. Though replacements interrupt the pattern of the slate roof and though one of the twin chimneys is chipped short, the house bespeaks solidity and endurance.

I pass through the iron gate and approach the house along its little path. I step carefully over and through the jumbled boards of the former porch and poke my head into the open doorway. A wooden staircase runs straight up from the landing to the center of the second floor; beside it, a hallway leads into what must be the kitchen. To my left is a closed door, but there is an open one on my right.

I call out, but my voice is swallowed by the house, so I open the door on the left. The bare floorboards creak as I step into the front room. The room—its paint and wallpaper peeling to reveal white, cracked plaster and, in places, bare lathe—stands completely empty except for two rocking chairs. A middle-aged couple looks up at me from the chairs but says nothing. Tentatively, I step toward them and hold out the child. They make no movement or sound, but merely turn to look back over their shoulders.

I follow their gaze to the closed doorway in the back corner of the room. The door opens, and a young girl walks into the room and over to me. The girl of thirteen has ancient-looking gray eyes and holds out her hands. I hand her the sleeping boy. She uncovers his face and smiles, and then walks over to the couple and shows them the child. They look at the baby and then back at me. Both rise.

"It's a fair trade," says the man, and the family walks from the room.

I am alone.

NOTES

Introduction

1. The scenes from the June 30 hearing are fictionalized but closely modeled after the account in James H. Day, *Lynched! A Fiendish Outrage! A Terrible Retribution!* (Celina, OH: A. P. J. Snyder, 1872), 11–19.

2. The excerpts from newspapers and other contemporary sources are transcribed from the originals; I have corrected any obvious spelling errors, but I have left all variant spellings of personal names, such as the many versions of "Secaur."

3. Daniel Mahoney's vignettes are fictional, but he was a real neighbor of the Kimmels, living off the northeastern corner of Tama and Erastus-Durbin Roads; 1870 US Census, "Daniel Mahony," Liberty Township, Mercer County, Ohio; 1880 US Census, "Daniel Mahoney," Liberty Township, Mercer County, Ohio; Estray Book of Liberty Township, Mercer Co., Ohio, Mercer County District Library, Celina, Ohio; Record of Birth for Dennis Mahoney, May 7, 1871, Mercer County, Ohio, Birth Registers 1867–1883 1:74–75, accessed December 20, 2017, FamilySearch; Record of Birth for Daniel Mahoney, October 8, 1875, Mercer County, Ohio, Birth Registers 1867–1883 1:170–171, accessed December 20, 2017, FamilySearch; *History of Mercer County, Ohio, and Representative Citizens*, ed. S. S. Scranton (Philadelphia: Griffin & Gordon, 1888), 233; Daniel Wolf to Daniel Mahaney, Deed Record, February 12, 1844, Mercer County Recorder, Mercer County Courthouse, Celina, Ohio, K:484; Mercer County Auditor to G.W. Meisner, Deed Record, October 25, 1860, Mercer County Recorder, Mercer County Courthouse, Celina, Ohio, 2:276; Daniel Mahoney to Maria Prior, Mortgage Record, March 2, 1863, Mercer County Recorder, Mercer County Courthouse, Celina, Ohio, 6:264; Thomas R. Miller to Thomas R. Swander, Deed Record, November 8, 1871, Mercer County Recorder, Mercer County Courthouse, Celina, Ohio, 19:153; Thomas Swander to A. J. Ricker, Deed Record. July 26, 1879, Mercer County Recorder, Mercer County Courthouse, Celina, Ohio, 33:275; Hanna Sullivan to Geo. W. Howell, Quit Claim Deed Record, May 11, 1881,

Mercer County Recorder, Mercer County Courthouse, Celina, Ohio, 26:100. To save space, I have simplified the citations for scans of census entries that I located online via the Ancestry database.

Chapter 1: Murder

1. This scene is fictional, but all the participants are real people, documented in the 1870 census returns for the neighborhood and Chas. A. McConahy, *Map of Mercer County Ohio: From Recent & Original Surveys* (Philadelphia: Chas. A. McConahy, 1876).

2. Day, *Lynched!*, 5; Leaving time from Day, ibid., 13.

3. Ibid., 5.

4. Ibid.

5. McConahy, *Map of Mercer County Ohio*. The plot map shows Stephens as owning the next house along the road, just past the Burrville Road intersection.

6. "At Home and Abroad," *Mercer County Standard*, July 4, 1872. The column discusses the hot weather, which extended at least through the middle of the month, as the same column on July 18 states, "Oh! terrible warm."

7. Day, *Lynched!*, 5. See also ibid., 11, reprinted from "The Liberty Township Murder Case," *Mercer County Standard*, July 4, 1872.

8. "A Little Girl Murdered," *Van Wert Bulletin*, June 28, 1872.

9. Day, *Lynched!*, 7.

10. "A Little Girl Murdered," *Van Wert Bulletin*.

11. Ibid. Other details of the location of the body in Day, *Lynched!*, 11, reprinted from "The Liberty Township Murder Case," *Mercer County Standard*.

12. Day, *Lynched!*, 11.

13. Ibid., 13–14.

14. Ibid., 11–13. Other descriptions of the condition of the body, sometimes quite graphic, are found in "Child Found Dead," *Mercer County Standard*, June 27, 1872, and "The Liberty Township Murder Case," *Celina Journal*.

15. Day, *Lynched!*, 8.

16. As with the earlier crossroads scene with Mary Ellen Kimmel, the participants in this fictional conversion are real people, based upon census returns and the 1876 plot map.

17. "The Secaur Murder," *Indiana Herald*, July 10, 1872.

18. Day, *Lynched!*, 10. See also "A Horrible Murder Perpetrated!" *Mercer County Standard*, July 4, 1872.

19. Ibid., 17, adapted from "The Liberty Township Murder Case," *Mercer County Standard*.

20. Ibid., 14–15, reprinted from "The Liberty Township Murder Case," *Mercer County Standard*; Ibid., 10, reprinted from "A Horrible Murder Perpetrated!" *Mercer County Standard*; Ibid., 15, reprinted from "The Liberty Township Murder Case," *Mercer County Standard*.

21. This excerpt was reprinted from the July 1 *Fort Wayne Gazette*.

22. Day, *Lynched!*, 10–11, and "The Secaur Murder," *Indiana Herald*. The Mercer County Jail Register lists his discharge date as July 5, but that date is clearly altered on the ledger. Mercer County Jail Register, Mercer County Jail, Celina, Ohio.

23. Ibid., 11–16, reprinted from "The Liberty Township Murder Case,"
Mercer County Standard.

Chapter 2: Understanding

1. Day, *Lynched!*, 20–22, revised from "The Liberty Township Horror!,"
Mercer County Standard, July 11, 1872. Also described in an untitled story on
page three of the *Celina Journal*, July 11.
2. Ibid., 20. See also "The Murder of Mary Secour!," *Celina Journal*, July 11,
1872.
3. Ibid., except for the information about Jacob paying the recognizance fee.
4. Day, *Lynched!*, 25–26.
5. Ibid.
6. Ibid., 26; "The Liberty Township Horror!," *Mercer County Standard*, July
11, 1872; "The Murder of Mary Secour!," *Celina Journal*, July 11, 1872; *Mercer
County Jail Register*, 1–2.
7. Ibid., 32.
8. John Sitterly, quoted in Day, *Lynched!*, 13.
9. Elias May, quoted in Day, *Lynched!*, 14.
10. Computed. Assuming a normal walking speed of around three miles
per hour (it was very hot, and Mary was dressed for church, but the walk was
down a flat-if-dusty road), Mary should have arrived at church (a little more
than two and a half miles from the Sitterly house) a little before ten o'clock,
which would have been in time for Sunday school (if held before the regular
service).
11. George Smitley and Thomas Wright, quoted in Day, *Lynched!*, 14.
12. Computed.
13. George Smitley and Thomas Wright, quoted in Day, *Lynched!*, 14.
14. George Smitley, quoted in Day, *Lynched!*, 14.
15. Computed. Fifteen minutes (at a run) to thirty minutes (at a walk) to
travel through the woods between the Kimmel house and the murder site. Day
reports Henry Hinton as saying, "It is about one mile and three-quarter from
Kimmel's house to where the murder was committed. A person could go from
Kimmel's there, all the way through the woods, except at the road crossing."
Day, *Lynched!*, 13.
16. Computed.
17. George Kimmel, quoted in Day, *Lynched!*, 17.
18. Absalom Kimmel, quoted in Day, *Lynched!*, 26.
19. Computed.
20. George Kimmel, quoted in Day, *Lynched!*, 17.
21. Elias May, quoted in Day, *Lynched!*, 14.
22. Computed.
23. Andrew Kimmel, quoted in Day, *Lynched!*, 16.
24. George Kimmel, quoted in Day, *Lynched!*, 17.
25. Absalom Kimmel, quoted in Day, *Lynched!*, 26.
26. Ibid.
27. Day, *Lynched!*, 14.
28. Ibid., 17.
29. Ibid., 15, 18.

30. Ibid., 15, 18.

31. Ibid., 15.

32. Ibid., 18.

33. Ibid., 15, 18.

34. Ibid., 15.

35. Ibid., 18.

36. Ibid., 15–16.

37. Ibid., 16.

38. Ibid., 17–19.

39. Andrew's confession appears in ibid., 16–17; George's in ibid., 17, 19; Jacob's in ibid., 20; Absalom's in ibid., 25–26.

40. Ibid., 20.

41. Ibid., 30.

42. Ibid., 25.

43. I. F. Raudabaugh, journal. Raudabaugh's handwritten account of the lynching provides eyewitness notes from the lynching site—most likely, from the looks of them, scribbled into the back of a notebook at the scene--along with other comments on the case written at greater leisure the next day. I have used the convenient term *journal*, though the document has no separate dated entries or page numbers.

44. Richard Maxwell Brown, *Strain of Violence* (New York: Oxford University Press, 1975), 21; James Elbert Cutler, *Lynch-Law: An Investigation into the History of Lynching in the United States* (Montclair, NJ: Patterson Smith, [1905] 1969), 41–59.

45. Brown, *Strain of Violence*, 21; Cutler, *Lynch-Law*, 128.

46. Michael J. Pfeifer, *Rough Justice: Lynching and American Society, 1874–1947* (Urbana, IL: University of Illinois Press, 2004), 12; Cutler, *Lynch-Law*, 90–96; Leonard L. Richards, *Gentlemen of Property and Standing: Anti-Abolition Mobs in Jacksonian America* (New York: Oxford University Press, 1970), 6–8, 12–14.

47. Arthur F. Raper, *The Tragedy of Lynching* (New York: New American Library, [1933] 1969), 1, 25; Cutler, *Lynch-Law*, 150–152; Brown, *Strain of Violence*, 309–310, 315; Christopher Waldrep, *The Many Faces of Judge Lynch: Extralegal Violence and Punishment in America* (New York: Palgrave Macmillan, 2002), 97; Frank Shay, *Judge Lynch: His First Hundred Years* (New York: Ives Washburn, 1938), 69.

48. Pfeifer, *Rough Justice*, 42, 63.

49. Waldrep, *The Many Faces of Judge Lynch*, 94.

50. John W. Caughey, *Their Majesties the Mob* (Chicago: University of Chicago Press, 1960), 10–13; Raper, *The Tragedy of Lynching*, 5; Shay, *Judge Lynch*, 77.

51. Caughey, *Their Majesties the Mob*, 19; Waldrep, *The Many Faces of Judge Lynch*, 95–96; Amy Louise Wood, *Lynching and Spectacle: Witnessing Racial Violence in America, 1890–1940* (Chapel Hill, NC: University of North Carolina Press, 2009), 9.

52. Richards, *Gentlemen of Property and Standing*, 9; Waldrep, *The Many Faces of Judge Lynch*, 95.

53. Raper, *The Tragedy of Lynching*, 23.

54. Cutler, *Lynch-Law*, 193–194; Waldrep, *The Many Faces of Judge Lynch*, 88–90, 92–94, 97.

55. Cutler, *Lynch-Law*, 152.

56. Cutler, *Lynch-Law*, 198; Wayne Gard, *Frontier Justice* (Norman: University of Oklahoma Press, 1949), v; H. Jon Rosenbaum, and Peter C. Sederberg, "Vigilantism: An Analysis of Establishment Violence," in *Vigilante Politics*, ed. H. Jon Rosenbaum and Peter C. Sederberg (Philadelphia: University of Pennsylvania Press, 1976), 10; Shay, *Judge Lynch*, 67.

57. Caughey, *Their Majesties the Mob*, 6–9.

58. Wood, *Lynching and Spectacle*, 27; Pfeifer, *Rough Justice*, 2, 8, 94; Raper, *The Tragedy of Lynching*, 46; Rosenbaum and Sederberg, "Vigilantism," 7.

59. Brown, *Strain of Violence*, 108–109, 145–148; Caughey, *Their Majesties the Mob*, 10; Pfeifer, *Rough Justice*, 15, 110.

60. Caughey, *Their Majesties the Mob*, 9, 15.

61. Pfeiffer, *Rough Justice*, 111; Brown, *Strain of Violence*, 152–154; Waldrep, *The Many Faces of Judge Lynch*, 93.

62. Wood, *Lynching and Spectacle*, 8–9, 24; Pfeifer, *Rough Justice*, 3, 44, 46–47, 66; Rosenbaum and Sederberg, "Vigilantism," 7.

63. Brown, *Strain of Violence*, 104, 162–167; Pfeifer, *Rough Justice*, 50; Richards, *Gentlemen of Property and Standing*, 5, 118, 149.

64. Brown, *Strain of Violence*, 88.

65. Pfeifer, *Rough Justice*, 53.

66. Brown, *Strain of Violence*, 88–89.

67. Day, *Lynched!*, 3–4.

68. "Child Found Dead," *Mercer County Standard*, June 27, 1872; Day, *Lynched!*, 4–5.

69. "Child Found Dead," *Mercer County Standard*; "A Little Girl Murdered," *Van Wert Bulletin*, June 28, 1872.

70. "Child Found Dead," *Mercer County Standard*; "A Little Girl Murdered," *Van Wert Bulletin*; "Horrible Crime," *Cincinnati Commercial Tribune*, July 3, 1872; "The Liberty Township Murder," *Celina Journal*, July 4, 1872; Day, *Lynched!*, 4–5; Raudabaugh, journal.

71. "Horrible Crime," *Cincinnati Commercial Tribune*.

72. Day, *Lynched!*, 4–5; See also Raudabaugh, journal.

73. "The Liberty Township Murder," *Celina Journal*.

74. Ibid.; "Horrible Murder in Mercer County, *Cincinnati Commercial Tribune*, June 30, 1872.

75. Day, *Lynched!*, 4–5.

76. Ibid., 4.

77. 1830 United States Census, "Strouse May," Colerain Township, Ross County, Ohio; 1830 United States Census, "Eli Hinton," Colerain Township, Ross County, Ohio; 1840 United States Census, "Strouse May," Colerain Township, Ross County, Ohio; 1840 United States Census, "Elias Hinton," Colerain Township, Ross County, Ohio; 1840 United States Census, "Thomas Hinton," Colerain Township, Ross County, Ohio; 1850 United States Census, "Strouse May," Colerain Township, Ross County, Ohio; 1850 United States Census, "Elias Hinton," Colerain Township, Ross County, Ohio; 1850 United States Census, "Thos E. Hinton," Colerain Township, Ross County, Ohio.

78. Headstone Photo and Burial Record in Liberty Chapel Cemetery, Liberty Township, Mercer County, Ohio, "Thomas E. Hinton," Find a Grave website, accessed January 3, 2015, http://www.findagrave.com; Marriage Record for

Strouse May and Polly Cox, December 30, 1822, Ross County, Ohio, Ohio Marriages, 1800–1958, accessed December 16, 2017, https://www.familysearch.org/.

79. Marriage License and Record for Joseph Secaur and Susannah May, September 15, 1843, Ross County, Ohio, Marriage Records 1840–1852, Vol. E–F, 116, accessed December 16, 2017, FamilySearch.

80. 1850 United States Census, "Jonas Seacoy," Colerain Township, Ross County, Ohio; 1850 United States Census, "Joseph W. Seacoy," Colerain Township, Ross County, Ohio; John Kimmel to Straus May, Deed Record, September 30, 1850, Mercer County Recorder, Mercer County Courthouse, Celina, Ohio, 17:471; 1860 United States Census, "Elias N. May," Liberty Township, Mercer County, Ohio; Strouse May to Wenzel Hocker, Deed Record, January 13, 1871; Mercer County Recorder, Mercer County Courthouse, Celina, Ohio, 17:472; F. M. Hinton to Elias N. May, Deed Record, July 18, 1861, Mercer County Recorder, Mercer County Courthouse, Celina, Ohio, 5:52; G. W. Meizner to Jacob May, Mortgage Record, March 8, 1867, Mercer County Recorder, Mercer County Courthouse, Celina, Ohio, 10:79; Geo. W. Meizner to Mahala A. Dawson, Deed Record, February 20, 1872, Mercer County Recorder, Mercer County Courthouse, Celina, Ohio, 18:443; Certificate of Death for Byron Leisure May, February 4, 1947, Ohio Department of Health, accessed December 16, 2017, https://www.familysearch.org/; Certificate of Death for Calvin T. Secaur, March 71, 1931, State of Ohio Department of Health, Division of Vital Statistics, accessed December 16, 2017, https://www.familysearch.org/.

81. 1860 United States Census, "Jonas Seacoy," Colerain Township, Ross County, Ohio.

82. 1850 United States Census, "John L. Seacoy," Colerain Township, Ross County, Ohio; *Official Roster of the Soldiers of the State of Ohio in the War of the Rebellion, 1861–1866* (Cincinnati: The Ohio Valley Press, 1888), VII: 396.

83. 1850 United States Census, "Wm D. Seacoy," Colerain Township, Ross County, Ohio. I have not been able to find any evidence of a grown William. He may have died of a childhood disease, or he may have left home after reaching adulthood.

84. 1870 United States Census, "Elias Secoy," Black Creek Township, Mercer County, Ohio; 1880 United States Census, "Elias Secaur," Dublin Township, Mercer County, Ohio; 1900 United States Census, "Elias Secaur," Hopewell Township, Mercer County, Ohio; "Elias Secaur," Headstone in Liberty Chapel Cemetery, Liberty Township, Mercer County, Ohio. Photo by author. There is a real problem in determining his birth year since the 1870 census and his gravestone would indicate 1851, but the latter two census entries agree with 1853.

85. 1870 United States Census, "Calvin Secoy," Black Creek Township, Mercer County, Ohio; 1900 United States Census, "Calvin T. Secaur," Blue Creek Township, Paulding County, Ohio; 1910 United States Census, "Calvin T. Secaur," Hopewell Township, Mercer County, Ohio; 1920 United States Census, "Calvin T. Secaur," Hopewell Township, Mercer County, Ohio; 1930 United States Census, "Calvin T. Secaur," Hopewell Township, Mercer County, Ohio; Headstone Photo and Burial Record in Friends Chapel Cemetery, Mercer County, Ohio, "Calvin Theodore Secaur," Find a Grave website, accessed January 3, 2015, www.findagrave.com.

86. Day, *Lynched!*, 3; 1870 United States Census, "Mary A. Seers," Liberty Township, Mercer County, Ohio; "Mary Arabelle Secaur." Headstone in Liberty Chapel Cemetery, Liberty Township, Mercer County, Ohio; photo by author; 1870 United States Census, "William M. Seacort," Black Creek Township, Mercer County, Ohio; 1880 United States Census, "Marion Secour," Dublin Township, Mercer County, Ohio; 1900 United States Census, "Marion Secaur," Hopewell Township, Mercer County, Ohio; Certificate of Death for Marion Secaur, October 18, 1915. State of Ohio Department of Health, Division of Vital Statistics, accessed December 16, 2017, https://www .familysearch.org/.

87. *Official Roster*, VII: 396.

88. Raudabaugh, journal.

89. 1870 United States Census, "Mary A. Seers," Liberty Township, Mercer County, Ohio.

90. 1870 United States Census, "Elias Secoy," Black Creek Township, Mercer County, Ohio; 1870 United States Census, "Calvin Secoy," Black Creek Township, Mercer County, Ohio.

91. Day, *Lynched!*, 5.

92. 1870 United States Census, "William M. Secort," Black Creek Township, Mercer County, Ohio.

93. 1870 United States Census, "Joseph Seers," Liberty Township, Mercer County, Ohio.

94. "C. B.," would seem to be Cornelius, who still lived with his parents near Joseph and his young family back in 1850. I have not located Cornelius in the 1860 or 1870 censuses, but he does show up in an 1875 account book for Miller and Swander's hardware store in Shanesville. Account book, Shanes Crossing Historical Society, Rockford, Ohio.

95. Betty Pond Snyder, *Pioneer Pond People Plus Robinson and Allied Families* (Foster City, CA: B. P. Snyder, 1992), 213.

96. Marriage License and Record for Joseph Secaur and Sarah Odell, April 10, 1873, Fairfield County, Ohio, Ohio Marriage Records 1869–1874, vol. 3, 395, accessed December 16, 2017, https://www.ancestry.com/.

97. The boys were Richard O. (born February 6, 1874), Joseph W. (born October 15, 1875), Charles H. (born April 11, 1877), Eugene (born February 13, 1879), and Robert Brown (born August 16, 1881). 1880 United States Census, "Joseph Secaur," Madison Township, Fairfield County, Ohio; 1900 United States Census, "Sarah Secaur," Basil, Liberty Township, Fairfield County, Ohio; Certificate of Death for Richard Secaur, April 21, 1941, State of Ohio Department of Health, Division of Vital Statistics, accessed December 16, 2017, https://www.familysearch.org/; Certificate of Death for Joseph W. Secaur, June 26, 1931, State of Ohio Department of Health, Division of Vital Statistics, accessed December 16, 2017, https://www.familysearch.org/; World War I Draft Registration Card for Charles H. Secaur, Franklin County, September 12, 1918, accessed December 16, 2017, https://www.ancestry.com/; Marriage License and Record for Eugene M. Secaur and Nora Irene Dressler, March 12, 1902, Franklin County, Ohio, Marriage Index and Records 1901–1902, vol. 33, 227, accessed December 16, 2017, https://www.ancestry.com/; Certificate of Death for Robert Brown Secaur, January 8, 1935, State of Ohio Department of Health, Division

of Vital Statistics, accessed December 16, 2017, https://www.familysearch.org/;
untitled, *Lancaster Gazette*, September 29, 1881.

98. Fictional, though my "reading" of Joseph is based on the documentary record.

99. Day, *Lynched!*, 30.

100. This vignette is fictional, but the conversations portrayed are likely to have occurred in some form.

101. Day, *Lynched!*, 9.

102. "A Horrible Murder Perpetrated!," *Mercer County Standard*.

103. "Horrible Crime," *Cincinnati Commercial Tribune*, July 3, 1872.

104. "The Brutal Murder at Celina," *Cincinnati Gazette*, July 3, 1872.

105. "The Brutal Murder at Celina," *Van Wert Bulletin*,

106. *History of Van Wert and Mercer Counties: With Illustrations and Biographical Sketches of Some of Its Prominent Men and Pioneers* (Wapakoneta, OH: R. Sutton, 1882), 423.

107. Day, *Lynched!*, 7.

108. Ibid., 14.

109. 1870 United States Census, "Henry Hinton," Liberty Township, Mercer County, Ohio; 1870 United States Census, "Elizabeth Hinton," Liberty Township, Mercer County, Ohio; McConahy, *Map of Mercer County Ohio*.

110. 1870 United States Census, "Lydia Hinton," Liberty Township, Mercer County, Ohio; 1880 United States Census, "Lydia Hinton," Liberty Township, Mercer County, Ohio; Marriage License and Record for Jacob Hinton and Lydia A. Baucher, February 23 and 24, 1870; Mercer County, Ohio, Marriage Records 1861–1875, vol. 3, 24, accessed December 61, 2017, https://www.ancestry.com/.

111. McConahy, *Map of Mercer County Ohio*.

112. Raudabaugh, journal.

113. McConahy, *Map of Mercer County Ohio*; "Elizabeth Kimmel," Federal Land Patent, Mercer County, Ohio, Certificate Number 11515, June 1, 1845, accessed December 20, 2017, http://glorecords.blm.gov; "Samuel Kimmel and William," Federal Land Patent, Mercer County, Ohio, Certificate Number 17050, June 1, 1852, accessed December 20, 2017, http://glorecords.blm.gov; F. M. Hinton to H. V. Hinton, Deed Record, August 14, 1865, Mercer County Recorder, Mercer County Courthouse, Celina, Ohio, 15:175.

114. *History of Van Wert and Mercer Counties*, 423.

115. Ibid.

116. George W. Hinton, *Hinton Family History* (Hinton Family Association, 1971), 195; Lyle S. Evans, ed., *A Standard History of Ross County* (Chicago: Lewis Publishing, 1917), 195, 435; Isaac J. Finley and Rufus Putnam, *Pioneer Record and Reminiscences of the Early Settlers and Settlement of Ross County, Ohio* (Cincinnati: Robert Clark, 1871), 101.

117. Evans, *A Standard History of Ross County*, 195, 743.

118. Hinton, *Hinton Family History*, 195; 1860 United States Census, "T. E. Hinton," Hopewell Township, Mercer County, Ohio; 1860 United States Census, "F. W. Hinton," Hopewell Township, Mercer County, Ohio.

119. John Franks to John C. Hinton, Deed Record. June 23, 1856, Mercer County Recorder, Mercer County Courthouse, Celina, Ohio, V:459; J. C. Hinton to Thomas E. Hinton, Deed Record, December 30, 1859, Mercer County

Recorder, Mercer County Courthouse, Celina, Ohio, 6:216; John C. Hinton
to F. M. Hinton, Deed Record, December 30, 1859, Mercer County Recorder,
Mercer County Courthouse, Celina, Ohio, 3:253.

120. Hinton, *Hinton Family History*, 195; Marriage License and Record for
Henry Hinton and Alpha Ann Rutlege, May 13 and 16, 1861, Mercer County,
Ohio, *Marriage Records 1861–1875* 3:5, accessed December 16, 2017, https://www
.ancestry.com/.

121. Hinton, *Hinton Family History*, 195; *Official Roster* V:120, VII:396.

122. "Elizabeth Kimmel," Federal Land Patent, Mercer County, Ohio,
Certificate Number 11515, June 1, 1845, accessed December 20, 2017,
http://glorecords.blm.gov.

123. This is a guess, since John Franks, the owner of this land since 1846,
does not show up as a resident of Liberty Township in the 1850 census. I would
imagine that this prime real estate was rented out and homesteaded, but I have
no proof.

124. "The Rail Road Election," *Mercer County Standard*, June 27, 1872.

125. 1870 United States Census, "Elizabeth Hinton," Liberty Township,
Mercer County. The literacy reporting in the census returns should be viewed
skeptically, as people shift in their status from census to census, and not in the
direction one would imagine. For example, Lydia Hinton, Henry's sister in law,
is listed as a school teacher in 1870 but illiterate in 1880.

126. Hinton, *Hinton Family History*, 195.

127. Ibid.; *Official Roster*, VII:396.

128. *Official Roster*, VII:381, 396.

129. Ibid., VII:381.

130. Kevin B. McCray, *A Shouting of Orders: A History of the 99th Ohio Volunteer
Infantry Regiment* (Philadelphia: Xlibris, 2003), 142.

131. *Official Roster*, VII: 396.

132. Photo of headstone for "Thomas E. Hinton," Liberty Chapel Cemetery,
Mercer County, Ohio, accessed December 20, 2017, https://www.findagrave
.com/memorial/31862502#view-photo=14308663.

1870 United States Census, "Henry Hinton," Liberty Township,
Mercer County, Ohio; 1870 United States Census, "Elizabeth Hinton," Liberty
Township, Mercer County, Ohio; McConahy, *Map of Mercer County Ohio*;
J. C. Hinton to Thomas E. Hinton, Deed Record, December 30, 1859, Mercer
County Recorder, Mercer County Courthouse, Celina, Ohio, 6:216; F. M. Hinton
to H. V. Hinton, Deed Record, August 14, 1865, Mercer County Recorder,
Mercer County Courthouse, Celina, Ohio, 15:175.

133. "Ruth E., daug. of H. V. and A. A. Hinton." Headstone in Liberty Chapel
Cemetery, Liberty Township, Mercer County, Ohio. Photo by author.

134. "The State of Ohio vs. Henry Kimmel," Mercer Common Pleas file for
February Term 1871, Vol. C, 313, Microfilm, Mercer County Court of Common
Pleas Office, Mercy County Courthouse, Celina, Ohio.

135. 1870 United States Census, "Andrew Henkle," Liberty Township, Mercer
County, Ohio; 1870 United States Census, "Henry Kimmel," Liberty Township,
Mercer County, Ohio.

136. Ralph Beaver Strassburger, *Pennsylvania German Pioneers: A Publication
of the Original Lists of Arrivals In the Port of Philadelphia From 1727 to 1808*

(Baltimore: Genealogical Publishing, [1934] 1975), I:722, 3:833. The *Crawford* carried ninety-eight male passengers over the age of sixteen out of 214 total passengers, so there is a good chance that the whole family was among the passengers. Only the male heads of households signed the passenger lists. The "Facsimile Signatures Volume" of Strassburger's book shows "Joh. Jacob Kummel" signing his own name, unlike some of his fellow passengers. See also Marianne S. Wokeck, "German Settlements in the British North American Colonies," in *In Search of Peace and Prosperity: New German Settlements in Eighteenth-Century Europe and America*, ed. Hartmut Lehmann, Hermann Wellenreuther, and Renate Wilson (University Park: Pennsylvania State University Press, 2000), 84–85, 191–216, 247; I. Daniel Rupp, *A Collection of Upwards of Thirty Thousand Names of German, Swiss, Dutch, French and other Immigrants in Pennsylvania From 1727 to 1776* (Baltimore: Genealogical Publishing, [1896] 1975), 385; Aaron Spencer Fogleman, *Hopeful Journeys: Immigration, Settlement, and Political Culture in Colonial America, 1717–1775* (Philadelphia: University of Pennsylvania Press, 1996), 73, 77; Frank Reid Diffenderffer, *The German Immigration into Pennsylvania Through the Port of Philadelphia from 1700 to 1775 and The Redemptioners* (1900; repr., Baltimore, MD: Genealogical Publishing Company, 2003), 150–151.

137. Timothy W. Kimmel, letter to author, May 8, 1999. Solid evidence of when the Kimmels moved is lacking, but we do know from baptismal records that Jacob Kuemmel and his wife, Margaretha, had a son, Christian Friedrich, baptized by Balthasar Meyer in this area on September 1, 1772. See Paul Miller Ruff, *Balthasar Meyer's Baptisms, Westmoreland County, Pennsylvania, 2 August 1772 to 4 June 1792* (Greensburg, PA: P.M. Ruff, 1997), Entry 10; Jacob Kimmel is not listed among taxable inhabitants of Bedford County in 1773 (before Westmoreland separated off). This implies to me that they were not property owners at that point. *Returns of Taxables for the Counties of Bedford (1773 to 1784), Huntingdon (1788), Westmoreland (1783, 1786), Fayette (1785, 1786), Allegheny (1791), Washington (1786) Census of Bedford (1784), and Westmoreland (1783)*, ed. William Henry Egle (Wm. Stanley Ray, State Printer of Pennsylvania, 1898), 7–53, 405.

138. Paul W. Myers, *Westmoreland County in the American Revolution* (Apollo, PA: Closson Press, 1988), 206, 215, 222; John N. Boucher, *Old and New Westmoreland* (New York: American Historical Society, 1918), 1: 375; Lewis Clark Walkinshaw, *Annals of Southwestern Pennsylvania* (New York: Lewis Historical Publishing, 1939), 2, 107; George Dallas Albert, *History of the County of Westmoreland, Pennsylvania* (Philadelphia, PA: L. H. Everts, 1882), 459; Edgar W. Hassler, *Old Westmoreland: A History of Western Pennsylvania During the Revolution* (Pittsburg, PA: J. R. Weldin, 1900), 11, 14–15, 25–26, 63–65; John N. Boucher, *History of Westmoreland County, Pennsylvania*, vol. I (Chicago: Wilson Publishing, 1906), 137–138. See also Henry Melchior Muhlenberg Richards, *The Pennsylvania-German in the Revolutionary War 1775–1783* (Baltimore, MD: Genealogical Publishing Company, [1908] 1978), 184; Richards claims the regiment "contained a very small number of Pennsylvania-Germans, so small as not to warrant the insertion of its interesting services."

139. Dale Van Every, *A Company of Heroes: The American Frontier, 1775–1783* (New York: William Morrow and Company, 1962), 200; Hassler, *Old*

Westmoreland, 61–68; Boucher, *History of Westmoreland County*, 138; Louise Phelps Kellogg, "Orderly Book of the Eighth Pennsylvania Regiment," in *Frontier Advance on the Upper Ohio, 1778–1779* (Madison: Wisconsin Historical Society, 1916), 431–459.

140. Manpower in the regiment dropped from 420 in April to 212 in December. Robert E. Cairns, "History of the 8th Pennsylvania Regiment 1776–1783," *Military Collector & Historian* 59, no. 4 (Winter 2007): 248–260; Myers, *Westmoreland County*, 127; "Rangers on the Frontiers—1778–1783," *Pennsylvania Archives*, ed. William Henry Egle (Harrisburg, PA: State Printer of Pennsylvania, 1897), 3rd ser., 23:222, 23:320. Truby commanded the Eighth Company of the Second Battalion of the Westmoreland County Militia, a unit formed up in 1777. "Revolutionary War Militia Organization: Westmoreland Co., PA," Pennsylvania Historical & Museum Commission, accessed January 17, 2014, http://www.portal.state.pa.us.

141. "A Muster Roll of Capt'n Casper Waldhauer Company in the Sixth Regiment of Westmoreland County on Their Touer of Duty at Crooket Crik at Clarks Station & Other Stations," *Pennsylvania Archives*, ed. Thomas Lynch Montgomery (Harrisburg, PA: Harrisburg Publishing, 1907), 6th ser., V:780; "A Pay Roll of Capt. Gasper Waldhair Company of Westmoreland County Militia at Clarks & Other Stations," *Pennsylvania Archives*, ed. Thomas Lynch Montgomery (Harrisburg, PA: Harrisburg Publishing, 1907), 6th ser., V: 782; untitled statement certifying "Andrew Kimmel hath served a thauer of Dutey," signed by Casper Waldhauer, Capt., *Pennsylvania Archives*, ed. Thomas Lynch Montgomery (Harrisburg, PA: Harrisburg Publishing, 1907), 6th ser., V: 822; "Inhabitants of Westmoreland to Gen. William Jack," *Pennsylvania Archives*, ed. John B. Linn and William H. Egle (Harrisburg, PA: Clarence M. Busch, 1896) 2nd ser., IV: 55–56; Gordon S. Wood, *Empire of Liberty: A History of the Early Republic, 1789–1815* (Oxford: Oxford University Press, 2009), 138–139; "Proclamation," *The Papers of George Washington*, ed. David R. Hoth and Carol S. Ebel (Charlottesville: University of Virginia Press, 2011), 16: 531–534. Washington actually mobilized the militia on September 9. James Thomas Flexner, *George Washington: Anguish and Farewell (1793–1799)* (Boston: Little, Brown, 1972) 169; Frank E. Vandiver, *How America Goes to War* (Westport, CT: Praeger, 2005), 2–4.

142. Timothy W. Kimmel, letter to author, May 8, 1999; 1810 United States Census, "Andrew Kimmele," Hempfield Township, Westmoreland County, Pennsylvania; 1820 United States Census, "Andrew Kimill," Black Lick Township, Indiana County, Pennsylvania.

143. 1830 United States Census, "Andrew Kimble," Plum Creek Township, Armstrong County, Pennsylvania; *Armstrong County Pennsylvania: Her People, Past and Present* (Chicago: J. H. Beers, 1914), 195.

144. "John and Rachel Kimmel Family German Bible," transcription by Timothy Kimmel from copies scanned October 1998 by Chris Beard of Reynoldsburg, Ohio, accessed May 20, 2014, http://www.kimmelfamily.net/Bible-John1792.htm.

145. 1840 United States Census, "John Kimel," Salt Creek Township, Holmes County, Ohio; 1840 United States Census, "Abram Kimel," Salt Creek Township, Holmes County, Ohio. Prior to 1850, the census returns only recorded the

name of heads of families; everyone else shows up as numbers within age ranges. By aligning the census listings with family trees and other records, it is possible to tease out who may be hiding behind those numbers. John Kimmel (forty-eight) was the oldest of Henry's brothers. In his house lived his wife, Rachel (thirty-nine), sons William (twenty) and John (twelve), and daughters Elizabeth (nineteen), Sarah Anne (fourteen), and Rachel (nine). With Abraham Kimmel, Henry's just-older brother (twenty-five), lived their sister, Catherine (sixteen), and mother, Elizabeth (sixty-four). "John and Rachel Kimmel Family German Bible." There is no record of a Kimmel who purchased or sold land in Salt Creek Township during this period.

146. David Fry to John Kimmel, Deed Record, January 4, 1840, Mercer County Recorder, Mercer County Courthouse, Celina, Ohio, J: 180.

147. Carolyn Brandon and Mary Brandon, eds., *1827 and 1843 Quadrennial Enumeration of Adult White Males of Mercer County, Ohio* (Celina: Mercer County Chapter of Ohio Genealogical Society, 2004).

148. "Elizabeth Kimmel," Federal Land Patent, Mercer County, Ohio, Certificate Number 11515, June 1, 1845, accessed December 20, 2017, http://glorecords.blm.gov.

149. "William Kimmel and John Kimmel," Federal Land Patent, Mercer County, Ohio, Certificate Number 15111, June 1, 1848, accessed December 20, 2017, http://glorecords.blm.gov. I am not sure if William moved to Mercer County right away after his marriage. There is no record of William buying or selling land in Holmes County, and my guess is that he was renting or simply living on land owned by one of his wife's relatives. The Frys had been original settlers as far back as 1815, and they'd been buying and selling land in Salt Creek Township since William's father-in-law, Frederick, started in 1837. Around 1848, there was a series of sales between family members in one of those efforts at clearing up ownership of a parcel. One sale, dated May 2, 1848, was witnessed by an "A. W. Kimmel." I really don't know who this is, unless, possibly, William had an unused first name beginning in *A*, possibly in honor of his grandfather. Eli M. Fry to George Fry, Deed Record, May 2, 1848, Holmes County Recorder, Millersburg, Ohio, 17: 325; "John Kimmel," Federal Land Patent, Mercer County, Ohio, Certificate Number 15865, February 1, 1849, accessed December 20, 2017, http://glorecords.blm.gov.

150. John Kimmel to Straus May, Deed Record, September 30, 1850, Mercer County Recorder. Mercer County Courthouse, Celina, Ohio, 17:471; "John and Rachel Kimmel Family German Bible."

151. "Samuel Kimmel and William," Federal Land Patent, Mercer County, Ohio, Certificate Number 17050, June 1, 1852, accessed December 20, 2017, http://glorecords.blm.gov.

152. William Kimmel to Elizabeth Berry, Deed Record, April 28, 1853, Mercer County Recorder, Mercer County Courthouse, Celina, Ohio, R: 355. The estray book lists William as Township Clerk until at least April 1853, and he transferred his father's 1842 animal markings to himself on April 14, 1853. Estray Book of Liberty Township, Mercer Co., Ohio. Mercer County District Library, Celina, Ohio.

153. 1860 United States Census, "Abraham Kimmel," Huntington Township, Huntington County, Indiana. Abraham's youngest son, Montgomery, is listed

as six years old and born in Ohio, so the family must have moved sometime after his birth in 1854.

154. Marriage License and Record for Samuel Chivington and Sarah Kimmel, March 12, 1846, Mercer County, Ohio, Marriage Records 1838–1852, vol. ABC, 187, accessed December 16, 2017, https://www.ancestry.com/; Marriage License and Record for Henry Kimmel and Susan Hines, March 12 and 18, 1846, Mercer County, Ohio, Marriage Records 1838–1852, vol. ABC, 187, accessed December 16, 2017, https://www.ancestry.com/; Marriage License and Record for Abraham Kimmel and Elizabeth Updyke, August 14 and 26, 1846, Mercer County, Ohio, Marriage Records 1838–1852, vol. ABC, 193, accessed December 16, 2017, https://www.ancestry.com/.

155. Estray Book of Liberty Township, Mercer Co., Ohio, Mercer County District Library, Celina, Ohio.

156. Don Yoder, "The Pennsylvania Germans: Three Centuries of Identity Crisis," in *America and the Germans: An Assessment of a Three-Hundred-Year History*, ed. Frank Trommler and Joseph McVeigh (Philadelphia: University of Pennsylvania Press, 1985), 1: 40–65.

157. Wokeck, "German Settlements," 191–216. See also Wokeck, Marianne S. *Trade in Strangers: The Beginnings of Mass Migration to North America* (University Park: Pennsylvania State University Press, 1999), 5, 16.

158. Hermann Wellenreuther, "Image and Counterimage, Tradition and Expectation: The German Immigrants in English Colonial Society in Pennsylvania, 1700–1765," in *America and the Germans: An Assessment of a Three-Hundred-Year History*, ed. Frank Trommler and Joseph McVeigh (Philadelphia: University of Pennsylvania Press, 1985), 1: 85–105; Fogleman, *Hopeful Journeys*, 12, 74–77, 80–83, 149; Mark Haberlein, "Communication and Group Interaction among German Migrants to Colonial Pennsylvania," in *In Search of Peace and Prosperity: New German Settlements in Eighteenth-Century Europe and America*, ed. Hartmut Lehmann, Hermann Wellenreuther, and Renate Wilson (University Park: Pennsylvania State University Press, 2000), 156–171; Wokeck, "German Settlements," 191, 208, 214–216; William T. Parsons, *The Pennsylvania Dutch: A Persistent Minority* (Boston: Twayne, 1976), 61, 115; Stephanie Grauman Wolf, "Hyphenated America: The Creation of an Eighteenth-Century German-American Culture," in *America and the Germans: An Assessment of a Three-Hundred-Year History*, ed. Frank Trommler and Joseph McVeigh (Philadelphia: University of Pennsylvania Press, 1985), 1:66–84.

159. Wokeck, "German Settlements," 191.

160. Yoder, "The Pennsylvania Germans," 48–49; Parsons, *The Pennsylvania Dutch*, 68.

161. Wokeck, "German Settlements," 205.

162. Parsons, *The Pennsylvania Dutch*, 83–84.

163. *Armstrong County*, 11; St. John de Crevecoeur, *Letters from an American Farmer* (n.p.: Fox, Dunfield & Co., 1904), 81–82.

164. R. Douglas Hurt, *The Ohio Frontier: Crucible of the Old Northwest, 1720–1830* (Bloomington: Indiana University Press, 1996), 253; see also Jack Larkin, *The Reshaping of Everyday Life: 1790–1840* (New York: Harper & Row, 1988), 11.

165. Hurt, *The Ohio Frontier*, 250.

166. John A. Jakle, *Images of the Ohio Valley: A Historical Geography of Travel, 1740–1860* (New York: Oxford University Press, 1977), 96–97.

167. Jakle, *Images of the Ohio Valley*, 111.

168. Ibid., 99.

169. Hurt, *The Ohio Frontier*, 254. Larkin, 11.

170. Jakle, *Images of the Ohio Valley*, 111.

171. Hurt, *The Ohio Frontier*, 351, 362.

172. Jakle, *Images of the Ohio Valley*, 96–97; Hurt, *The Ohio Frontier*, 211, 356, 395.

173. Hurt, *The Ohio Frontier*, 350–352.

174. Jakle, *Images of the Ohio Valley*, 115.

175. Hurt, *The Ohio Frontier*, 266.

176. Ibid., 373–375.

177. Larkin, *The Reshaping of Everyday Life*, 35, 289.

178. Jakle, *Images of the Ohio Valley*, 112; Larkin, *The Reshaping of Everyday Life*, 128.

179. Emily Foster, ed., *The Ohio Frontier: An Anthology of Early Writings* (Lexington, KY: University Press of Kentucky, 1996), 190, 193.

180. Foster, *The Ohio Frontier*, 161.

181. Larkin, *The Reshaping of Everyday Life*, 123, 125.

182. J. Merton England, "Introduction," in John M. Roberts, *Buckeye Schoolmaster: A Chronicle of Midwestern Rural Life 1853–1865*, ed. J. Merton England (Bowling Green, OH: Bowling Green University Popular Press, 1996), 8.

183. Foster, *The Ohio Frontier*, 198; Hurt, *The Ohio Frontier*, 272.

184. Larkin, *The Reshaping of Everyday Life*, 288.

185. Ibid., 281–282.

186. Quoted in Foster, *The Ohio Frontier*, 208–209; Snyder, *Pioneer Pond People*, 213.

187. "The State of Ohio vs. Henry Kimmel," 1–2. This file of materials is located on a microfilm in the Mercer County Clerk of Courts Office in the Mercer County Courthouse, Celina, Ohio. The documents in the file are numbered, so I will use those numbers in my references.

188. "The State of Ohio vs. Henry Kimmel," 1–2.

189. Ibid., 3–5.

190. Ibid., 6–7.

191. Ibid., 8–10; 1870 United States Census, "Jacob Wright," Liberty Township, Mercer County, Ohio; 1870 United States Census, "Jacob Harmon," Liberty Township, Mercer County, Ohio; 1870 United States Census, "Daniel Mahony," Liberty Township, Mercer County, Ohio; 1870 United States Census, "Peter Davis," Hopewell Township, Mercer County, Ohio; "The State of Ohio vs. Henry Kimble," 11–14; 1870 United States Census, "Anthony Flake," Willshire Township, Van Wert County, Ohio; "The State of Ohio vs. Henry Kimble," 15–16; 1870 United States Census, "Joseph Wells," Liberty Township, Mercer County, Ohio; 1870 United States Census, "Elias May," Liberty Township, Mercer County, Ohio; 1870 United States Census, "Jacob Hinton," Liberty Township, Mercer County, Ohio; 1870 United States Census, "Henry Hinton," Liberty Township, Mercer County, Ohio; 1870 United States Census, "Anthony Mertz," Liberty Township, Mercer County, Ohio; 1870 United States Census, "Geo. W. Mizner," Liberty Township, Mercer County, Ohio. George Mizner

(or Meizner—name is spelled variously in census documents) is listed as a Methodist preacher on the 1870 census report, and his father, William, lives on a back-quarter of Joseph Wells's land.

192. "The State of Ohio vs. Henry Kimmel," 17–19; "Court Proceedings," *Mercer County Standard*, March 9, 1871.

193. Day, *Lynched!*, 16.

194. Ibid., 24–25.

195. Ibid., 30.

196. "Frequently Asked Questions on Intellectual Disability," American Association on Intellectual and Developmental Disabilities website, accessed January 2, 2015, http://aaidd.org; See also American Psychiatric Association, *Diagnostic and Statistical Manual of Mental Disorders*, 5th ed. (Washington, DC: American Psychiatric Publishing, 2013).

197. Robert M. Hodapp and Elisabeth M. Dykens, "Behavioral Effects of Genetic Mental Retardation Disorders" in *Handbook of Intellectual and Developmental Disabilities*, ed. John W. Jacobson, James A. Mulick, and Johannes Rojahn (New York: Springer Science and Business Media, 2007), 115–131.

198. Elizabeth L. Brennan, "A Matter of Difference: A Contextual Perspective on the History of Children with Mental Retardation in the United States," in *Children with Disabilities in America: A Historical Handbook and Guide*, ed. Elizabeth J. Sanford and Philip L. Safford (Westport, CT: Greenwood Press, 2006), 65–86.

199. Brennan, "A Matter of Difference," 67.

200. James W. Trent, *Inventing the Feeble Mind: A History of Mental Retardation in the United States* (Berkeley: University of California Press, 1994), 20.

201. Brennan, "A Matter of Difference," 66.

202. Ibid., 67.

203. Day, *Lynched!*, 30.

204. American Psychiatric Association, *Diagnostic and Statistical*, 35.

205. Day, *Lynched!*, 30.

206. US National Library of Medicine, *Genetics Home Reference*, accessed February 6, 2014, http://ghr.nlm.nih.gov/.

207. Day, *Lynched!*, 30.

208. American Psychiatric Association, *Diagnostic and Statistical*, 35.

209. 1870 United States Census, "Absalom Kimmel," Liberty Township, Mercer County, Ohio.

210. American Psychiatric Association, *Diagnostic and Statistical*, 35.

211. Ibid., 34–35.

212. Ibid., 34.

213. Day, *Lynched!*, 24–25.

214. Perske quoted in Gary N. Siperstein, Jennifer Norins, and Amanda Hohler, "Social Acceptance and Attitude Change," in *Handbook of Intellectual and Developmental Disabilities*, ed. John W. Jacobson, James A. Mulick, and Johannes Rojahn (New York: Springer Science and Business Media, 2007), 133.

215. Siperstein, Norins, and Hohler, "Social Acceptance," 134.

216. Robert W. Heffer, Tammy D. Barry, and Beth H. Garland, "History, Overview, and Trends in Child and Adolescent Psychological Assessment," in

Assessing Childhood Psychopathology and Developmental Disabilities, ed. Johnny L. Matson, Frank Andrasik, and Michael L. Matson (New York: Springer Science and Business Media, 2009), 4.

217. Kagendo Mutua, James Siders, and Jeffrey P. Bakken, "History of Mental Disabilities," in *History of Special Education*, ed. Anthony F. Rotatori, Festus E. Obiakor, and Jeffrey P Bakken (Bingley, UK: Emerald Group Publishing, 2011), 91.

218. Philip L. Safford and Elizabeth J. Safford, "Children Being Different, Difficult, or Disturbed in America," in *Children with Disabilities in America: A Historical Handbook and Guide*, ed. Elizabeth J. Safford and Philip L. Safford (Westport, CT: Greenwood Press, 2006), 88.

219. Philip M. Ferguson, "The Legacy of the Almshouse," in *Mental Retardation in America: A Historical Reader*, ed. Steven Noll and James W. Trent Jr. (New York: New York University Press, 2004), 46.

220. Brennan, "A Matter of Difference," 70.

221. Penny L. Richards, "'Beside Her Sat Her Idiot Child': Families and Developmental Disability in Mid-Nineteenth-Century America," in *Mental Retardation in America: A Historical Reader*, ed. Steven Noll and James W. Trent Jr. (New York: New York University Press, 2004), 65, 67. Trent, 7.

222. Trent, *Inventing the Feeble Mind*, 7.

223. Ferguson, "The Legacy of the Almshouse," 40; Trent, *Inventing the Feeble Mind*, 7.

224. Ferguson, "The Legacy of the Almshouse," 40, 52–55.

225. Brennan, "A Matter of Difference," 74, Trent, *Inventing the Feeble Mind*, 19.

226. Steven Noll and James W. Trent Jr., "Introduction," in *Mental Retardation in America: A Historical Reader*, ed. Steven Noll and James W. Trent Jr. (New York: New York University Press, 2004), 1.

227. Trent, *Inventing the Feeble Mind*, 19.

228. Samuel G. Howe, "A Selection from Report Made to the Legislature of Massachusetts," in *Mental Retardation in America: A Historical Reader*, ed. Steven Noll and James W. Trent Jr. (New York: New York University Press, 2004), 24.

229. Howe, "Legislature of Massachusetts," 24.

230. Safford and Safford, "Children Being Different," 89.

231. Mutua, Siders, and Bakken, "Mental Disabilities," 97.

232. Safford and Safford, "Children Being Different," 89; Trent, *Inventing the Feeble Mind*, 16, 21.

233. Noll and Trent, "Introduction," 3.

234. Brennan, "A Matter of Difference," 71.

235. Quoted in Brennan, "A Matter of Difference," 74.

236. Trent, *Inventing the Feeble Mind*, 18. William B. Fish, "A Thesis on Idiocy," in *Mental Retardation in America: A Historical Reader*, ed. Steven Noll and James W. Trent Jr. (New York: New York University Press, 2004), 27–39.

237. Richards, "Her Idiot Child," 65, 70, 72, 73, 78.

238. Richards, "Her Idiot Child," 68; see also 65, 69.

239. Ibid., 65.

240. The date of this fictionalized event is accurate, according to the few surviving court documents. The details are fictional.

Chapter 3: Lynching

1. This short piece is a fictionalization based on the many versions of the jailbreak. I have attempted to match the tone of the pro-lynching narratives found in the newspapers.
2. Day, *Lynched!*, 20–22.
3. Ibid., 27–28.
4. This narrative, while fictionalized, is based on a careful and judicious reading of the many accounts of the lynching. Other than the thoughts of Jake and some of the dialogue, this is as close to accurate as I can make it.
5. The mob initially took the three young men to the murder site, but when the owner of the property objected, the crowd decided to head to the Kimmel farm, instead. Day, *Lynched!*, 28.

Chapter 4: Aftermath

1. Reprinted from the *Wapakoneta Democrat*, "The Tragedy in Mercer County—Our Opinion of the Example, & c."
2. Reprinted from the *Lancaster, Indiana, Eagle*.
3. See also "Local and Miscellaneous," *Celina Journal*, November 21, 1872.
4. 1880 United States Census, "Samuel Kimmel," Dublin Township, Mercer County, Ohio; Deed Record, Samuel Kimmel and Sarah Jane Kimmel to Thomas Beaghler and Gilbert Beaghler, Deed Record, February 18, 1882, Mercer County Recorder, Mercer County Courthouse, Celina, Ohio, 41:34; 1900 United States Census, "Samuel Kimmel" Lake Township, Harper County, Kansas; "Samuel Kimmel," *Kansas: A Cyclopedia of State History, Embracing Events, Institutions, Industries, Counties, Cities, Towns, Prominent Persons, Etc.*, vol. 3 (Chicago: Standard Publishing Company, 1912), 290–291.
5. "Marriage License and Record for William Kimmel and Lydia Tester, November 17 and 18, 1882, Mercer County, Ohio," Marriage Records 1875–1880, vol. 4, 115, accessed December 16, 2017, https://www.ancestry .com/; 1880 United States Census, "Lydia Kimmel," Black Creek Township, Mercer County, Ohio. Lydia's connection to Sarah is tenuous but probable. The "Bevington Family Tree" lists Lydia's father, John, and Sarah's father, David, as sons of Jacob Tester, a link other family trees fail to make. "Bevington Family Tree," accessed January 15, 2015, https://www.ancestry .com/. In the 1850 census, David Tester and his family are listed in German Township in Allen County, just to the northeast of Mercer County. 1850 United States Census, "David Tester," German Township, Allen County, Ohio. Unfortunately, Jacob Tester and the rest of his family are not found in the township listing for that census. Both families do show up there in 1860, however. 1860 United States Census, "J. Tester," German Township, Allen County, Ohio. Meanwhile, David moved on to Mercer County. 1860 United States Census, "David Tester," Dublin Township, Mercer County, Ohio. Both Jacob and David were buried in Stringtown Cemetery, which is located southwest of Rockford. Headstone Photo and Burial Record in Stringtown Cemetery, Rockford, Ohio, "David Tester," accessed January 3, 2015, http://www.findagrave.com.

6. Carl Kimmel and Mary Krugh, interview by author, Van Wert, Ohio, May 29, 1999.

7. "Marriage License and Record for Jacob Kimmel and Mary Chivington, August 26 and September 3, 1878, Mercer County, Ohio," Marriage Records 1875–1880, 110, accessed December 16, 2017, https://www.ancestry.com/.

8. 1880 United States Census, "Jacob Kimmel" Wilmington Township, Waubaunsee County, Kansas. An odd note about Jacob and Mary: living with Susan Kimmel's family in 1880 is three-year-old Viola Chivington (1880 United States Census, "Viola Chivington," Dublin Township, Mercer County, Ohio), but Jacob married Mary Elizabeth Chivington on September 3, 1878. Their first three children are listed as being born in Missouri in 1883, 1889, and 1890 (1900 United States Census, "Jacob Kimmel," Black Creek Township, Mercer County, Ohio). So, it is possible that Jacob and Mary Elizabeth headed out to Missouri without a daughter bearing Mary's last name.

9. "Jacob Kimmel," *Hoye's City Directory* (Kansas City, Missouri: Hoye Directory Company, 1884), 290; "Mrs. Mary Kimmel," *Hoye's City Directory* (Kansas City, Missouri: Hoye Directory Company, 1885), 331; "Jacob Kimmel," *Hoye's City Directory* (Kansas City, Missouri: Hoye Directory Company, 1886), 458; "Jacob Kimmel," *Hoye's City Directory* (Kansas City, Missouri: Hoye Directory Company, 1888), 397; "Jacob Kimmell," *Hoye's City Directory* (Kansas City, Missouri: Hoye Directory Company, 1889), 383; "Jacob Kimmel," *Hoye's City Directory* (Kansas City, Missouri: Hoye Directory Company, 1891), 367.

10. 1900 United States Census, "Jacob Kimmel," Black Creek Township, Mercer County, Ohio.

11. 1910 United States Census, "Jacob Kimmel," Harper City, Liberty Township, Blackford County, Indiana; 1920 United States Census, "Jacob Kimmel," Harper City, Liberty Township, Blackford County, Indiana; Headstone Photo and Burial Record in Hartford City Cemetery, Hartford City, Indiana, "Jacob Kimmel," accessed January 3, 2015, http://www.findagrave.com.

12. 1880 United States Census, "George Kimble," Dublin Township, Mercer County, Ohio.

13. 1900 United States Census, "George Kimball," Rockford Village, Dublin Township, Mercer County, Ohio; 1910 United States Census, "George Kimball," Dayton City, Dayton Township, Montgomery County, Ohio; 1920 United States Census, "George Kimble," Celina Village, Jefferson Township, Mercer County, Ohio.

14. Missouri Birth & Death Records Database, "Charles Kruimel," Missouri Digital Heritage, accessed December 1, 2014, https://www.sos.mo.gov/mdh.

15. Marriage Record for John A. Kimmel and Alvena Derr, September 23, 1905, Leavenworth County, Kansas," Kansas, Marriages, 1840–1935, accessed March 14, 2015, https://www.familysearch.org/.

16. 1900 United States Census, "John Derr," Leavenworth City, Leavenworth County, Kansas; 1910 United States Census, "Alvina Kimmel," village of New South Memphis, Shelby County, Tennessee.

17. 1910 United States Census, "Jon A. Kimmel," village of New South Memphis, Shelby County, Tennessee; 1910 United States Census, "Jn. Derr," village of New South Memphis, Shelby County, Tennessee; "John A Kimmel,"

R.L. Polk & Co.'s Memphis City Directory (Memphis, TN: R. L. Polk, 1908), 823; "John A Kimmel," *R.L. Polk & Co.'s Memphis City Directory* (Memphis, TN: R. L. Polk, 1910), 787; "John Derr," *R.L. Polk & Co.'s Memphis City Directory* (Memphis, TN: R. L. Polk, 1910), 411.

18. 1930 United States Census, "John Kimmel," Dublin Township, Mercer County, Ohio.

19. Headstone Photo and Burial Record in Riverside Cemetery, Rockford, Ohio, "John A. 'Peck' Kimmel," accessed January 3, 2015, http://www.findagrave.com.

20. 1860 United States Census, "Mary E. Kimble," Liberty Township, Mercer County, Ohio; 1870 United States Census, "Mary E. Kimmel," Liberty Township, Mercer County, Ohio.

21. 1880 United States Census, "Mary E. Felver," Black Creek Township, Mercer County, Ohio.

22. 1900 United States Census, "Clark Felver," Dublin Township, Mercer County, Ohio.

23. Obituary for "Clark Felver," clipping without publication information; Clark is listed as being interred in the cemetery near Fountain Chapel, the same cemetery where Mary Ellen's parents were buried, but his name appears on a headstone shared with "Mary E." in Riverside Cemetery. "Mary E. Felver," Headstone in Riverside Cemetery, Rockford, Ohio, photo by author.

24. 1860 United States Census, "Eve Kimble," Liberty Township, Mercer County, Ohio; 1870 United States Census, "Sarah Kimmel," Liberty Township, Mercer County, Ohio; 1880 United States Census, "Sarah A. Kimble," Dublin Township, Mercer County, Ohio.

25. "Obituary of Wm. Kimmell," clipping without publication information.

26. 1930 United States Census, "Anna McKay," Rockford Village, Dublin Township, Mercer County, Ohio; 1920 United States Census, "Anna McKay," Rockford Village, Dublin Township, Mercer County, Ohio; 1910 United States Census, "Annie McKay," Superior Township, Chippewa County, Michigan.

27. 1900 United States Census, "David McKay," Superior Township, Chippewa County, Michigan.

28. 1900 United States Census, "Belle D. Kimble," Dublin Township, Mercer County, Ohio.

29. 1900 United States Census, "Alice Tester," Dublin Township, Mercer County, Ohio; "Marriage License and Record for Wilson Tester and Alice Kimmel, November 17 and 18, 1882, Mercer County, Ohio," Marriage Records 1875–1880, vol. 5, 170, accessed December 16, 2017, https://www.ancestry.com/. Oddly, Clark Felver is listed as the person requesting the marriage license for his sister-in-law.

30. 1910 United States Census, "Alice Tester," Rockford Village, Dublin Township, Mercer County, Ohio; 1920 United States Census, "Alice Tester," Rockford Village, Dublin Township, Mercer County, Ohio; 1920 United States Census, "Wm M. Kimmell," Rockford Village, Dublin Township, Mercer County, Ohio.

31. 1910 United States Census, "Jennie Atkinson," Dublin Township, Mercer County, Ohio; 1910 United States Census, "William Kimmel," Dublin Township, Mercer County, Ohio; 1930 United States Census, "Jennie Atkinson,"

Dublin Township, Mercer County, Ohio; 1930 United States Census, "Ferdellus Kimmel," Dublin Township, Mercer County, Ohio.

32. 1910 United States Census, "Helen Atkinson," Dublin Township, Mercer County, Ohio; 1920 United States Census, "Helen Atkinson," Dublin Township, Mercer County, Ohio.

33. Certificate of death for Jennie Atkinson, June 25, 1945, Ohio Department of Health, accessed December 20, 2017, https://www.familysearch.org/.

34. I have been unable to locate the original story from either the London or Boston periodicals of this name.

35. "The Heart-Rending Story of Little Mary Belle Secaur's Terrible Fate in This County in June 1872," *Mercer County Standard*, March 26, 1874.

36. "The Secaur Tragedy," *Mercer County Standard*, March 26, 1874.

37. Untitled, *Mercer County Standard*, April 9, 1874.

38. "Did Thomas Bradwell Douglass Die in Denver?," *Mercer County Standard*, April 9, 1874. Evidently, Callen provided the *Standard* with a copy of the article that originally appeared in the *Daily Times*: "Did Thomas Bradwell Douglass Die in Denver?," *Denver Daily Times*, March 31, 1874.

Chapter 5: Grieving

1. All five vignettes in this chapter are fictional, though the characters are real.